BUDDHISM AND THE SENSES

Buddhism *and the* Senses

A Guide to the Good and Bad

EDITED BY Robert DeCaroli AND Donald S. Lopez Jr.

NATIONAL MUSEUM of ASIAN ART
Smithsonian

Wisdom

Wisdom Publications
132 Perry Street
New York, NY 10014 USA
wisdomexperience.org

Library of Congress Cataloging-in-Publication Data is available at https://lccn.loc.gov/2023044397

ISBN 978-1-61429-890-8 ebook ISBN 978-1-61429-903-5

28 27 26 25 24 5 4 3 2 1

Designed by Gopa & Ted 2.

Printed on acid-free paper that meets the guidelines for permanence and durability of the Production Guidelines for Book Longevity of the Council on Library Resources.

Printed in Malaysia.

In the same way, Mañjuśrī, regardless of their malevolent or benign intentions, if anyone so much as beholds the tathāgatas in painted forms or statues, their eyes will become pure through that root of virtue. Even down to those born in the abode of animals, regardless of their malevolent or benign intentions, if anyone hears the words *buddha*, or *tathāgata*, or *protector of the world*, their sense of hearing will become pure through that root of virtue. If anyone catches the scent of their qualities, regardless of their malevolent or benign intentions, their nose will become pure through that root of virtue. If anyone tastes the flavor of their teaching, regardless of their malevolent or benign intentions, their tongue will become pure through that root of virtue. If anyone makes physical contact with them, regardless of their malevolent or benign intentions, their body will become pure through that root of virtue.

—*Introduction to the Domain of the Inconceivable Qualities and Wisdom of the Tathāgatas* (*Tathāgataguṇajñānācintyaviṣayāvatāranirdeśa*)

Contents

Director's Note ix

Foreword

Exhibiting the Senses:
Encountering the Buddha at the National Museum of Asian Art
Debra Diamond xi

Introduction
Robert DeCaroli and Donald S. Lopez Jr. 1

Sight

Avoiding Eye Contact: The Negative Aspects of Sight in Early South Asian Buddhism
Robert DeCaroli 19

Seeing Splendor and Envisioning Hell: The Moral Economy in Thai-Buddhist Merit-Making
Melody Rod-ari 43

Sound

Bewildering Sounds of the Bardo
Kurtis R. Schaeffer 65

The Sound of Music
Donald S. Lopez Jr. 89

SMELL

What Is *Bad* about Bad Smell? Relativity, Relationship, and Revelation in the Buddhist Olfactory Imagination
LINA VERCHERY 107

Thus Have I Smelled
JOHN S. STRONG 125

TASTE

Bad Taste: The Case of the Five Pungent Vegetables
JAMES ROBSON 145

Sweetness and Power: The Buddhist Transformation of Taste
D. MAX MOERMAN 167

TOUCH

Infectious Touch and the Buddha's *Seven Zombies Spell* (*Saptavetāḍaka-dhāraṇī*)
BRYAN J. CUEVAS 183

A Science of Pleasurable Touch? Sex Rules in the Vinaya
REIKO OHNUMA 205

INDEX 225

CONTRIBUTORS 237

Director's Note

In 2017, the groundbreaking exhibition *Encountering the Buddha: Art and Practice across Asia*, generously funded by the Robert H. N. Ho Family Foundation, opened at the National Museum of Asian Art. Introducing and examining some of the principles of Buddhism for a museum audience, the exhibition displayed more than two hundred artworks spanning two millennia.

Building on the themes of the exhibition, a scholarly meeting was convened in 2021. Organized by Debra Diamond, Elizabeth Moynihan Curator for South and Southeast Asian Art at the National Museum of Asian Art; Robert DeCaroli, Professor of South and Southeast Asian Art History at George Mason University; and Donald S. Lopez Jr., Arthur E. Link Distinguished University Professor of Buddhist and Tibetan Studies at the University of Michigan, the meeting brought together a group of experts who have transformed the study of Buddhism. The essays in this volume are based on lively discussions that addressed several multisensory facets of Buddhist practices, ranging from an analysis of the perfumed fragrance of the Buddha to the taste of monastic cuisine.

The scholarly meeting and this volume, produced in collaboration with the museum's Freer Research Center and Wisdom Publications, reflect the ongoing commitment of the National Museum of Asian Art to foster a more nuanced understanding of Buddhism. We are deeply grateful to the Ho Foundation for supporting this publication and for providing the National Museum of Asian Art with the opportunity to share *Buddhism and the Senses* with the wider academic community.

Chase F. Robinson
Dame Jillian Sackler Director
Arthur M. Sackler Gallery and Freer Gallery of Art
Smithsonian's National Museum of Asian Art

Exhibiting the Senses: *Encountering the Buddha* at the National Museum of Asian Art

DEBRA DIAMOND

THE EXHIBITION *Encountering the Buddha: Art and Practice across Asia* (October 2017–January 2022) was the heart of a multiyear, multipartite project at the National Museum of Asian Art. The goals of the project, which in addition to the exhibition included print publications, digital features, and public programs, were to conceptualize, realize, and study effective strategies for museum presentations of Buddhist art and traditions.[1]

After putting together the lineaments of the project, I was joined by the co-curators Robert DeCaroli and Rebecca Bloom in 2015–16. Together we studied the museum's collections of Buddhist art, made many short lists, and brainstormed innovative display strategies and conceptual frameworks.[2] Our challenge was to illuminate Buddhist artworks and histories that spanned centuries and ranged geographically from Japan to Afghanistan. We were equally committed to creating an exhibition that was meaningful to both practicing Buddhists and visitors who had no knowledge of Buddhism.

Inspired by a turn within Buddhist studies toward finding commonalities among traditions, we explored and contextualized the exhibition objects through the lenses of art and practice. Our art-focused labels encouraged visitors to simultaneously discern transregional motifs and local traditions, and to marvel at the ways that artists inflected meaning and created beauty. Practice included considerations of how objects have agency, how devotees and communities engage with objects, how material

FIG. 1. A clip from the three-channel installation *The Texture of Practice: Sri Lanka's Great Stūpa*. National Museum of Asian Art, Smithsonian Institution, filmmaker Stanley J. Staniski. To see more, go to https://asia-archive.si.edu/exhibition/the-texture-of-practice-sri-lankas-great-stupa.

culture embodies key Buddhist concepts, and how art museums collect and frame objects created within Buddhist contexts.

Art museums traditionally focus on the visual. Precious objects are displayed on pedestals or in vitrines, and paintings are hung at eye level for visual delectation and close study. Incorporating the material *practice* of Buddhism into the exhibition, however, immediately begged the question of how to incorporate other senses, sensory experiences, and contexts.

The images and captions on these pages reveal the means through which we incorporated the awareness of the position and movement of one's own body (proprioception) and hearing into the exhibition, as well as the ambient environments of a Tibetan shrine and a Sri Lankan stūpa.

We emphasized the somatic experience of visitors. For example, we included a wall-size map (7.25 ft. × 6.5 ft.) studded with small light boxes. In each box, glowing photographs of Buddhist sites grabbed the attention of visitors, who often stretched their arms up to point to the Erdene Zuu Monastery in Mongolia, or crouched down to look at Borobudur Stupa in Java. By physically engaging the map with their entire bodies, visitors internalized the notion that Asia is vast and varied. We also created numerous small seat-

FIG. 2. The dense layering and uplighting in the Tibetan Buddhist shrine reconstruction privileged context and ambience. We allowed for darkness and shadows in order to approximate how sculptures and thangkas appear in some Himalayan shrines. It surprised visitors expecting to see individual objects with the clarity typical of art museums. National Museum of Asian Art, Smithsonian Institution, photo by Colleen Dugan. To enter the virtual shrine room and hear the Gyuto monks, go to https://asia.si.edu/interactives/sacred-spaces/shrine-room.html.

ing areas scattered with relevant books, which encouraged contemplation, further learning, and the simple, but not unimportant, act of resting.

Creating sensorial experiences grounded in Buddhism was more complicated, as we were keenly aware that every culture and tradition not only elaborates its own conceptions of the senses but also brings different sensorial components to religious practices. We most overtly gestured toward that multiplicity by contrasting a Vajrayāna shrine with the Ruwanwelisaya stūpa. The former was re-created, densely packed with objects, somewhat theatrically lit to mimic the flickering light of butter lamps, and accompanied by the chanting of monks (fig. 2).[3] The latter is a three-channel digital film that captures the Sri Lankan stūpa over the course of a day from sunrise to moonrise and features ambient sounds (fig. 3).[4]

Both installations were experiential. So as to not dilute their sensory impact, we placed all interpretative materials outside the two gallery spaces. The two immersive installations proved to be the most popular aspects of

Fig 3. The soundtrack levels of *The Texture of Practice* installation were set to allow the ambient sounds to pervade the space outside the room. One of the film's flickering screens was clearly visible behind a vitrine of stūpa-shaped objects from China, Tibet, and Indonesia. Long shots of the Ruwanwelisaya stūpa were periodically visible to visitors. The spatial gap between film and vitrine allows visitors to apprehend relationships between devotion, meaning, scale, and place without overdetermining the context or attributing present-day practices to historical objects. National Museum of Asian Art, Smithsonian Institution, photo by Colleen Dugan.

the exhibition; visitors spent the longest time in these spaces and praised them in exit interviews. Our Audience Study suggests, moreover, that their impact reverberated: visitors rated the objects in vitrines more highly than anticipated, as superior in quality and rarity, which we interpret as a result of their adjacency to the context-rich installations.

It was important to set the sound levels of each immersive to allow the chanting and ambient soundtracks to seep into different sections of the main gallery. Due to the breadth of the exhibition and the nascent state of sensory studies in Buddhist disciplines, the exhibition's use of sound was not historicized to the same extent as were its contributions to aesthetics and practice. However, the different soundtracks established that not all Buddhist practices sound alike, and they also underscored a diversity

FIG. 4. An installation of four fragmentary buddha heads engaged the viewers somatically. The heads were installed at eye level, giving visitors a sense of the height of the now lost bodies. Labels to the right and left of the quartet exemplified our curatorial approach. One label focused on the *lakṣaṇas* (physical attributes of the Buddha) that were deployed by artists across geographic and temporal spans; the other explained why broken buddha statues are valued in art museums but not in Buddhist contexts. National Museum of Asian Art, Smithsonian Institution, photo by Colleen Dugan.

(monastic-lay, geographic, temporal, etc.) that was otherwise inevitably contained by their location within a single exhibition.

The exhibition's multi-layered engagement with the visual, the aural, and the somatic resonated powerfully with visitors, encouraging closer looking and fostering a deeper connection to content. Indeed, over 62 percent of visitors reported losing track of time during their visit.

One of the most fulfilling and productive aspects of working on *Encountering the Buddha* was that it consistently fostered new ways of communicating with diverse publics as well as new discoveries and new research. Due to the generosity and flexibility of the Robert H. N. Ho Family Foundation grant, we were able to pivot during the pandemic, when the museum was largely closed to the public. We not only re-catalogued our Tibetan collection in this period but we also created an enduring immersive experience by commissioning the composer Philip Glass and his ensemble to respond to

Fig. 5. Reflections are common when spot-lit objects are displayed in vitrines within dark-colored rooms. Here, the contrast between the rough iron surface of two Ming dynasty *louhans* (arhats) and their illusory reflections emphasizes the tactility of the sculptures while conjuring thoughts of the immaterial. National Museum of Asian Art, Smithsonian Institution, photo by Colleen Dugan.

Fig. 6. The placement of a gilt-copper Padmasambhava (eighteenth century, Central Tibet) within its own vitrine immediately outside the shrine room contrasts the display strategy of post-Enlightenment art museums and the liturgical requirements of Tibetan Buddhist shrines. National Museum of Asian Art, Smithsonian Institution, photo by Colleen Dugan.

Encountering the Buddha. The resulting film by Arturo Béjar, which combines transcendent music with footage of the exhibition and a discussion with the composer, is exalting.[5]

Our exploratory engagement with the senses continued with an exciting and eye-opening colloquium with eminent scholars in the summer of 2021. Their discussions, now published in this volume, are both a fitting end to the project's five years of beauty, dialogue, and discovery and a promise of continued learning and deep insight.

Notes

1. The project was generously funded by the Robert H. N. Ho Family Foundation. Its individual elements were diverse and included the museum handbook *Paths to Perfection: Buddhist Art at the Freer|Sackler* (2017); a collaboration with Donald S. Lopez Jr. and the University of Michigan that led to an exhibition section on pilgrimage centered on *Hyecho's Journey: The World of Buddhism* (Lopez 2017) that included digital features for different age groups (http://hyecho-buddhist-pilgrim.asian.lsa.umich.edu/about.php); the virtual publication/app *Sacred Spaces: Tibetan Buddhist Shrines* on domestic, monastic, and roadside shrines (https://asia.si.edu/interactives/sacred-spaces); a lecture series organized by Robert DeCaroli at the National Museum of Asian Art ("Encounters with Buddhism," 2019); and an exhibition-inspired concert by the Philip Glass Ensemble (https://www.youtube.com/watch?v=CqaIJvNcJcE). The most complete links to these offerings can be found at https://asia.si.edu/exhibition/encountering-the-buddha-art-and-practice-across-asia/.
2. Our process was collaborative: we settled on the framework in consultation with the museum director, Julian Raby, the project adviser, Donald S. Lopez Jr., and a cross-departmental team of museum colleagues.
3. The Gyuto Monks Tantric Choir, from the recording *The Perfect Jewel: Sacred Chants of Tibet*, HRT15022, courtesy of Smithsonian Folkways Recordings.
4. *The Texture of Practice: Sri Lanka's Great Stupa*, ambient sound, no narration, 10:05 minutes, is a film made for the exhibition by Stanley J. Staniski; producer, Debra Diamond; content advisers and location coordinators, Lakshika Senarath Gamage and Sriyani Senarath Gamage; editor, Penny Trams; sound recordist and camera assistant, Janith Jayasekara; production assistant, Sachin Sanjeev.
5. *Art in Practice: Encountering the Buddha with the Philip Glass Ensemble*, https://www.youtube.com/watch?v=CqaIJvNcJcE.

Bibliography

The Freer Gallery of Art and the Arthur M. Sackler Gallery. 2017. *Paths to Perfection: Buddhist Art at the Freer|Sackler.* Edited by Debra Diamond. Washington, DC: Giles.

Jay, Martin. 2011. "In the Realm of Senses: An Introduction." *The American Historical Review* 116.2: 307–15.

———. 2014. *Sensational Religion: Sensory Cultures in Material Practice.* Edited by Sally M. Promey. New Haven, CT: Yale University Press.

Lopez, Donald S., Jr. 2017. *Hyecho's Journey: The World of Buddhism.* Chicago: University of Chicago Press.

Introduction

ROBERT DECAROLI & DONALD S. LOPEZ JR.

WHEN THE EMPEROR AŚOKA'S SON was born, the child's eyes were so beautiful that he was named Kuṇāla, after a bird renowned for its striking eyes. When the boy had grown, his father took him to a wise monk for training in the Dharma. The monk warned Kuṇāla that his eyes, captivating to all who saw him, could be a source of suffering: "Reflect constantly, O prince, that the eye is by its nature perishable, that it is the source of a thousand sorrows; becoming too attached to it, many ordinary men commit actions that make their misfortune."

Aśoka had several wives, one of whom lusted after Kuṇāla, telling him, "At the sight of the ravishing look in your eyes, of your beautiful body, of your charming eyes, all my body burns like dried straw that the forest fire consumes." As in the biblical story of Joseph, Kuṇāla resisted her advances, and like Potiphar's wife, Aśoka's queen plotted her revenge. When Kuṇāla was sent by his father to quell a rebellion in another city, she forged a letter in the name of the emperor, ordering that Kuṇāla be arrested and that his eyes be plucked out.

So virtuous was Kuṇāla and so beautiful were his eyes that the people resisted, only consenting when Kuṇāla insisted that they carry out what he believed was his father's command. When the first eye was plucked out and placed in his palm, the prince declared, "Why thus do you not see shapes as you did a moment ago, crude globe of flesh? How mistaken and how blameworthy, the insane who become attached to you, saying: 'It is me.'" Upon reciting these words, Kuṇāla became a stream enterer, the first of the four stages of enlightenment.

Kuṇāla was a skilled musician with a beautiful singing voice. Now blind and destitute, he returned to the capital, playing his lute and singing his songs in the streets of the city. He was reunited with his father when Aśoka heard a familiar voice that sang, "If your mind, indulged in sin, is tormented by the sufferings of existence and if you desire happiness in this world, hasten to renounce forever the objects of the senses."[1]

This story appears in the *Legend of Aśoka* (*Aśokāvadāna*), a work that is difficult to date. Following the convention of estimating the dates of Indian Buddhist texts based on the date of their translation into Chinese, we can note that such a translation was made around 300 CE, some five hundred years after the reign of the famous emperor. The story told here was translated from the Sanskrit into French by Eugène Burnouf in 1844, making it one of the earliest Buddhist Sanskrit texts to appear in a European language. Little in the legend is regarded as historically accurate. Our interest here, however, is not so much the historical evidence, but those eyes, things of captivating beauty in one moment, objects of revulsion gruesomely cupped in the palm of a blinded prince in the next.

This story, and this volume, suggest that Buddhism has a complicated relation with the five senses, careening between the extremes of indulgence and rejection, delight and disgust, rarely finding a middle way. Buddhist texts describe the visual beauties of various pure lands, where the trees are made of gold and their leaves are made of jewels, making music when rustled by the wind. They also describe horrific visions of charnel grounds, where all manner of ghouls devour the decomposing dead. Buddhist texts describe the most beautiful sound, the voice of the Buddha. They also describe a hell in which beings are born with weapons in their hands, killing each other in hand-to-hand combat. When all are dead, a voice from the sky shouts, "Revive," and it all begins again, killing and being killed for millions of years. Buddhist texts describe all manner of fragrances. Indeed, one of the eight types of non-humans is the *gandharva*, a kind of celestial musician said not to consume solid food but to live on fragrances; the beauty of their music and the miracle of their olfaction suggests that the Sanskrit term should be translated as something more elegant than "odor eater." Buddhist stories are particularly obsessed with a type of sandalwood called *gośīrṣa*, said to be cool to the touch; incense was used not only as an offering to the gods above but to mask the odors of the all-too-human world below. The Buddha's last meal was a delicacy called "pig's delight," which caused him to suffer a bout of dysentery that led to his death. Tantric texts declare that buddhahood is achieved through the bliss of orgasm, yet a nun is expelled from the order if she allows a man to touch her clothed body anywhere between the collarbone and the knee. What, then, are the Buddhist views of the five senses?

The Abhidharma

The Buddhists were one of several philosophical schools in ancient India, each of which had theories to explain sense experience. For the Sāṅkhya school, there are twenty-four principles (*tattva*) that constitute the material world. Five of them are the five senses. The Jains argued that all elements of the material world have sense experience, with humans and animals having all five senses, flying insects having four (lacking hearing), crawling insects having three (lacking hearing and sight), worms having only two (touch and taste), and inanimate objects having only the sense of touch. Thus in Jainism, not only do plants have consciousness, but rocks, water, fire, and wind do as well; they are sentient. We note here that sight and hearing are unique to humans and animals; they are also especially prized in Buddhism.

The most systematic description of sense experience in Buddhist literature is found in the Abhidharma, that section of the canon devoted to psychology, ontology, cosmology, and epistemology. Here we find the five senses and their functions described in detail, in descending order from their location on the body: eye, ear, nose, tongue, and body. Sense perception for each of the five is produced from the interaction of three conditions. The first, called the "dominant condition" (*adhipatipratyaya*), is the physical sense organ itself. The Buddhists describe five organs (each called an *indriya*, or "power") composed of subtle matter (and therefore invisible) that make sense perception possible. Each has its own shape. Hence the sense organ of the eye, located in the pupil, is shaped like a cumin flower; the sense organ of the ear is shaped like the end of a twisted roll of birchbark paper; the sense organ of the nose is shaped like two hollow needles, one in each nostril; the sense organ of the tongue is shaped like many tiny half-moons. The sense organ of the body is the shape of the body itself. If a sense organ is damaged, perception by that sense is not possible. It is these five sense organs, each physical, that come in contact with the five objects of the senses.

The second condition is called the "immediately preceding condition" (*samanantarapratyaya*). This is the moment of consciousness immediately prior to the sense experience, necessary because most schools of Buddhism famously do not believe in a permanent self that provides a foundation for consciousness. Instead, the person is a series of moments of consciousness, a continuum of cause and effect that has no beginning in time and that ends only with the achievement of nirvāṇa. Thus, in order for a sense object to be experienced, there must be a previous moment of consciousness, any kind of consciousness, for the moment of sense experience to follow. The third and most obvious cause of sense experience is the object, called the "object condition" (*ālambanapratyaya*): the form, sound, smell, taste, or object of touch experienced by the sense consciousness. When these three conditions come together, the sense consciousness is produced. From that contact comes feeling, either pleasurable, painful, or neutral.

Buddhist philosophy makes a sharp distinction between mind and matter, or in the language of the tradition, consciousness (*vijñāna*) and form (*rūpa*). Thus, one of the persistent questions in Buddhist epistemology is whether something that is material (a sense object) can be directly perceived by something that is immaterial (a sense consciousness). Those schools that answer this question in the negative posit the existence of something called the "aspect" (*ākara*), a kind of image that the physical object projects toward the sense organ. It is this immaterial image that the immaterial sense organ perceives. But even the advocates of the aspect disagree on exactly what the aspect is and how it works.[2]

It is also in the Abhidharma literature that one finds the most systematic classification of the objects of each of the senses.[3] Like other schools of Indian philosophy, Buddhism has something of a fetish for enumeration (likely derived from its origins as an oral tradition that relied heavily on memorization). And so here we find some lists. Thus, the eye consciousness perceives colors and shapes. There are four primary colors—blue, red, yellow, and white—and eight secondary colors—cloud, smoke, dust, mist, shadow, sunlight, light, and darkness. We would not think of these eight as colors but perhaps as conditions that affect the perception of colors. There are eight shapes: long, short, round, square, high, low, even, and uneven. Yet even in this apparently banal list there is a Buddhist message: what we see with the eyes are not people or things that we like or dislike; what we see are simply colors and shapes onto which our mind projects all manner of meanings.

There are four kinds of sounds. The first are sounds made by a living being (or literally, "sound caused by elements connected with consciousness"), such as the sound of the voice or the clapping of hands. The second are sounds not made by a living being ("sound caused by elements not connected with consciousness"), like the sound of water or the sound of wind. The third are sounds that convey some meaning, such as speech. The fourth are sounds that do not convey meaning. Each of these is further divided into the pleasant and the unpleasant. These categories of sound are obviously not mutually exclusive. Thus, there are meaningful sounds made by a living being that are pleasant, such as the words of the Buddha, and there are meaningful sounds made by a living being that are unpleasant, such as harsh words. There are meaningless sounds made by a living being that are pleasant, such as the sound of snapping fingers, and there are meaningless sounds made by a living being that are unpleasant, like the sound of someone being struck with a fist.

Because of the extraordinary powers of a buddha, there are meaningful sounds not made by a living being that are pleasant; the example that is given is the rustling of the leaves taking the form of the words of the Dharma through the power of a buddha. A buddha is also able to make the leaves of a tree take the form of a reprimand; this would be the unpleasant category. More common are sounds not caused by a living being, which can be pleasant (like the sound of a drum) or unpleasant (like the sound of a landslide).[4]

There are six tastes or flavors: sweet, sour, salty, pungent, bitter, and astringent; umami is not mentioned. There are four odors: good, bad, excessive, and not excessive. Objects of touch are of eleven types: earth (solidity), water (wetness), fire (heat), wind (motility), smooth, rough, heavy, light, cold, hunger, and thirst. It is noteworthy that pleasurable and painful (or good and bad), found in the list of sounds and flavors, do not appear in the list of objects of touch. This suggests that good and bad sounds and flavors are naturally good or bad, while physical pleasure and pain are feelings that result from contact with objects of touch, feelings that are the result of past karma. One of the Buddhist examples of the suffering of change is that feelings of warmth and cold can quickly change from pleasurable to painful.

The Creation Myth

What has been provided here is the technical description of the senses and their function, a topic known only to scholar-monks, a tiny fraction of the Buddhist community over the long history of Buddhism. Perhaps a better source of insight into Buddhist attitudes toward the senses is to be found not in philosophy but in narrative, the myriad stories depicted in words and in art across the Buddhist world, the stories that Buddhists know. As is the case with other religions, particular insights can be gained from the creation myth.

If Buddhism has a legend of the fall, it is found in a text called the *Account of Origins* (*Aggañña Sutta*). Here, shortly after the formation of the world, hosts of angelic beings arrive in the sky above to populate it, brought there by their past karma. They can fly, they are luminous, they have no need to eat and so have no organs to excrete waste, they are without gender and without genitals. At that time, the surface of the earth is covered with a frothy substance. Eventually, one of these beings swoops down, scoops a drop of the frothy substance with its finger, and touches the finger to its tongue. It tastes sweet. Enjoying the flavor, it swoops down for another taste. The other beings soon follow, eventually consuming the sweet substance by the handful. Because they are consuming this food, their bodies come to lose their luster, causing the sun and the moon to appear in the sky. Because they are consuming this food, their bodies become heavy, no longer able to fly. Soon, organs appear on their bodies to excrete waste. Male and female sex organs appear. Eventually, a male and female put them to use. Their coupling disgusts the other beings, who throw clods of dirt at them, causing the couple to flee to the forest, returning later to build a dwelling so that they can engage in sex in private. The frothy surface turns into a kind of vine and then into a naturally growing rice that can be harvested each day. When the beings begin to horde rice, it stops growing naturally and has to be cultivated. Soon there is a need for labor, plots of land, and private property, and for a king to adjudicate disputes.[5]

This is the Buddhist story of the fall, where gender, sexuality, the built environment, private property, and rulership are all seen as the unfortunate outcome of one being touching a sweet substance to its tongue. The sin, in this case, was not tasting the substance. The sin was going back for more. From the perspective of the Garden of Eden, it wasn't the first bite. It was the second.

In the Buddhist description of the function of the sense organs, contact between a sense organ and a sense object creates a feeling, a feeling that can be pleasant, unpleasant, or neutral. That feeling is beyond our control; it is the result of past karma. If Buddhism has free will, it comes in our response to that feeling; we can become attached to that feeling—loving the pleasant and hating the unpleasant—or we can remain equanimous and unattached. Attachment to sense experience binds us in the cycle of rebirth; non-attachment frees us from it. This is evident from one of the many descriptions of the Buddha's enlightenment:

> That pleasure and delight arise owing to forms, that is the attraction, that is the addiction, of forms. The nature of the eye is impermanent, bound to suffering, subject to change and death. That is the affliction of forms . . . But when I truly understood these six internal sense fields, their attraction and addiction as such, their affliction as such, liberation from them as such, my enlightenment could be called true enlightenment, unsurpassed in the world with its *devas*, Māras, and Brahmās, among *devas*, human beings, Brahmās, *samaṇas*, and Brahmins. Then knowledge and insight arose within me: "My liberation of mind is unshakable. This is my final existence. Never again will there be rebirth for me."[6]

The Buddha makes the point even more bluntly in this famous passage from the Saṃyutta Nikāya: "The eye is impermanent . . . The ear is impermanent . . . The nose is impermanent . . . The tongue is impermanent . . . The body is impermanent . . . The mind is impermanent. What is impermanent is suffering. What is suffering is nonself. What is nonself should be seen as it really is with correct wisdom thus: 'This is not mine, this I am not, this is not my self.'"[7] And should we think that such an attitude is limited to India, we find this passage in an early Chinese Buddhist apocryphon called the *Scripture on the Fifty Contemplations* (*Wushi jiaoji jing*): "If a bodhisattva can guard his eyes so that visible forms do not appear . . . guard his ears so that sounds do not appear . . . guard his nose so that scents do not appear . . . guard his mouth so that tastes do not appear . . . guard his body so that bodily sensations do not appear, so that they return to extinction, [he in this manner] plants the sprouts of the Way."[8]

There is likely another lesson to be drawn from the Buddhist creation myth. When we examine the celestial beings more closely, they begin to look like monks and nuns—that is, monks and nuns who can fly. Monks and nuns shave their heads (and sometimes eyebrows) and wrap their bodies in robes to remove physical signs of gender and to hide their sex organs, organs that, according to the monastic code, are never to be put to use. In the early days of the Buddhist community, monks and nuns had no homes, living in the open, sometimes sheltered by a tree. Monks and nuns are also prohibited from tilling the soil and hence cultivating crops. Instead, food that they did not cultivate appears, not unlike the naturally growing rice of the story, in their begging bowls each morning. All of this suggests that in the perfect Buddhist world, there is little need for the pleasures of the senses; instead, we should hover above the world. This is confirmed in Buddhist descriptions of the pure lands, the heavenly "buddha fields" that abound in the Buddhist universe. In the most famous of these, the Land of Bliss (Sukhāvatī) of the buddha Amitābha, there is no need for physical food; its inhabitants simply visualize whatever food they would like to eat and their body is sustained as if they had eaten it. There is also no need for sex or traditional birth. In fact, there are no women present in this monastic realm. After their death in this world, the devotees of Amitābha appear in his world, emerging fully formed from a lotus.

The Three Realms

The Buddhist cosmos has three realms, in descending order.[9] The first is the formless realm, so-called because the beings reborn there have no senses;

they are only minds, blissfully absorbed in their objects. Its four heavens are named after those objects: infinite space, infinite consciousness, nothingness, and neither perception nor non-perception. Below (in the sense of level of concentration rather than location, since the formless realm has no location) is the realm of form, so-called because those reborn there retain some attachment to form, the object of the sense of sight. It has four levels, often simply called the first, second, third, and fourth concentrations. The gods of the realm of form have no need for food and so have only three senses: sight, hearing, and touch. The beings who inhabit the formless realm and the realm of form are classified as gods in Buddhism; those states are attained only through achieving the requisite deep level of meditation during their previous life as a human. If one achieves, for example, the second level of concentration of the realm of form through meditation practice in this life, one is reborn as a god of the realm of form in the next life.

Thus, the gods of these two realms have no senses in one realm and three senses in the other. It is only in the third realm, the lowest realm, our realm, that beings have five senses. It is called the "realm of desire," so-called because its inhabitants are attached to pleasing objects of sight, hearing, taste, smell, and touch. The gods of this realm, inhabitants of six heavens located either on the surface of the central mountain Meru or in the sky above it, are more familiar, in part because their sensory pleasures are simply magnified versions of our own. Indeed, the heavens of the realm of desire are essentially a fantasy land of human longing.

The gods live in palaces in a wonderland where everything is beautiful, serenaded by celestial musicians, garlanded with fragrant flowers, dining on ambrosia, and having rapturous sex. We learn in the story of the Buddha's cousin Nanda that the karmic result of keeping the vow of celibacy as a human is rebirth as a god who has centuries of sex with women so beautiful that when the Buddha takes Nanda to heaven to see them, he has to put a force field around the young monk to prevent him from dying of desire. The gods of the six heavens enjoy lifespans measured in the billions of years.

But the realm of desire is located in saṃsāra and so even its heavens are marked by impermanence, suffering, and no self. We learn that five signs portend the death of a god: their beautiful robes become stained, the garlands of flowers around their neck begin to wither, they begin to perspire, their body begins to smell, and their throne becomes uncomfortable. As we think about the five senses, we note that all of these signs, signs that occur for the first time in billions of years for a god but for humans are simply a daily annoyance, are all sensory, all physical, with the stains and withered flowers seen by the eye, the body odor smelled by the nose, the sweat and the discomfort felt by the body.

Thus, in the realm of desire, whether as a god or as a human, it is this attachment that dooms us to beginningless and potentially endless rebirth in saṃsāra. It is therefore not surprising that so much of Buddhist literature is devoted to overcoming that attachment. Its primary means of doing so is by deprecating sense experience, especially by showing that those things that bring us sensual pleasure in fact lead to all manner of physical and mental pain.

A Festival of the Senses

This does not mean that the senses have no positive purpose. In the nineteenth chapter of the *Lotus Sūtra*, we find a remarkable festival of the senses, which begins when the Buddha declares, "If sons or daughters of a virtuous family preserve this *Lotus Sūtra*, recite, explain, and copy it, they will attain eight hundred qualities of the eye, twelve hundred qualities of the ear, eight hundred qualities of the nose, twelve hundred qualities of the tongue, eight hundred qualities of the body, and twelve hundred qualities of the mind. These qualities will adorn the six sense faculties, purifying them all."[10] Fortunately, he does not list all of them, but the entire chapter is devoted to their enumeration, in prose and verse. With their eyes, they will be able to see the entire cosmos and all the beings that inhabit its realms, from the heavens to the hells. With their ears, they will hear all the sounds of the cosmos and all the beings in it. They will hear beautiful music but not become attached to it. They will hear the voices of the gods and the screams of the denizens of hell. They will hear bodhisattvas reciting the *Lotus Sūtra*. The senses of sight and hearing described here are variations on the well-known "divine eye" and "divine ear" of Indian literature, in Buddhism, listed as two of the six forms of super knowledge (*abhijñā*). Here, however, the Buddha repeatedly specifies that the powers gained by the expounders of the *Lotus*

Sūtra are not gained through attaining deeps states of meditation but are powers bestowed to the eyes and ears that they were born with, magically enhanced by their devotion.

The sense of smell, not the subject of particular attention in Buddhist literature, is enhanced in wondrous ways in this chapter of the *Lotus Sūtra*. As one might expect in the baroque world of the Mahāyāna, devotees of the sūtra will be able to detect and identify the fragrance of all manner of flowers, trees, and incense throughout the universe. They will also be able to identify all manner of humans, gods, and animals by their scent, recognizing not only who they are but where they are. They can smell gold and jewels and know where they are buried, they can smell jewelry and know its value. They can smell a woman and know if she is pregnant, knowing the sex of the child, whether the birth will be easy, and whether the child will be happy. Through their sense of smell, they know where monks are and what they are doing, whether they are meditating or reciting the sūtra.

The powers of the tongue gained by the expounders of the *Lotus Sūtra* not only allow them to discern all flavors but also provide them with an ability to preach the Dharma in a way that will attract all manner of gods and humans. Indeed, their eloquence will even attract the attention of the buddhas. The powers of the body are even more strange, with the bodies of the sūtra's devotees becoming not only as clear as crystal but also becoming a crystal ball, where they, and they alone, can see the entire world and all the beings in it.

There is much that one could say about this remarkable passage. We can note, however, that the vastly enhanced sensory powers bestowed upon the devotees of the *Lotus Sūtra* do not offer enhanced sensory pleasure. Instead, they offer knowledge. The sense of sight allows them to see all of the inhabitants of the universe, from the hells to the buddha fields. The sense of hearing allows them to hear the voices of those inhabitants, with special mention given to their ability to hear the *Lotus Sūtra* being taught. Their sense of smell allows them to experience the fragrance of all manner of flowers and trees, but this is described not as a form of pleasure but a form of knowledge. Indeed, their sense of smell allows them to identify things, sentient and insentient, knowing what they are, where they are, what value they possess, and, in the case of pregnant women, the destiny of their unborn children. The chapter's description of the sense of taste makes no mention of sublime flavors; instead it describes the enhanced eloquence of the tongue to preach the Dharma. And the enhancement of the body sense says nothing about sensual pleasure or even about the tactile, instead turning the opaque body into a clear crystal where the universe can be observed.

The Path

The senses of sight, hearing, and touch receive the most attention in Buddhist literature, perhaps because these are the most important senses for the monks who are the authors of that literature. Buddhist texts, and especially Buddhist philosophy, are filled with the language of sight and sound. Indeed, progress on the path to enlightenment makes repeated reference to the senses of seeing and hearing. We think immediately of the Pāli term *vipassanā*, in which the intensifier *vi-* is added to a word that means sight, creating the word commonly rendered in English as "insight." There is "right view" (*samyagdṛṣṭi*), one of two sense words (along with "right speech") among the eight elements of the noble path. A common term for a philosophical position in classical Indian literature is *darśana*, "view." In the *Diamond Sūtra*, we find this famous passage: "A shooting star, a clouding of the sight, a lamp, an illusion, a drop of dew, a bubble, a dream, a lightning flash, a thunder cloud: this is the way one should see the conditioned." Each of these is something that we see; the message of the passage is to see everything in this way: fleeting, deceptive, unreal.

Reminding us again that Buddhism began, and in many ways remains, an oral tradition, the first of the three levels of wisdom is the "wisdom arisen from hearing" (*śrutamayīprajñā*). When a monk or nun is described as learned, the term that is often translated is *bahuśruta*, literally "heard much." Bahuśrutīya is the name of one of the eighteen schools of mainstream Buddhism. This is not to say, however, that smell and taste are unimportant. Again, we find the motif of pleasure and renunciation, with the fragrances of flowers and incense, both in this world as well as the various heavenly realms and pure lands, described. Yet we also find the monastic code prohibiting monks and nuns from using perfumes. All manner of worldly and divine feasts are described, perhaps most famously the vegetarian feasts (sometimes called "maigre feasts") of Chinese Buddhism, offered to monks on festival days. The most important of these in East Asia was the so-called Ghost Festival, which derives from the story of the monk Maudgalyāyana (Mulian in Chinese) who found it impossible to offer food to his mother, who had been reborn as a hungry ghost. The Buddha informed him that the only way to feed the dead was to feed monks, with the merit produced by the gift being transformed into sustenance for the departed.[11]

Yet in the monastic code we find the rule that monks must consume whatever food is placed into their begging bowl, no matter how disgusting. Buddhaghosa's *Path of Purification* (*Visuddhimagga*) contains a lengthy chapter devoted entirely to the repulsiveness of food, where he describes chewing and swallowing: "When thus mashed up and besmeared, this peculiar compound now destitute of the [original] colour and smell is reduced to a condition as utterly nauseating as a dog's vomit in a dog's trough. Yet, notwithstanding that it is like this, it can still be swallowed because it is no longer in range of the eye's focus."[12] This emphasis on the disgusting qualities of human sense experience is not without purpose. These passages discourage identification with physical form and encourage escape from worldly rebirth. Indeed, earlier in the text he describes each of five sense organs as engines of disgust, describing the body as "the home of disease, the basis of painful states, perpetually oozing from the nine orifices like a chronic open carbuncle, from both of whose eyes eye-filth trickles, from whose ears comes ear-filth, from whose nostrils snot, from whose mouth food and bile and phlegm and blood, from whose lower outlets excrement and urine, and from whose ninety-nine thousand pores the broth of stale sweat seeps."[13]

The extremes that we observe in Buddhist attitudes toward the senses is nowhere more acute than in the case of the body and its sense of touch. The body is described as a site of danger and disgust, often in starkly misogynistic terms, throughout Buddhist literature.[14] In order to overcome lust, the Buddha prescribed meditation on the foulness of the human body, a practice that required monks to go to a charnel ground and stare at corpses in various states of decomposition, including the bloated, the livid, the festering, the cut up, the gnawed, the scattered, the hacked and scattered, the worm-infested, and the skeleton.

As is well known, the Buddhist monastic code is said to have developed organically, with the Buddha making rules only after a deed was performed by a monk or nun that he considered objectionable. Four deeds, called "downfalls" (*pārājika*), were considered sufficiently serious to require expulsion: killing, stealing, sexual intercourse, and lying (about spiritual attainments). Thus, the rule requiring celibacy was only established after the monk Sudinna had sexual intercourse with his former wife at his mother's request. But what could have occasioned a monk to commit murder? It seems that the Buddha recommended corpse meditation as a particularly effective means of overcoming lust, on one occasion leaving the community of monks to meditate in charnel grounds. When he returned, he found the ranks of the saffron robed considerably diminished and asked Ānanda where the other monks were. Ānanda replied that they had become so disgusted with their own bodies that they regarded it as like the carcass of an animal hung around their neck. To relieve themselves from this burden, they convinced another monk to slit their throats. The Buddha then declared that henceforth killing a human would result in expulsion from the community.[15] He also suggested that monks meditate on their breath.

Still, Buddhist texts, both mainstream and Mahāyāna, describe the human body in often stomach-churning detail. At the conclusion of his discussion of "meditation on the foul" (Pāli, *asubhabhāvanā*), where ten stages of the decomposition of a corpse are recommended as objects for developing concentration (Pāli, *jhāna*), Buddhaghosa declares that, despite our best efforts, the body's disgusting nature is impossible to hide. And yet we continue to seek delight in delusion:

> But by rubbing out the stains on its teeth with tooth sticks and mouthwashing and all that, by concealing its private parts under several cloths, by daubing it with various scents and salves, by pranking it with nosegays and such things, it is worked up into a state that permits of its being taken as "I" and "mine." So men delight in women and women in men without perceiving the true nature of its characteristic foulness, now masked by this adventitious adornment. But in the ultimate sense there is no place here even the size of an atom fit to lust after.

> And then, when any such bits of it as head hairs, body hairs, nails, teeth, spittle, snot, excrement, or urine have dropped off the body, beings will not touch them; they are ashamed, humiliated, and disgusted. But as long as any one of these things remains in it, though it is just as repulsive, they take it as agreeable, desirable, permanent, pleasant, self, because they are wrapped in the murk of ignorance and dyed with affection and greed for self.[16]

This Book

Our senses are so central to the way that we understand our lives and the world around us that we rarely think to doubt them or consider how cultural and historical factors shape our interpretation of the experience they provide. Our perceptions can have a deeply personal aspect that also colors our responses. We are conditioned by our own experiences, and those assumptions can carry over into our work, including the work of scholarship. Acknowledging these inherently human biases is a necessary starting point for historicizing the role of the senses.

The reader will have noted above in the discussion of sense experience in the Abhidharma literature that only one categorization of the senses occurs repeatedly, the simple dyad of good and bad, variously rendered as pleasant or unpleasant. We assume, therefore, that that dyad was familiar to the ancient authors of the Abhidharma. We also note that it is familiar to us, in a very different time and a very different place, as we say or think to ourselves on a daily basis: This looks good. This looks bad. That sounds good. That sounds bad. This smells good. This smells bad. That tastes good. That tastes bad. This feels good. This feels bad. Thus, inspired both by the Abhidharma and by our shared experience, the present volume considers the five senses, each in two instantiations: the good and the bad. However, as will be clear from the essays, good and bad are often a matter of perspective. Fatty and sugary foods are good insofar as they are delicious, but modern medicine often identifies them as bad because of their detrimental effects on the body, especially when eaten in excess. These complications are not just found in contemporary sources, they also characterize the views of authors writing in the past, and the essays in this volume reflect some of that ambiguity.

For example, in Rod-ari's essay on miraculous and menacing sculptural imagery in Southeast Asia, are the scenes of hell "bad" because they are terrifying, or "good" because they dissuade people from negative actions that lead to rebirth in those hells? Does Schaeffer's study of music inspired by the liminal state of the bardo count as a negative because the bardo itself is frightening? Presumably, the composer and audience for the work might choose to describe the work's experimental sounds in positive terms. Likewise, sexual acts are generally pleasurable and might therefore be considered positive. Indeed, in some forms of Buddhist tantric practice, the bliss of sexual intercourse is essential for the achievement of buddhahood. Yet many of Ohnuma's Vinaya sources view any sexual activity in almost criminal terms. It would not be difficult to list additional examples from the volume, but the point is clear. In each instance context is key. Because of this religiously and historically contingent ambiguity, individual contributors to this volume were free to define the positive or negative aspects of each sense as they deemed appropriate within their studies. The results, both within individual essays and in dialogue with other works in the volume, reveal the tensions within the scholarship and shed light on the discourse of the senses within Buddhism itself.

Just as sense experience is suppressed in Buddhism, the study of sense experience was largely repressed in Buddhist studies for decades. It is striking how closely scholars of Buddhism have seemed to conform to the monastic code. Thus, apart from the reading of the texts, little attention was paid to the visual. Apart from the sound of the chanting of scriptures, there was little attention to sound. Apart from scent of incense burning on the altar of a temple, there was little mention of smell. Apart from occasional discussions of vegetarianism, there was little mention of taste. And because of both academic prudishness and the complex of Buddhist restrictions around sex, there has been little mention of touch. We said above that there has been little attention to the visual. That is only true when we exclude art history from Buddhist studies, as has so often been the case. It is therefore likely significant that the impetus for this volume, a book that seeks to overcome the Buddhological suppression of the senses, was occasioned by an exhibition of Buddhist art.

This collection of essays is a recognition and celebration of this new direction, a direction that has been vital for humanizing Buddhist history. Grounded in human experience and sensation, the essays collected here seek to contribute meaningfully to the forward momentum. The concept and organization of this project is thus meant as an invitation to the reader to think about the senses in a focused way. By foregrounding aspects of practice and sensory experience, the essays together seek to shift our understanding of Buddhism from the conceptual to the practical, from the idealized to the human, from the abstract to the grounded, from the mind to the body. It is our hope that this volume will encourage further work on the experience of Buddhist practice, in the broadest sense of that term.

Notes

1. Burnouf 2010, 386. For a more recent translation, see Strong 1983. There are two versions of the story of Aśoka preserved in Chinese. The first is the *A yu wang zhuan* (*Aśokāvadāna*), translated in the late third century by the Parthian monk An Faqin. The second is the *A yu wang jing* (*Aśokasūtra*) translated by Saṅghapāla in 512. The latter text has been translated into English by Li Rongxi 1993.
2. Changkya Rölpai Dorjé 2019, 157–59.
3. The following description is drawn from the most famous of the Abhidharma texts, the *Treasury of Abhidharma* (*Abhidharmakośa*) by the fourth-century Indian monk Vasubandhu. See La Vallée Poussin 1988, vol. 1, 55–150.
4. Hopkins 1983, 227.
5. For a translation and study of the *Aggañña Sutta*, see Collins 1993.
6. Nakamura 2000, 205–6.
7. Bodhi 2000, 2.1133.
8. Greene 2017, 69.
9. An influential description of the Buddhist cosmos is found in the third chapter of the *Treasury of Abhidharma* (*Abhidharmakośa*) by Vasubandhu. See La Vallée Poussin 1988, vol. 2, 365–550.
10. Kubo and Yuyama 2007, 251.
11. Teiser 1996.
12. Buddhaghosa 2010, 341.
13. Buddhaghosa 2010, 183.
14. Wilson 1996.

15. Horner 1949, 116ff.
16. Buddhaghosa 2010, 183–84.

Bibliography

Bodhi, Bhikkhu, trans. 2000. The *Connected Discourses of the Buddha: A New Translation of the Saṃyutta Nikāya*. 2 vols. Oxford: Pali Text Society.

Buddhaghosa. 2010. *The Path of Purification (Visuddhimagga)*. Translated by Bhikkhu Ñāṇamoli. Kandy: Buddhist Publication Society.

Burnouf, Eugène. 2010. *Introduction to the History of Indian Buddhism*. Translated by Katia Buffetrille and Donald S. Lopez Jr. Chicago: University of Chicago Press.

Changkya Rölpai Dorjé. 2019. *Beautiful Ornament of Mount Meru: A Presentation of Classical Indian Philosophy*. Translated by Donald S. Lopez Jr. Somerville, MA: Wisdom Publications.

Collins, Steven. 1993. "The Discourse on What Is Primary (*Aggañña Sutta*)." *Journal of Indian Philosophy* 21.4: 301–93.

Greene, Eric M. 2017. "Doctrinal Dispute in the Earliest Phase of Chinese Buddhism—Anti-Mahāyāna Polemics in the *Scripture on the Fifty Contemplations*." *Journal of the International Association of Buddhist Studies* 40: 63–109.

Hopkins, Jeffrey. 1983. *Meditation on Emptiness*. London: Wisdom Publications.

Horner, I. B., trans. 1949. *The Book of Discipline (Vinaya-Piṭaka), Vol. 1 (Suttavibhaṅga)*. London: Luzac and Co.

Kubo, Tsugunari, and Akira Yuyama, trans. 2007. *The Lotus Sutra*. rev. 2nd ed. Berkeley, CA: Numata Center for Buddhist Translation and Research.

La Vallée Poussin, Louis de. 1988. *Abhidharmakośa Bhāśyam*, vols. 1 and 2. Translated by Leo Pruden. Berkeley, CA: Asian Humanities Press.

Li Rongxi, trans. 1993. *The Biographical Scripture of King Aśoka*. Berkeley, CA: Numata Center for Buddhist Translation and Research.

Nakamura, Hajime. 2000. *Gotama Buddha: A Biography Based on the Most Reliable Texts*, vol. 1. Tokyo: Kosei Publishing.

Strong, John S. 1984. *The Legend of King Aśoka: A Study and Translation of the Aśokāvadāna*. Princeton, NJ: Princeton University Press.

Teiser, Stephen F. 1996. *The Ghost Festival in Medieval China*. Princeton, NJ: Princeton University Press.

Wilson, Liz. 1996. *Charming Cadavers: Horrific Figurations of the Feminine in Indian Buddhist Hagiographic Literature*. Chicago: University of Chicago Press.

Avoiding Eye Contact: The Negative Aspects of Sight in Early South Asian Buddhism

ROBERT DECAROLI

IN THE MID-1960S Richard Gombrich documented Sri Lankan ceremonies performed to consecrate newly enshrined images of the Buddha.[1] Such rituals culminated with rites intended to "open the eyes" of the Buddha. This entailed inviting a specialist to paint in the eyes of the statue, a cause for celebration in the local community. Gombrich's monastic informants did not fully approve of these rituals because they understood the image as merely an inert reminder of the Buddha. Their attitude might be characterized as resigned tolerance, seeing the ritual as misguided but essentially harmless.[2] By contrast, the local artists and broader community took the consecration ceremony very seriously. Skilled specialists (*sittaru*) were called in to paint the eyes. They did so by using a mirror to avoid direct eye contact with the Buddha's gaze. The power of the image's vision was considered so potent that, even after taking these precautions, the craftsman was blindfolded and led from the temple so that he would first look upon a waterpot or other prepared vessel that could be symbolically sacrificed, thus dissipating the residual power.[3] Such care and such potency certainly imply that the Buddha, or some measure of his identity, was resident in the completed statue. Gombrich characterized the dichotomy between the knowledge of the Buddha's absence and the efficacious power of his image as a tension between cognitive and affective ways of thinking, both of which were embedded in the Sri Lankan Buddhist worldview of the 1960s.[4]

It might be tempting to characterize this dichotomy as one between the educated saṅgha and the parochial laity, or more broadly as traditional practices confronting newer modes of scientific rationalism informed by modernism and the colonial experience. Although such powerful cultural and political forces must have certainly played a role in the participants' understanding of the event, tensions over the presence or absence of the Buddha are far older than the modern period. Whether ancient or modern, however, questions about vision—both the devotees' and the Buddha's—have remained central to the debate over his presence.

There has never been a single Buddhist way to understand the Buddha's images. Multiple, often contradictory, views of what it means to see an image of the Buddha have been present in Buddhism since the inception of the image tradition. In fact, because of the way the depictions of the Buddha were intentionally avoided prior to the start of the first century CE, one must conclude that this topic was an issue even before the creation of the earliest Buddha images. Artists, donors, and members of the saṅgha justified avoiding his depiction in various ways, some of which I have discussed elsewhere.[5]

Does his depiction imply his presence and accessibility? Might images undercut the finality of nirvāṇa, and if not, then how can image use be an effective mode of religious practice? In these and other ways, the tension over the presence of the Buddha is, in part, connected to the importance of vision in Buddhism. This concern also manifests in textual sources as a desire to regulate how people understand their interactions with figural artwork.[6] For better or worse, vision, more than any other sense, has the power to impact how we behave. A natural corollary of this is the recognition that some aspects of sight must be regulated.

My primary goal is to explain how the formalized ritual use of vision and eye contact (*darśana*) led to a change in the way statues of the Buddha were made after centuries of uniformity and consistency. This change was contingent on the increased use of sculpture as a focus for Brahmanical rituals that gained popularity in fourth-century South Asia and was eagerly embraced by the Gupta royalty. Before elaborating, however, an overview of how vision was regulated by the Buddhist community will be helpful.

Not for the Eyes of the Saṅgha

It is no exaggeration to state that almost every rule in the Buddhist codes of behavior (Vinaya texts) for the saṅgha is predicated on a monk, nun, layperson, or god witnessing improper behavior and reporting it to the Buddha. Nothing escapes scrutiny. All manner of monastic behavior—ranging from terrible acts of violence to the style of a monk's undergarments and the length of his nostril hairs—are regulated.[7] In many cases, blameworthy actions are forbidden because they are inherently contrary to the Buddha's teachings. In other instances, however, as in the case of the underwear and nose hairs, rules appear to have been set in place exclusively to prevent public misconceptions or disapproval. In these cases, one might easily assert that concerns over public perception of the behavior prompted the rule rather than any inherently immoral quality of the act itself.

This is particularly apparent in rules related to monks undertaking menial chores and physical labor. Gregory Schopen has noted how the Mūlasarvāstivāda Vinaya requires monks to avoid being seen by the public when performing activities that might be associated with pollution or people of low social status.[8] Manual labor, smithing, leather working, and cutting hair were all permissible, and at times necessary, activities. But in each case monks were allowed to perform them only in private, away from the gaze of the public. Such activities were to be done privately in order to preserve the community's positive image and not generate negative public opinion. In other words, some activities that were permissible for the saṅgha were not suitable viewing for the public.

Just as there were things the public should not see monks or nuns doing, certain sights acceptable for the lay community were forbidden to the saṅgha. There is a rule, for example, that limits the subject matter used for adorning the monastery. This rule is found in the Mūlasarvāstivāda Vinaya as well as in the Chinese version of the Sarvāstivāda Vinaya.[9] As is standard for Vinaya texts, the restriction is predicated by a story that explains and justifies it. In both versions, a monk is feeling wistful and begins to draw an image of the young bride he left in order to join the saṅgha. At this inopportune moment a senior monk sees the image and scolds the amateur artist—ultimately bringing the matter to the Buddha. This leads to the pronouncement of a rule forbidding monks from creating images of living beings. This passage seems primarily intended to counter the titillating aspects of figural art that may be contrary to celibate monastic life; however, it is also likely that it was intended to prevent public disapproval.

For example, the Sarvāstivāda Vinaya contains rules explicitly preventing the decoration of stūpas with images of "men and women coupling."[10] In the Cullavagga of the Pāli Vinaya, similar concerns are expressed. It contains a general restriction on any representations of men or women used as decoration in monastic dwellings. In both of these cases there is good reason to think that public perception played a role in the formalization of the rule. The Pāli Vinaya makes this apparent by framing the rule with a story about guests in the monastery who are shocked to see depictions of people on the walls of a monk's residence and begin to question the legitimacy of the entire Buddhist monastic community.[11] Presented in this fashion, the Buddha's restriction would seem to have as much to do with external perceptions as internal discipline. Either way, these rules identify visual imagery that was suitable for the laity but deemed inappropriate for members of the monastic community.

This is certainly not the only rule in the Vinaya requiring saṅgha members to control their gaze. As is well known, members of the monastic community were always expected to conduct themselves with proper decorum, and this was especially true when traveling outside the monastery. At these times they were required to direct their eyes downward.[12] This restriction is emphasized in the *Mahāparinibbāna Sutta.* When the disciple Ānanda asks the Buddha how monks should act toward the women they encounter while on pilgrimage, he instructs monks to simply not see them.[13] The self-control required to regulate their vision was seen as conducive to both monastic practice and the positive public perception of the saṅgha. In short, appearances mattered. What members of the monastic community saw and what they allowed others to see them doing were of deep concern to the writers of the monastic codes. It is also clear that a great deal of this concern goes beyond the moral implications of actions and aims to forestall any criticism by witnesses. What an individual sees can impact their thinking. The visual, therefore, holds great potential for misunderstandings that can place both the individual and the Buddhist institution at risk.

Seeing the Buddha

The Buddhist relationship with sight is a complex one. In many South Asian contexts, vision and sight were (and continue to be) synonymous with understanding.[14] For example, in the *Divine Stories* (*Divyāvadāna*), a monk wishes to see the Buddha's physical body (*rūpakāya*) to complement his understanding of the Buddha's teachings, or Dharma body (*dharmakāya*). For the monk in the story, seeing both aspects of the Buddha's nature ultimately benefits his spiritual advancement.[15] Being in the presence of a living buddha is frequently described as one of the greatest possible karmic rewards, because seeing and hearing a buddha preach provides an unparalleled opportunity for insight and awakening. For those not fortunate enough to live in the time of a buddha, systems of internal visualization were created to replicate the experience.

The Pāli tradition introduced a meditative process known as *buddhānussati* (Skt. *buddhānusmṛti*). In this form of meditation one "recollects the Buddha"—that is, one envisions the image of the Buddha in one's mind so as to benefit from being in the Buddha's presence as he preaches. In some cases, this practice has been linked to the use of images, but typically physical images are not required.[16] In fact, the meditative practice reveals some mistrust of physical forms and the attachments they may engender. Sessions of *buddhānusmṛti* conclude with the practitioner reversing the process of embodiment and systematically dismissing the Buddha's form. This exercise may confirm the value in seeing the Buddha's form but also provides a firm reminder of his absence.

The viewer's mindset when looking at an image is often presented as the key to positive or negative outcomes. For example, Andy Rotman has written at length about a concept known as *prasāda* and its role in the *avadāna* literature. He describes it as a state in which external stimuli—typically seeing the Buddha's image—inspire acts of generosity and kindness. This compassionate mindset, which Rotman describes as a kind of arousal, automatically places one in the proper mental state for performing meritorious acts.[17] In other words, what one sees affects one's attitudes and one's actions. This potentially opens the way to great karmic rewards, or might just as easily inspire wicked deeds and the negative karma they engender. Vision is a two-edged sword and was therefore subject to great deal of (occasionally contradictory) regulation and commentary. Although *prasāda* might be understood as an essentially positive form of vision, I discuss it here because it is one of several rationales that allowed for the use of images without necessitating the Buddha's presence or attention. In other words, the statue could be inert, the Buddha could remain absent in nirvāṇa, and the use of images could still bear results for the devout because the simple act of looking at it inspires (or actively produces) acts of good karma.

While vision could occasionally be conducive to attaining religious goals, it was more often understood as an impediment or potential source of attachments. The difference between a negative or positive outcome was largely contingent on the viewer's frame of mind. Therefore, defining how viewers should understand an image of the Buddha was of particular concern to Buddhist authors, but they provide little consensus on the correct approach. The views of Buddhist writers were often at odds with one another. Some Buddhists strongly rejected the idea of the Buddha acting through an image, others conditionally accepted it, and others were not troubled by these implications at all.[18] In many cases the critics saw the use of images as introducing potential risk, and a few even characterize it as dangerously misguided.[19]

The development of the Buddhist image tradition at the start of the first century CE introduced new categories of visual imagery and new problems for Buddhist authors. One of the most impactful challenges faced by the Buddhist community involved the common understanding of images as more than just passive objects. Images, including those of the Śākyamuni, were credited with a substantial degree of agency in early South Asian religions.[20] This is seen most clearly in the ways Buddhist legal codes grappled with how to manage the presence of images in monasteries. Images of the Buddha were treated as independent entities with several legal rights, including the ability to receive gifts and own property.[21] This agency ascribed to images meant that there was not only great concern over how devotees understood Śākyamuni's images and what images might imply about impermanence, but also concern over what, if anything, the statues themselves might see.

In the early years of the Common Era, the brahman community also struggled with this topic. Many brahmins were hostile to those who attempted to depict the Vedic gods in physical form, and these arguments often paralleled those found in Buddhist sources. The Pūrva Mīmāṃsā school, for example, was strongly averse to the use of any images in ritual practice. They rejected the possibility of divine embodiment and argued that all references to gods' "bodies" were entirely metaphorical. A less extreme position was held by the Vedānta thinkers, however. This philosophical school, particularly the Advaita Vedānta branch, took a more moderate approach and allowed for the possibility that gods might embody themselves if they desired to do so.[22]

Many early Brahmanical sources held exceptionally negative views of those who used images in worship. This is exemplified by the *Manusmṛti*, or *Laws of Manu*, a Brahmanical legal text often attributed to the second century CE, which marginalizes and demeans *devalakas*, temple priests who attend images. They, along with doctors and butchers, are to be excluded from funerary rituals and from all rites directed to the Vedic gods or ancestors. This disdain for people who would normally hold high status is explicitly connected to their central role in devotional acts involving figural representations of the gods.[23] However, these passages also reveal that enough brahmins were participating in image-based devotion to warrant commentary by concerned traditionalists.

By the fourth century the brahman priests' prevailing attitude toward images began to change. The Gupta period saw the rise of royally supported, temple-based Hinduism and the increased prominence of both *bhakti* (devotional worship) and *darśana* (eye contact with the divine, often mediated through an image). This shift in religious practice posed challenges to both Vedic traditionalists and to Buddhists. It solidified ideas about images and created expectations of an immediate and personal encounter with the object of devotion mediated though the image. As is probably apparent, this approach was directly contrary to longstanding Buddhist views on images that insisted on the Buddha's absence and the fundamental nature of impermanence.

A Buddhist response to this increasingly dominant Hindu mindset can be seen in buddha images created in the Gupta territories. This change starts in the fourth century and is first apparent in North India, centered on the Mathurā region. Specifically, artists introduced a new manner of representing the Buddha's eyes that broke eye contact with the viewer and, in so doing, also broke with standard visual forms that had remained consistent over prior centuries.

The Buddha's Eyes: Origins and Alterations

The earliest images of the Buddha were created primarily in two regions of South Asia, Mathurā (in north-central India) and Gandhāra (in what is now mostly Pakistan). Although the images of Śākyamuni from both regions share similar iconography, they are stylistically quite distinct. The most important of these differences for the present discussion is the way artists represented his eyes. Gandhāran buddhas typically exhibit partially-closed eyes with heavy lids.[24] By contrast, the standard Mathurā types had large, wide-open eyes, which were derived from the eyes depicted on statues of *yakṣas* and other terrestrial deities. The Mathurān artists drew on familiar, large-scale figural forms when sculpting the earliest buddhas, so the similarities to images of *yakṣas* are most likely a byproduct of their production (figs. 1 and 2). In comparing this *yakṣā* from Vidiśā (located near Mathurā) with a second century CE image of Śākyamuni that was produced in Mathurā and installed in a monastery at Sarnath, we can note the large, staring eyes, the frontal stance that rests equally on both feet, the broad shoulders, and the fist balled at the hip that grasps either a flask or the outer monastic robe.[25] These so-called *kapardin*-style figures from Mathurā (of which the Sarnath image is a late example) are arguably the earliest Śākyamuni images (ca. first century CE) and are invariably sculpted with prominent, open eyes and clearly defined upper and lower eyelids (fig. 3). I have intentionally referred to these figures as Śākyamuni rather than as buddha images because when they bear inscriptions, they are identified as bodhisattvas. Ju-Hyung Rhi has argued convincingly that they are intended to represent Śākyamuni before his enlightenment and thus before attaining buddhahood.[26]

By contrast, the earliest inscribed Gandhāran Śākyamuni images are typically identified as buddhas despite being iconographically identical to the Mathurān bodhisattvas. This regional difference is made particularly apparent in one image that bears inscriptions identifying it as both a buddha and a bodhisattva, each in a different language. Both Bishwa Nath Mukherjee and Gregory Schopen have discussed this bi-scriptural inscription from the base of a Mathurān sculpture.[27] The Brāhmī portion (typical of Mathurā inscriptions) identifies the figure as a "bodhisattva," whereas the Kharoṣṭhī portion (used in Gandhāran inscriptions) uses the term "buddha." The implication is that two Buddhists might see the same image and understand it in different ways. There is substantial evidence of contact and exchange between the regions, however, and these differences

FIG. 1. Yakṣa, Besnagar, c. 100 BCE, Archaeological Museum, Vidiśā, photo by author.

FIG. 2. Bodhisattva image donated by *bhikṣu* Bala, Sarnath, second century CE, Sarnath Museum, photo by author.

Fig. 3. Head of Kapardin-style Śākyamuni, Chauhara Tila, Mathurā district, first century CE, Government Museum Mathurā, photo by John C. Huntington, courtesy of the John C. and Susan L. Huntington Photographic Archive of Buddhist and Asian Art.

in nomenclature appear to have eroded over time, with the term "buddha" becoming applied more universally.

This contact occurred most intensely over the long periods of time when both regions were part of the same empires, most notably during the periods of Śaka and Kuṣāṇa control (c. mid-second century BCE to fourth century CE). An interesting and very early example of this artistic exchange was noted by Johanna van Lohuizen-de Leeuw. She identified Mathurān influence on some Gandhāran images of Śākyamuni with only one shoulder covered (typical for Mathurān images of the *kapardin* style) and wide-staring eyes.[28] Conversely, Rhi notes that robes covering both shoulders (associated with Gandhāran-style images) appear on some Mathurān sculptures after the late second century CE.[29] It must be noted, however, that most of the Mathurān images with Gandhāran-style robes still retained their wide-open eyes (fig. 4).

By the fourth century, however, the heavy lids become increasingly common, eventually giving way to a new type of buddha image whose eyes are half closed in a manner akin to what is seen in the earlier northwestern (Gandhāran) sculptures. Some of the clearest examples of this transition

FIG. 4. Standing Śākyamuni, Manoharpura, Mathurā district, first–third centuries CE, Government Museum Mathurā, photo by John C. Huntington, courtesy of the John C. and Susan L. Huntington Photographic Archive of Buddhist and Asian Art.

can be seen in Sarnath. Compare the eyes of an early fifth-century buddha head with those of an earlier image (fig. 2 and fig. 5) and the differences are immediately apparent. The prominent, staring eyes are occluded behind drooping eyelids. It does not seem that the artist intended to close the Buddha's eyes entirely, but the eyelid disrupts normal eye contact and indicates that the gaze is directed downward, even in the absence of a clearly indicated pupil. Although these two well-known examples make a strong contrast, there is some variation and experimentation apparent in the way the eyes were rendered during the early fourth century. In all cases, however, the eyelids are lowered enough to impede the image's forward gaze, marking a pervasive change from earlier practices.

As noted previously, the shift to buddhas with downcast eyes is most apparent in territories held by the Gupta empire. While it is plausible to

Fig 5: Head of the Buddha, Sarnath, fifth century CE, Sarnath Museum, photo by author.

assume that this change was inspired by Gandhāran-style buddhas, one must still ask why at this point, after centuries of consistency, did Mathurān artists alter the way they represented the Buddha. As noted earlier, the regions had been in contact long before the Gupta period. Prior artists must have been aware of the differences yet chose not to adopt them.

Notably, only the Buddha is singled out with a change in appearance. Gupta images of gods and bodhisattvas continue to exhibit the wide-open eyes that had been characteristic of Mathurān-style images for centuries.[30] The consistency in the images of other religious figures suggests that the change relates to something unique about the nature of a buddha.[31] How do we explain this? The reasons for the development appear to have stemmed from both concerns arising within Buddhism and forces impacting it from outside.

In the Eyes of the Buddha

The timing of this transition in the appearance of the Buddha, after roughly four centuries of iconographic consistency, requires some explanation. As alluded to earlier, I believe this innovation was a response to the emergence of temple-based Hinduism and the codification of ritual practices centered on *darśana* and *bhakti*, which developed in this same period. These modes of Hindu worship emphasized the inherent links between images and the divine, particularly in ritual contexts. Most typically (as expressed primarily in Vedānta literature), the deity in Hindu ceremonies was not seen as being identical to the image but was understood to temporarily inhabit the image during the course of the ceremony.[32] The immediacy and accessibility provided by such practices had great appeal. This popularity must have presented a significant challenge to Buddhist modes of image use and their general insistence on the total and permanent absence of the Teacher. At a minimum the rise of temple-based devotion must have resurfaced old concerns held by those elements in the Buddhist community who disapproved of image use and feared that it might lead to doctrinal misunderstanding.

Although temple-based devotion involving acts of offering and veneration had already been around for centuries, these challenges appear to have become particularly potent with the Gupta's royal support of, primarily, Vaishnava temple construction and of the brahman priests who oversaw these rites. As criticism of these image-centered rituals declined among the brahman community, the monastic traditions were alone in holding to older modes of image use. While such devotional practices had been common in other contexts for centuries, as attested by the widespread use of the devotional terminology in inscriptions, this period seems to mark an important transition to systematized, temple-based practices overseen directly, and exclusively, by the brahman priesthood.[33]

Newly built, royal-sponsored religious architecture, as exemplified at fourth–fifth century CE sites like Deogarh and Udayagiri, formalized and sanctioned temple-based modes of Brahmanical religious practice. Specifically, these rock-cut and free-standing structures enshrined the images into which the brahman priests invited the deity to be present through the ritual (*pūjā*). These rites were the culmination of a complex process by which the axis of the old Vedic rituals, which sent prayers up to the gods in heaven, were inverted, and the deity was now made present on earth through the intermediary of the image.

At the Gupta court's religious center at Udayagiri, the deities' eyes are prominently on view, both inside and outside the rock-cut shrines.[34] Although the erosion is significant enough to have effaced the eyes of some images, all the extant examples are wide-eyed. This is true of the deities preserved outside Cave 6, the massive Varaha (who is in profile), and the *eka-mukhaliṅga* in Cave 4 (fig. 6). These prominent eyes were not only a continuation of earlier artistic style but also played a primary role in acts of devotion.

Central to these Hindu forms of worship was the ritualized connection between the worshipper and the divine that was mediated through the eyes of an image or cult icon, which serves as a focus of devotion. Specifically, *darśana* is an important component in devotional worship wherein the

FIG 6. Mukhaliṅga, Udayagiri Cave 4, fifth century CE, photo by John C. Huntington, courtesy of the John C. and Susan L. Huntington Photographic Archive of Buddhist and Asian Art.

devotee makes eye contact with the divinity by gazing upon the eyes of a ritually prepared image. To support these practices, the representation and creation of a deity's eyes became an important and highly regulated aspect of Hindu image production. Consider, for example, the *Citrasūtra* of the *Viṣṇudharmottara Purāṇa* (sixth–eighth centuries CE), a manual instructing artists and priests how to properly create and prepare images of the gods. It represents the views of a fully mature, Brahmanical, image-based system of devotion. Given the increased centrality of *darśana* over the centuries, it is not surprising that the text stipulates that the eyes of gods must always be prominent and level. By contrast, in its description of poorly made images, the text states that "(in the case of idols to be worshipped) . . . a downward or oblique gaze should be avoided" because such images incur grief and misfortune.[35]

Yet this is precisely what the Buddhists do. In the fourth century, just as *darśana* is becoming institutionalized in royally-supported temples, the Buddhists of Mathurā, Sarnath, and other parts of North India introduce buddha images with half-closed eyes that eventually replace the earlier style entirely. Because of their introspective demeanor—appearing to focus on a point a few inches beyond the nose—it might be tempting to assume this new style of buddha represents him engaging in deep meditation. This interpretation is unlikely, however. It is complicated by the frequent presence of downward-looking buddhas in narrative contexts in which the Buddha is explicitly not meditating (fig. 7). Many post-fourth-century examples represent the Buddha in the midst of preaching, making a boon-granting gesture (*varada mudrā*), and other activities that are not typically meditative acts and that involve direct interaction with others.

It might also be argued that the downward gaze of the images was intended to facilitate eye contact with images placed at high vantage points. This too seems unlikely. First, no other images, Hindu or Buddhist, make a similar accommodation based on the presumptive position of the devotee. The eyes are left wide to accommodate all, regardless of their position relative to the statue. Second, although it can be challenging to reconstruct the context for free-standing images, rock-cut examples are found at a wide variety of heights. Late-fifth-century examples from cave sites such as Nāsik (Caves 14, 15, 17) and Kānherī (Caves 2, 4, 90) include images placed very

Fig. 7. The First Sermon, Sarnath, fifth century CE, Sarnath Museum, photo by author.

close to the ground and well below the eye level of even seated devotees.[36] Further, most large or elevated images would require the devotee to be standing directly under to the Buddha's nose to have any chance of catching his eye. We need to look elsewhere for an explanation.

Both the specificity of this change, limited almost exclusively to images of buddhas, and the narrative contexts that preclude meditation, narrow the likely motivations that underly this innovation. In short, the move toward a buddha with an oblique gaze appears to be a firm denial of *darśana* and an affirmation of the Buddha's absence. The lowered gaze of the Buddha intentionally disrupts eye contact and, by extension, any assumptions of contact with the Buddha himself. This simple alteration denies the presence of the Buddha in his image by preventing the fourth century's primary manner of engaging with images. Although we know that images of the Buddha were often believed to have agency and potency, there seems to have been a limit to this acceptance. Unlike their Hindu counterparts, these images explicitly do not mediate between the devotee and a divine subject. With a subtle iconographic shift, the Buddhists were visibly denying his treatment as a god.

That this alteration is most apparent in the same regions that house the earliest Hindu temples seems more than coincidental. As grand, brahman-controlled temples became increasingly powerful, they redefined image-based devotion in the region. These developments are physically embodied by the Daśāvatāra Temple at Deogarh, a Gupta temple constructed to facilitate *pūjā* and *darśana*. Dating to the late fifth or early sixth century, this free-standing Vaiṣṇava temple is adorned with spectacular relief sculpture. The eyes of the figures can be difficult to read because they all bulge slightly outward, and in the absence of incised or painted pupils they are often misread as being closed. Given the well-known narrative content of the reliefs, however, we must assume that most of the eyes are indeed open. This includes the reclining Viṣṇu image resting on the back of the great serpent (*nāga*) Śeṣa depicted on the south side of the temple (fig. 8). The deity's eyes are more clearly open than any of the surrounding figures. This is in striking contrast to the Buddha images that invariably look down even in narrative contexts. In this case the reverse is apparent. The Puranic accounts tell us that Viṣṇu was sleeping, but here his eyes are open.[37]

The newly dominant Hindu devotional practices centered on *darśana* must have posed a challenge to traditional Buddhist forms of image use, and this challenge required a response. In rebuttal, the eyes of the Buddha changed. He no longer engaged the viewer directly with his forward stare. These changes in iconography interfered with *darśana* and refuted any notion of the Buddha's divinity, affirming his complete absence in nirvāṇa.

According to most early South Asian Buddhist traditions, nirvāṇa was a permanent state, totally apart from the world. The prevalent ritual logic of *darśana* threatened to undermine this finality. If catching the Buddha's eye through his image might be mistaken for a moment of *darśana*, then the experience itself had to be subverted. The subtle but innovative alteration in the Buddha's eyes changed centuries of artistic tradition, but in so doing decisively prevented any implications that one might make eye contact with the Buddha.

Fig. 8. Viṣṇu Anantaśayana, Daśāvatāra Temple, Deogarh, early sixth century CE, photo by John C. Huntington, courtesy of the John C. and Susan L. Huntington Photographic Archive of Buddhist and Asian Art.

The Buddha's image had to navigate between doctrinal requirements and societal expectations. It is clear, however, that not every Buddhist agreed on how best to do this. As might be expected, there are indications that not all Buddhists were troubled by the Buddha being compared to a divinity. This same period at the end of the third and the start of the fourth century saw the emergence of theories postulating the absolute immortality of the Buddha, in which he was characterized as an eternal being possessed of a body of adamant (*vajrakāya*).[38] The *Lotus Sūtra* (*Saddharma Puṇḍarika Sūtra*) states the near-immortality of the Buddha overtly by claiming that he only pretended to enter nirvāṇa so as to helpfully convey the urgency and self-reliance needed to escape rebirth. The sūtra asserts that, in actuality, the Buddha continues to exist in the world, possessing an immeasurable lifespan.[39] This claim marks an important distinction between Nikāya and Mahāyāna conceptions of both buddhahood and image use.

The legacy of these stylistic changes is uneven. Although they persisted in Sarnath and spread to other regions (including Southeast Asia), the late-fifth-century caves at Ajaṇṭā are less consistent in the use of half-closed eyes. These changes may be due to the rising prominence of Buddhist schools that were comfortable with the idea of buddhas remaining active in the world, but it might also be a byproduct of individual artistic style. Shrines to the Buddha are included at the back of *vihāras* starting in the late fifth century, suggesting an increased interest in his presence and proximity.[40] Yet the painted images at Ajaṇṭā demonstrate that even bodhisattvas and humans could have languid, heavy lids, and the clearly rendered pupils reveal that many figures avoid eye contact by looking obliquely away from the viewer.[41] The buddhas, both sculpted and painted, have lowered lids, but some disrupt eye contact more than others. One might argue that the need for rigorous attention to these details had relaxed in the intervening decades. Nevertheless, it is clear that the wide-eyed figures of earlier centuries remained out of fashion.

Just as early Buddhist authors found ways to justify and defend devotional practices even in the Buddha's absence, downturned eyes did not preclude all forms of devotional worship. Image use continued to be a powerful form of Buddhist religious practice, just as it had in earlier centuries. The seventh-century Chinese pilgrim Yijing, for example, reported on the mandatory daily lustrations and offerings made to buddha images in the great monastery of Nālandā. In his passage describing these practices, he accuses any who shirk this devotional responsibility as giving in to laziness and breaking the line of succession from teacher to pupil.[42] Far from being marginal, for Buddhists like Yijing devotional practices were central to the tradition. As made apparent by the account of the Sri Lankan eye-opening ceremony that began this chapter, aspects of these same tensions were still at play in the 1960s and are still playing out today.

From the Buddhist perspective, vision presents a number of potential pitfalls that vary significantly depending on who is doing the looking and how they interpret what they see. Perception is a nebulous thing, however. Cultural shifts and changes in public expectations can quickly change the meaning of old and familiar sights. When confronted with growing public expectations of *darśana* in fourth-century North India, the Buddha's open eyes risked taking on unwanted implications. Changes from outside Buddhism threatened the justifications that allowed for the use of images without compromising ideology.

Vision in Buddhist traditions is more than a simple sensory experience. It can have profound karmic repercussions. What one should or should not see varies among the laity and members of the saṅgha. In all cases, however, the way sights are interpreted (and the actions they inspire) are far more significant than the objects of sight themselves. While it might be apparent that monks generally should avoid looking at sexual imagery, even seeing images of the Buddha was not without risk. Drawing the wrong conclusions could lead devotees to engage in misguided practices that were fruitless at best and karmically damaging at worst. To protect against this, attention had to be paid to where the Buddha was looking, and sometimes the easiest solution was for the Buddha to simply look away.

Notes

1. There is textual evidence suggesting that versions of this "eye-opening" ritual (*nētra pinkama*) have been practiced since the fifth century. Gombrich 1966, 23–36.
2. Gombrich 1966, 25. He reports that the monks felt the ceremony was "nonsense" but "picturesque."
3. Gombrich 1966, 36.
4. Gombrich 1966, 23.
5. For a full discussion of Buddhist concerns about image use, see DeCaroli 2014, 29–50.
6. DeCaroli 2014, 30–43.
7. Horner 1997–2000, vol. 1, 116–50, addresses various forms of murder; vol. 5, 191–92, instructs on how not to tie a loincloth (including a fashion known as the "elephant's trunk"); and vol. 5, 186, discusses long nostril hairs, which make monks resemble worshippers of *piśācas* (flesh-eating demons).
8. Schopen 2014, 268.
9. Soper 1979, 148–49.
10. Soper 1979, 147. The distracted monk in the story is the Buddha's half-brother Nanda.
11. Horner 1997–2000, vol. 5, 121–213.
12. Horner 1997–2000, vol. 5, 299, and vol. 3, 122
13. Rhys Davids 1995, vol. 2, 154.
14. Eck 1998, 9–10.

15. Rotman 2008, 62. See also Cowell and Neil 1970, 18–20.
16. Harrison 1992, 220. See also Ehara, Thera, and Thera 1961, 141.
17. Rotman 2003, 557–58.
18. For a discussion of these positions, see DeCaroli 2014, 29–43.
19. See for example Conze 1995, 291. The author of the *Aṣṭasāharikā Prajñāpāramitā Sūtra* describes any persons who adhere to the form of the Buddha as "foolish and stupid" and compares them to a man chasing a mirage for water.
20. DeCaroli 2014, 66–77.
21. Schopen 1997b, 258–90.
22. See von Stietencron 1977, 126–38; and Davis 2000, 107–32.
23. For translations of this passage by Manu, see Burnell 1995, 62–63 and 66; and Olivelle 2004, 116–17.
24. Most Gandhāran buddhas from the first and second century exhibit heavy eyelids. The standing buddha from the Tokyo National Museum is an excellent example (http://www.art-and-archaeology.com/japan/precursor1.html).
25. For more on the early Sarnath image, see Schopen 1997a, 238–57.
26. Rhi 1994, 220–21.
27. Mukherjee 1980–82, 285–86; and Schopen 1987, 99–138.
28. van Lohuizen-de Leeuw 1979, 377–400.
29. Rhi 1994, 213.
30. See, for example, the fifth-century sandstone Viṣṇu (E.6) from Mathurā that is in the collection of National Museum, New Delhi (https://commons.wikimedia.org/wiki/File:Vishnu_sculpture.jpg), or the head of a bodhisattva (28.159.6) from the second half of the fourth century in the collection of the Metropolitan Museum of Art (https://www.metmuseum.org/art/collection/search/38556).
31. The Jainas struggled with very similar issues. For more, see Cort 2009.
32. Eck 1998, 44–55.
33. For more on the early use of devotional terminology—specifically the term *bhagavata*—see DeCaroli 2014, 180–83.
34. For a full analysis of Udayagiri, see Willis 2009, 10–73.
35. Mukherji 2001, 60.
36. Most of the examples are so-called intrusive images added to the site after their initial construction.
37. Pargiter 1904, 469–70.
38. Radich 2011–12.
39. Watson 1993, 227–29.
40. Schopen 1997b, 276.
41. The spectacular painted bodhisattvas flanking the entrance to the shrine at the back of Cave 1 provide good examples (https://en.wikipedia.org/wiki/Ajanta_Caves#/media/File:Bodhisattva_Padmapani,_cave_1,_Ajanta,_India.jpg).
42. Li Rongxi 2000, 135–37.

Bibliography

Burnell, Arthur Coke, trans. 1995 [1884]. *The Ordinances of Manu.* Edited by E. W. Hopkins. New Delhi: Munshiram Manoharlal.

Conze, Edward, trans. 1995 [1973]. *The Perfection of Wisdom in Eight Thousand Lines and Its Verse Summary.* San Francisco: Four Seasons Foundation.

Cort, John E. 2009. *Framing the Jina: Narratives of Icons and Idols in Jain History.* Oxford: Oxford University Press.

Cowell, Edward B., and Robert Alexander Neil, eds. 1970 [1886]. *Divyāvadāna: A Collection of Early Buddhist Legends.* Amsterdam: Oriental Press.

Davis, Richard H. 2000. "Indian Image-Worship and Its Discontents." In *Representation in Religion: Studies in Honor of Moshe Barasch*, edited by J. Assmann and A. I. Baumgarten, 107–32. Leiden: Brill.

DeCaroli, Robert. 2014. *Image Problems: The Origin and Development of the Buddha's Image in Early South Asia.* Seattle: University of Washington Press.

Eck, Diana L. 1998. *Darśan: Seeing the Divine Image in India.* New York: Columbia University Press.

Ehara, N. R. M., Soma Thera, and Kheminda Thera, trans. 1961. *The Path to Freedom (Vimuttimagga).* Colombo: Roland D Weerasuria.

Gombrich, Richard. 1966. "The Consecration of a Buddha Image." *Journal of Asian Studies* 26.1: 23–36.

Harrison, Paul. 1992. "Commemoration and Identification in *Buddhānusmṛti.*" In *In the Mirror of Memory: Reflections on Mindfulness and Remembrance in Indian and Tibetan Buddhism*, edited by Janet Gyatso, 215–38. Albany: State University of New York Press.

Horner, Isaline Blew, trans. 1997–2000 [1938–66]. *The Book of Discipline (Vinaya Piṭaka).* 6 vols. Oxford: Pali Text Society.

Li Rongxi, trans. 2000. *Buddhist Monastic Traditions of Southern Asia: A Record of the Inner Law Sent Home from the South Seas by Śramaṇa Yijing.* Berkeley: Numata Center for Buddhist Translation and Research.

van Lohuizen-de Leeuw, Johanna Engelberta. 1979. "New Evidence with Regard to the Origin of the Buddha Image." *South Asian Archaeology*: 377–400.

Mukherjee, Bishwa Nat. 1980–82. "On a Bi-scriptural Epigraph of the Kuṣāṇa Period from Mathurā." *Journal of Ancient Indian History* 13: 285–86.

Mukherji, Parul Dave, trans. 2001. *The Citrasūtra of the Viṣṇudharmottara Purāṇa.* New Delhi: Motilal Banarsidass and Indira Gandhi Centre for the Arts.

Olivelle, Patrick, trans. 2004. *Manu's Code of Law: A Critical Edition and Translation of the Mānava-Dharmaśāstra.* New York: Oxford University Press.

Pargiter, Frederick Eden, trans. 1904. *The Mārkaṇḍeya Purāṇa*, Calcutta: Asiatic Society of Bengal.

Radich, Michael. 2011–12. "Immortal Buddhas and Their Indestructible Embodiments: The Advent of the Concept of *Vajrakāya.*" *Journal of the International Association of Buddhist Studies* 34.1–2: 277–90.

Rhi, Ju-Hyung. 1994. "From Bodhisattva to Buddha: The Beginning to Iconic Representation in Buddhist Art." *Artibus Asiae* 54.3–4: 207–25.

Rhys Davids, Thomas William, trans. 1995 [1910]. *Dialogues of the Buddha Translated from the Dīgha Nikāya.* 3 vols. Oxford: Pali Text Society.

Rotman, Andy. 2003. "The Erotics of Practice: Objects and Agency in Buddhist *Avadāna* Literature." *Journal of the American Academy of Religion* 71.3: 557–58.

———, trans. 2008. *Divine Stories Divyāvadāna.* Part 1. Classics of Indian Buddhism. Boston: Wisdom Publications.

Schopen, Gregory. 1987. "The Inscription on the Kuṣān Image of Amitābha and the Character of the Early Mahāyāna in India." *Journal of the International Association of Buddhist Studies* 10.2: 99–138

———. 1997. *Bones, Stones, and Buddhist Monks: Collected Papers on the Archaeology, Epigraphy, and Texts of Monastic Buddhism in India.* Honolulu: University of Hawai'i Press.

———. 1997a. "On Monks, Nuns, and 'Vulgar' Practices: The Introduction of the Image Cult into Indian Buddhism." In *Bones, Stones, and Buddhist Monks*, 238–57.

———. 1997b. "The Buddha as an Owner of Property and Permanent Resident in Medieval Indian Monasteries." In *Bones, Stones, and Buddhist Monks*, 258–90.

———. 2014. "On Monks and Menial Laborers: Some Monastic Accounts of Building Buddhist Monasteries." In *Buddhist Nuns, Monks, and Other Worldly Matters: Recent Paper on Monastic Buddhism in India,* 251–75. Honolulu, University of Hawai'i Press.

Soper, Alexander. 1979. "Early Buddhist Attitudes toward the Art of Painting." *Art Bulletin* 32: 147–51.

von Stietencron, Heinrich. 1977. "Orthodox Attitudes towards Temple Service and Image Worship in Ancient India." *Central Asiatic Journal* 21: 126–38.

Watson, Burton, trans. 1993. *The Lotus Sutra.* New York: Columbia University Press.

Willis, Michael. 2009. *The Archaeology of Hindu Ritual: Temples and the Establishment of the Gods.* Cambridge: Cambridge University Press.

Seeing Splendor and Envisioning Hell: The Moral Economy in Thai-Buddhist Merit-Making

MELODY ROD-ARI

WHEN THE MONK VAKKALI was dying, the Buddha came to visit him, asking if he had any regrets. Vakkali said that his only regret was that he did not have the strength to come and see the Buddha. To this, the Buddha famously replied, "Enough, Vakkali. What is there to see in this vile body? He who sees the Dhamma, Vakkali, sees me; he who sees me sees the Dhamma."[1] Despite this, over the course of many centuries, Buddhists, longing to see the Buddha, have been creating, animating, and worshipping his image. However, this essay will argue that it is neither texts nor images that help to privilege the sense of sight in Buddhist practice. Instead, it is the moral imperative of merit-making. According to the Buddhist doctrines of cause and effect (karma), happiness in this life results from performing the virtuous deeds prescribed by the Buddha. Suffering is the result of failing to do so. Texts and images are central to what I call "the moral economy" of Buddhist merit-making. The positive karmic effects, extolled in texts, of sponsoring, copying, or crafting sūtras and images help to explain the development and sustained patronage of Buddhist art and architecture since antiquity. For example, sponsorship of sculpted images of the Buddha allows the Tathāgata to accept offerings, even after his *parinirvāṇa*, to support monasteries and temples for members of the saṅgha, who in turn perpetuate his Dharma. The moral economy of merit-making is self-fulfilling and self-sustaining.

What does it mean to see an image of the Buddha? In the stories in Andy Rotman's translation of the *Divyāvadāna*, the act of seeing (*darśana*) the

Buddha and witnessing the moral economy of merit-making generates faith (*śraddhā*) in the Buddha's teachings.[2] This ultimately reinforces the importance of giving (*dāna*), which sustains the saṅgha and the Dharma. To illustrate this in a Thai context, this essay examines legends associated with the sandalwood Buddha, which narrate the circumstances and benefits of constructing the "first" image of the Buddha. It then turns to the narrative *Phra Malai Klon Suat* ("Phra Malai, chanted version"), where the monk Phra Malai travels to hell and back to relate the important karmic rewards of merit-making by performing dāna.

The Moral Economy of Merit-Making

What makes someone a Buddhist? It is traditionally said that it is taking refuge in the Three Jewels (*triratna*): the Buddha, the Dharma, and the Saṅgha. Additionally, the practice of Buddhism is often divided into the three trainings (*triśikṣa*): ethics (*śīla*), meditation (*samādhi*), and wisdom (*prajñā*). For the Buddhist laity, ethics is most important. They are not required to take the hundreds of vows held by monks and nuns. If this was necessary, the population of self-identified Buddhists in the world would certainly plummet. This emphasis on *śīla* is corroborated by a 2018 survey by the National Statistical Service of Thailand on the *Conditions of Society, Culture, and Mental Health*, which found that nearly 94 percent of the population identified as Theravāda Buddhists and 55 percent of this cohort adhered to Buddhist precepts.[3] This means that, either temporarily or for life, they take up to five vows: not to kill, steal, lie, engage in sexual misconduct, or use intoxicants. These, however, are prohibitions. What do Buddhist laypeople actively do? I argue that what makes someone a Buddhist is indeed a belief in the Buddha's Dharma, and specifically a belief in and adherence to the laws of cause and effect that govern the Buddhist worldview, and that this belief encourages participation in the Buddhist moral economy that supports the saṅgha and ensures the posterity of Buddhism and its institutions. In other words, they take refuge in the Three Jewels. Nearly 92 percent of the survey participants gave alms to monks, proving the importance of merit-making through dāna.[4]

Reminders of the effects of karma can be witnessed and internalized every day, so that one's good fortune comes to be understood as the result of living life according to the Buddha's teachings; conversely, negative consequences can be understood as living in opposition to the Dharma. Here, Rotman's study of the *Divyāvadāna* is useful in illustrating how seeing and experiencing one's participation in the moral economy of Buddhism, and specifically merit-making, reinforces belief and trust in the Buddha's Dharma. In *Thus Have I Seen: Visualizing Faith in Early Indian Buddhism*, Rotman illustrates the importance of sight and belief to Buddhist practice through the "Koṭikarṇa-avadāna." In the story, the merchant Koṭikarṇa finds himself in a city surrounded by hungry ghosts. He asks the ghosts how they came to have such an unfortunate rebirth, and they respond: "Śroṇā, the people of Jambudvīpa are difficult to convince. You won't have śraddhā [faith] [in us]." Koṭikarṇa replies: "Friends, I can see what's before my eyes. Why wouldn't I have śraddhā [in you]?"[5] The text is clear here that seeing is believing. As Koṭikarṇa proceeds, he sees a man in a flying mansion making love to four nymphs, but as the sun rises the mansion and the nymphs disappear and the man is devoured by four dogs. Koṭikarṇa asks the man what deeds resulted in his unfortunate rebirth. The hungry ghost tells him that in his previous life he was a butcher and killed sheep by day, but that at night he lived by the Buddhist moral code (*śīlasamādāna*).[6] As a result, during the day he lives a life of suffering, but at night he lives a life of pleasure. The man requests that Koṭikarṇa go back to the human realm and tell his son, who is also a butcher, about the karmic results of such deeds.

> "Tell him, I have seen your father. He says that the consequence of this deed will be most undesirable. Stop this evil practice that goes against the true dharma!"
>
> "Friend, as you said before, 'The people of Jambudvīpa are difficult to convince.' He won't have śraddhā [in me]."
>
> "Śroṇā, if he doesn't have śraddhā [in you], tell him, 'Your father says that underneath the slaughtering pen, a pot full of gold is buried. Retrieve it and use it to enjoy yourself fully. And from time to time offer alms to the noble Mahākātyāyana and then direct the reward in our names. Maybe then this bad karma will diminish, give out, and finally be exhausted.'"[7]

Here the text is explicit, if the butcher's son does not have faith in Koṭikarṇa's account, he will at least believe in the tangible pot of gold that he can see with his own eyes. The *Koṭikarṇa-avadāna* illustrates Rotman's thesis that seeing generates faith, and that after the character gains faith, he is compelled to make an offering. Furthermore, the *Cūḷakammavibhaṅga Sutta* illustrates the importance of dāna in altering one's karma. The Buddha tells the brahman student Subha:

> Here, student, some man or woman does not give food, drink, clothing, carriages, garlands, scents, unguents, beds, dwellings, and lamps to ascetics or brahmins. Because of performing and undertaking such action . . . he is reborn in a state of misery . . . But if instead he comes back to the human state, then wherever he is reborn he is poor. This is the way, student, that leads to poverty, namely, one does not give food . . . and lamps to ascetics or brahmins.
>
> But here, student, some man or woman does gives food, drink, clothing, carriages, garlands, scents, unguents, beds, dwellings, and lamps to ascetics or brahmins. Because of performing and undertaking such action . . . he is reborn in a good station . . . But if instead he comes back to the human state, then wherever he is reborn he is wealthy. This is the way, student, that leads to wealth, namely, one gives food . . . and lamps to ascetics or brahmins.[8]

Like the *Koṭikarṇa-avadāna*, the *Cūḷakammavibhaṅga Sutta* describes how the laws of karma guarantee that each person experiences the fate merited by their actions. Both texts exemplify the benefits of giving, which leads to wealth and thus becomes visual proof of one's virtue and the veracity of the Buddha's teachings.

The First Portrait of the Buddha, the Sandalwood Statue

In the opening lines of the *Kosalabimbavaṇṇanā*, King Pasenadi of Kosala prepares "all the perfumes, garlands and the rest" to offer to the Buddha, echoing the words of the Tathāgata to Subha in the *Cūḷakammavibhaṅga Sutta.*[9] However, upon reaching Jetavana Monastery, he finds that the Buddha is gone. The king laments the absence of the Buddha and desires to have him present in the form of an image so that he can fulfill his duty as an exemplary "wheel-turning king" (*cakravartin*) by making offerings to him. When the Buddha returns, the king asks if he can have an image of him made. The Buddha agrees. This is the story of the first image of the Buddha, the sandalwood statue.

The story of the sandalwood Buddha appears in Buddhist texts at various times and in nearly all corners of the Buddhist world.[10] Despite variations in the different narratives, similar themes persist, such as the king's desire to construct the Buddha's portrait because of his absence—either the Tathāgata has entered *parinirvāṇa* or he is in Trāyastriṃśa Heaven (Pāli: Tāvatiṃsa) to preach to his mother, who has been reborn as a god. Other themes include the great merit bestowed upon individuals who sponsor or construct an image of the Buddha or who copy Buddhist texts, as well as a discussion of the merit accrued when worshipping an image of the Buddha.

The earliest sandalwood Buddha story appears in the diary of the early fifth-century Chinese monk Faxian. Later versions of the story appear throughout Asia, including the *Kosalabimbavaṇṇanā*, a fourteenth-century Pāli text from Sri Lanka.[11] In this version, King Pasenadi explains his desire for a portrait of the great teacher, saying to the Buddha: "So, for the benefit of the whole world I would like to have an image made in the likeness of the Tathagata."[12] The Buddha agrees and says that whoever constructs an image of him of any size and material will accrue great merit.[13] Returning to his residence, King Pasenadi orders a buddha figure made of sandalwood that displays the thirty-two marks and instructs that it is to be inlaid with gold and clothed in yellow robes. When it is finished, he invites the Buddha to see the figure. When the Buddha enters the shrine, the seated sandalwood statue rises to greet him; however, the Buddha restrains the statue from standing and explains that his work lies ahead: "Reverend sir, after me you will illumine my teaching. For the sake of the teaching, enduring five thousand years."[14] In accepting the sandalwood buddha as his successor, the Buddha effectively reiterates his famous saying: "He who sees the Dhamma sees me; he who sees me sees the Dhamma."

The text makes clear that the sandalwood statue is made because the Buddha himself will soon be gone. His absence will cause anguish in the king and his entourage, preventing them from taking part in merit-making rituals. In other words, the Buddha needs to be present as the focus and recipient of the ritual act. Indeed, across the Buddhist world, rituals depend on the presence of the Buddha, either in person, as an image, or represented by some other material sign that can be seen.[15] The text also makes clear that the benefits of constructing or sponsoring an image will be "incomparable bliss" and goes on to describe rewards such as avoiding rebirth in the hells and an assurance of rebirth into a wealthy family.[16] When questioned by Ānanda about the specific rewards and benefits of image-making, one of the Buddha's twenty-six responses is that "they never become frightened or terrified of rivals. Image-makers and copyists are born in a high family of great halls and great wealth, not in any other family."[17]

The story of the sandalwood statue traveled beyond China and Sri Lanka because it provides an effective guide to the benefits of image use and merit-making, both of which are important to lay practitioners and the saṅgha. One example from Chiang Mai, Thailand, is the Vaṭṭaṅgulirāja Jātaka.[18] As discussed by Donald Swearer in *Becoming the Buddha: The Ritual of Image Consecration in Thailand*, "In the Vaṭṭaṅgulirāja Jātaka, the legend of King Pasenadi and the construction of the sandalwood statue appears as the frame story of the present. In the story of the past, the Buddha narrates an incident from one of his previous lives as King Vaṭṭaṅguli where, as a consequence of having repaired the broken finger of a buddha statue when he was a merchant in Aggavati, he was able to defeat an army merely by lifting and bending his finger."[19]

In this version of the story, the benefits of image production and use are recounted in both the past and the present. By uniting these two events through a rebirth story of the Buddha, the author(s) of the text make clear that image use is important because it affords the practitioner access to the Buddha in his absence during any eon: past, present, or future. Furthermore, the Vaṭṭaṅgulirāja Jātaka also makes explicit that image production and preservation are important, as they allow worshippers to make offerings to the Buddha and thus fulfill their duty of merit-making and sustaining the Dharma.

Both the *Kosalabimbavaṇṇanā* and the Vaṭṭaṅgulirāja Jātaka mention a timespan of five thousand years. There are many predictions and prophecies in Buddhist texts about how long the teachings of Śākyamuni Buddha will remain in the world before they disappear. In the Thervavāda tradition, that period is five thousand years, measured from the Theravāda date of the Buddha's passage into nirvāṇa, 544 BCE. As in other predictions of the disappearance of the Dharma, it is a process that occurs in stages. For Theravādins, the fifth-century master Buddhaghosa's description is considered orthodox. He explains that by the end of the first millennium, it will no longer be possible to attain any of the four stages of enlightenment: stream enterer, once returner, never returner, or arhat. By the end of the second millennium, monks will no longer be able to keep their vows. By the end of the third millennium, all books of the canon will have disappeared. By the end of the fourth millennium, monks will marry and wear laymen's robes. At the end of the fifth and final millennium, the "nirvāṇa of the relics" will occur, when all the relics of the Buddha break out of their stūpas and assemble in Bodh Gayā, where, having been worshipped by the gods one last time, they will burst into flame. At this point, all remnants of Śākyamuni and his teachings will be gone.[20]

Thus the composition of the Vaṭṭaṅgulirāja Jātaka in the fifteenth century is quite significant, because the two thousandth anniversary of the Buddha's death was approaching and monks would soon not be able to keep their vows.[21] This anniversary was believed to have occurred in 1456–57. As Peter Skilling and Santi Pakdeekham have noted, making merit during this period of perceived decline in Southeast Asia generally, and Thailand specifically, was linked to the legend of the sandalwood Buddha.[22] In the Vaṭṭaṅgulirāja Jātaka, the Buddha is more emphatic than in the *Kosalabimbavaṇṇanā* when instructing the sandalwood buddha to remain seated: "Do not descend from your seat! Remain there—it will not be very long before the Tathāgata passes away. You must stay and protect the *śāsana* [teaching] for five thousand years."[23] As we will see, although this passage did not inspire a new iconic type of statuary in the fifteenth century, it did find enthusiasm among royal patrons during the late Ayutthaya period (seventeenth–eighteenth centuries) and in the nineteenth century during the Rattanakosin period. During this time, buddha statues referencing the

Fig. 1. *Standing Buddha*, approx. 1400–1700, Thailand. Wood. Asian Art Museum of San Francisco, F2002.8.13.a–b. H: 57¾ in. × W: 19¾ in. × D: 12 in. (H: 146.7 cm. × W: 50.2 cm. × D: 30.5 cm.). Photograph, Asian Art Museum of San Francisco.

legend of the sandalwood Buddha are depicted standing with the left arm bent at the elbow and raised at chest height, palm facing outward, while the right arm and hand is positioned straight down, beside the body.[24] This posture indicates the moment that the Buddha instructs the sandalwood figure to remain seated (fig. 1).

For the two-thousandth anniversary, laypeople sponsored monks to travel to Sri Lanka to be re-ordained, and the monks brought texts and relics back to Thailand, all of which resulted in a florescence of Buddhist writing and artistic patronage in the fourteenth and fifteenth centuries. Like the Vaṭṭaṅgulirāja Jātaka, the sponsored texts overwhelmingly included stories extolling the advantages of merit-making (Sanskrit *ānisaṃsa*; Thai *ānisong*) as well as chronicles and legends (Thai *tamnān*) that similarly illustrate the virtues of dāna. One such example is the story of the monk Phra Malai, which, like the story of the sandalwood Buddha, became synonymous with the period of decline.

Thai-Buddhist Merit-Making and the Story of Phra Malai

The earliest mention of a monk by the name of Malaya, on which the Thai name Phra Malai is based, is found in the *Mahāvaṃsa*, the "Great Chronicle" of Sri Lanka, dated between the fourth and sixth centuries CE, as well as in the writings of Buddhaghosa. There is also a later legend written in Pāli devoted to the monk entitled *Māleyyadevathera-vattu.*[25] However, the Phra Malai story was not introduced to Thailand until the fourteenth or fifteenth centuries, coinciding with the two thousandth anniversary.[26] The story, which narrates the great merit of Phra Malai and his visits to hell and heaven, was perfectly congruous with the religious, political, and social milieu of this period in Thai history. As noted in Bonnie Brereton's seminal study, *Thai Tellings of the Phra Malai: Texts and Rituals concerning a Popular Buddhist Saint*, the most well-known and popular version of the story is the *Phra Malai Klon Suat* ("chanted version"). It is recited orally in vernacular Thai during the annual Vessantara Festival as well as during funerals.[27]

The theme of merit-making and karma is central to all versions of the Phra Malai story. Phra Malai, like the merchant Koṭikarṇa in the *Koṭikarṇa-avadāna*, visits hell, where hungry ghosts plead with him to tell their relatives in the human realm to make merit on their behalf so that they may be reborn in heaven.[28] When Phra Malai returns to Jambudvīpa, he conveys their message, and almost immediately the hell-beings are reborn in heaven. The story also describes Phra Malai's visit to Trāyastriṃśa Heaven on the summit of Mount Meru at the invitation of Indra. While there, he meets Maitreya, who asks him how those in the human realm make merit, to which Phra Malai responds that worshippers make merit in many ways according to their abilities, such as casting images of the Buddha or presenting robes to monks. In response, Maitreya tells Phra Malai to tell the people in Jambudvīpa that if they wish to meet him, they should listen to the recitation of the entire Vessantara Jātaka in one day and one night, in addition to making offerings of one thousand candles, incense sticks, flowers, and other gifts to temples. Maitreya explains to Phra Malai that the deterioration of Buddhism will occur after the Buddha's teachings have been on Earth for five thousand years. This deterioration will cause suffering on

Earth. After seven days, a new society will emerge based on a commitment to morality. At that time, Maitreya will be born to the human realm. He tells Phra Malai that he had earned sufficient merit through the practice of dāna to be reborn as a buddha.

The *Phra Malai Klon Suat* differs from other versions in that it gives equal prominence to the splendors of heaven (rewards of dāna) and the visions of hell (consequences of karma).[29] Brereton argues that the oral format benefits from vignettes of karmic retribution, providing opportunities for monks to teach important moral lessons and for the audience to hear and visualize examples of karma that sometimes verge on the gruesomely comedic.[30] In one vignette, a government official is reborn in hell for being corrupt:

> There was another type of suffering ghost who was in great torment. He had testicles that were as huge as water jugs. They hung way down to the ground like a yam shoulder bag. Rotten and putrid, bloated and stinking, they were like slimy snails.
>
> Whenever he wanted to go somewhere, he'd fling them over his shoulder, stagger under their weight, and reel from side to side. When he wanted to sit down, they'd get pinched between his legs, and he'd have to stand up, and then sit down on top of them.[31]

The focus on both heaven and hell compliments the text's ritual use during the Vessantara Festival (Thai: *Thet Maha Chat* or *Bun Phra Wet*). The Vessantara Jātaka is the final rebirth story before the Buddha-to-be is reborn in Tuṣita Heaven and then as Prince Siddhārtha Gautama. The narrative extols the virtue and perfection of dāna by Prince Vessantara, who gives away not only all his possessions but also his small children and then his wife as well. Large scrolls of the Vessantara Jātaka that are paraded in the streets of a village community during the festival often include imagery related to the story of Phra Malai at the beginning of the scroll.[32] In one such example, Phra Malai is seen in hell addressing hungry ghosts sitting in a boiling caldron (fig. 2).

It is important to note that the parading of illustrated scrolls depicting scenes from the story is not the only visual element of the Vessantara Fes-

FIG. 2. Vessantara Jātaka, first half of the twentieth century, Thailand. The Walters Art Museum, Baltimore, 35.258. H: 29 15⁄16 in. × W: 22 1⁄16 in. (H: 76 cm. × W: 56 cm.). Photograph, The Walters Art Museum.

tival. Reenactments of the most famous scenes from the narrative, such as Vessantara's gift of his children to the Brahman Jujaka or the royal family's return from exile, bring home visually and viscerally the importance of dāna. The performance also serves as a source of entertainment. The date of the first dramatization of the Vessantara Jātaka in Thailand is not definitively known, but it is likely that there was interest in making the story available to a non-literate audience by the mid-fifteenth century. This is when King Trailok (Ayutthaya Kingdom, r.1448–84), whose reign coincided with the two-thousandth anniversary of the Buddha's death, sponsored the composition of the vernacular *Maha Chat Kham Luang* ("Great Birth Sermon") of the Vessantara Jātaka, which was intended to be recited.[33] Since the fifteenth century, numerous local, vernacular examples of the story have emerged that share the same basic narrative structure of the original Pāli version.[34]

In *Of Beggars and Buddhas: The Politics of Humor in the Vessantara Jātaka in Thailand*, Katherine Bowie reveals that in northern Thailand *tujoks*, or monks, who recite the Jujaka chapter of the Vessantara Jātaka in dramatic detail were once considered local "rock stars" for their performances of the story, and on occasion even dressed up as Jujaka.[35] Jujaka is the moral foil to Vessantara and is portrayed as a greedy old man married to a much younger woman, Amitatā. While retrieving water from a well for her husband, Amitatā is teased and harassed by the other village women and refuses to return. She asks Jujaka to acquire Vessantara's children as servants so that she would not have to endure continued indignities. Scenes of Jujaka in search of

Vessantara and chased by the family's protective dogs, as well as his tying up the children and taking them away, provide comedy and drama as they are popularly reenacted. Bowie interviewed the *tujok* Luang Poh Bunthong, who explained: "In the past there were monks who dressed as Puu Phraam [Jujaka]. They had a bag, with a bamboo salt container. They would wear a beard and walk with a cane. They wore their yellow robes underneath [their costume]. The more one dressed like Puu Phraam, the more people liked it."[36] The dramatization of the Vessantara Jātaka not only provides entertainment but is also an opportunity to invite the Buddha to local temples. In his study of *Bun Phra Wet* festivals, Leedom Lefferts argues that parading Vessantara Jātaka scrolls and performing the narrative with actors playing the part of Vessantara and his family are intended to bring the narrative to life for village participants. Moreover, participants—both actors and audience—are inviting Vessantara, and by extension the Buddha, into their community and their temple.[37]

The reading and chanting of the *Phra Malai Klon Suat* and the Vessantara Jātaka, coupled with their depictions in illustrated scrolls and in contemporary Thai Buddhist ceremonies, suggest that seeing the results of merit-making and the karmic consequences of the characters' bad actions in the stories are an important element of fostering and reinforcing faith in the Buddha's Dharma. Indeed, the 2018 survey referenced earlier found that Buddhists in Thailand overwhelmingly gave alms to monks, prayed, meditated, and maintained the Buddhist precepts on important Buddhist holy days, when such ceremonies took place, more than at other times in the year.[38]

Seeing Splendor and Envisioning Hell

When envisioning religious artworks, most of us imagine objects of splendor. And while many examples of heavenly imagery and radiant deities exist in Buddhism, such images can also be found alongside grisly images of hell realms and their inhabitants. Heavenly and hellish imagery in Buddhist traditions is meant to inspire, educate, and remind the worshipper how to be a good Buddhist. This explains the larger-than-life-size statues of a blood-soaked, naked man and woman climbing a thorn-covered tree as hungry

Fig. 3. *Hell Scene*, Wat Saen Suk, Bang Saen, Thailand, twentieth century. Photograph, author.

dogs lick their open wounds (fig. 3). As gruesome and disgusting as these scenes are, they should not be seen as bad, but rather as good, because they positively reinforce the teachings of the Buddha. This sculpture and other artwork at places like Wat Saen Suk, just outside of Bangkok, depict scenes from the *Phra Malai Klon Suat*. Brought to life as hellscapes, they remind visitors of the karmic effects of not following the Buddhist precepts, such as the prohibition on sexual misconduct. As Brereton writes, "Those men and women who are unfaithful to their spouses, and those women who give their husbands love potions to incite their desire, are forced by snarling dogs and sword-wielding hell wardens to climb a thorn tree to reach their lover, who is at the top."[39]

Stories about hell and hungry ghosts in both the *Phra Malai Klon Suat* and the *Koṭikarṇa-avadāna* contain detailed descriptions that are entertaining and easy to remember, making them effective educational tools. Scholastic texts in the Abhidharma Piṭaka also discuss the karmic effects of sexual misconduct, but they do so in a prescriptive manner rather than an engaging narrative format, making it neither entertaining nor particularly accessible to a lay practitioner.

"Hell parks" such as the one at Wat Saen Suk are popular among Buddhist families in Thailand as well as curious tourists. Both types of visitors knowingly or unknowingly support the saṅgha; their admission dollars go toward the upkeep of the monastery and the sustenance of the monks. Moreover, the photos they post on various social media platforms extend the reach of Wat Sean Suk, and thus the teachings of the Buddha, beyond traditional Buddhist communities. The name of the monastery, Wat Saen Suk, means "Temple of a Hundred Thousand Joys." This is not meant to be ironic; the grisly images in the hellscapes are intended to spark joy, not fear, inspiring the worshipper to take refuge in the Buddha's Dharma.

While it may be difficult to equate images of hell with happiness, it is easy to understand the function of heavenly imagery and sculptures of the Buddha. This is because such imagery is rooted in the lived experience and material aspirations of Buddhist practitioners. Images of heaven in Buddhist art often look like the earthly royal palaces of kings and queens, or the very temples that practitioners go to for worship. This can be seen, for example, in a nineteenth-century painting of the Buddha preaching in Trāyastriṃśa Heaven that depicts the Tathāgata seated in a pavilion that resembles contemporary Thai Buddhist architecture (fig. 4). Similarly, descriptions in texts of earthly utopias portray a fertile land with pots of gold that provide for the material well-being of all, not just the ruling class. Describing the utopia that will precede the advent of Maitreya, the *Phra Malai Klon Suat* says, "At that time, the people of Jambu will enjoy complete happiness, with plenty of silver, gold, wealth and material goods. Water will flow up one side of the bank and down the other; the ponds will always be filled to the top. The level of water will be neither too shallow nor too deep, but just enough so that a crow can drink just by tilting its head. It will always be full and so clear that you can see the fish."[40]

Conclusion

Images of the Buddha in Thai art are often gilded, reflecting both the material wealth and the enlightened state that result from the Buddha's teachings. We are reminded that in the *Kosalabimbavaṇṇanā*, King Pasenadi gave instructions that the first image of the Buddha be inlaid with gold.

Fig. 4. *Buddha Preaches in Indra's Heaven and Descends to Earth, with Hell Below*, painting on cloth, approx. 1850–1900, Thailand. Asian Art Museum of San Francisco, the Avery Brundage Collection, B60D108. H: 112 ½ in. × W: 35 in. (H: 285.8 cm. × W: 88.9 cm.). Photograph, Asian Art Museum of San Francisco.

This tradition continued over the millennia, long after the two-thousandth anniversary of the Buddha's nirvāṇa. As discussed above, during the nineteenth century in Thailand, there was particular interest in statues of the standing buddha refraining the seated sandalwood buddha from rising. The most significant example is in the collection of the Grand Palace in Bangkok, Thailand.[41]

In the nineteenth century, Thailand was at a political and religious crossroads. Neighboring countries to the north, south, east, and west had been colonized or annexed by the British and the French. In an effort to deflect the perception of being primitive or superstitious and thus in need of colonization, three kings of the Chakri dynasty—Nangklao (r. 1824–51), Mongkut (r. 1851–68), and Chulalongkorn (r. 1886–1910)—began the process of modernizing the Thai monarchy and demythologizing Thai Buddhism. Central to their efforts was the reinterpretation of the Jātakas, which had long served as the key source of teachings for the Thai practice of Theravāda Buddhism.[42] As noted by Patrick Jory in his study of the Thai monarchy, it was the Jātaka texts generally, and the Vessantara Jātaka specifically, that had served as the source for conceptualizing authority and political organization among Thai Buddhists since the Sukhothai period (1238–1438).[43] Early efforts to modernize Buddhism in the nineteenth century can be seen in the adoption of new *mudrās* (gestures) and postures (Thai *pang*) for buddha images. King Nangklao (r. 1824–51) learned of King Trailok's commission of a complete set of sculptures depicting the Jātaka stories and was inspired to undertake a similar project. However, he believed that the hybrid and animal forms of the Buddha-to-be as described in the Jātakas were unsuitable for worship.[44] Nangklao asked his uncle, Prince Paramanuchit Chinorot, who was a Buddhist monk and who later became Somdet Saṅgharāja (Supreme Patriarch), to develop new iconic types based on sacred texts to depict the Buddha's historical life.[45] One of the thirty-three new postures that he developed, or rather reintroduced, is seen in the *Buddha Subduing the Sandalwood Image* sculpture.[46] It can be argued that the revival of this iconic type, first seen during the Ayutthaya period, had taken on a new meaning. Now, in the nineteenth century, the historical Buddha (the "real" Buddha) restrains the unseen sandalwood image (the replica, the idol) from standing. This posture or iconic type was a metaphor for the authentic Buddhism that the Thai monarchy was promoting. With the twenty-five-hundredth anniversary of the Buddha's passing less than a century away, it was still not the right time for the seated sandalwood buddha to stand.

While many scholars have noted that King Mongkut (r. 1851–68) and his son King Chulalongkorn (r. 1868–1910) sought to demythologize Thai Buddhism, this process began during the reign of their predecessor, King Nangklao, albeit to a much lesser degree. Nangklao preferred the *Paṭhama Sambodhi* ("The Buddha's Supreme Enlightenment"), the story of the Buddha's final lifetime, over the Jātaka stories of his previous lifetimes, seeing it as more historical and less mythological. The *Paṭhama Sambodhi* describes the Buddha's enlightenment, recounting his final incarnation from Prince Vessantara into Prince Siddhārtha, his journey of renouncing lay life, his temptation by Māra, and finally, his attainment of enlightenment and his preaching the Dharma. The most well-known version in

Thailand (*Pathom Somphot*) was compiled by Paramanuchit Chinorot in 1845 and includes expanded chapters on the Buddha's *parinirvāṇa*, the distribution of relics, the Buddha's prediction of the coming of Maitreya, the binding of Māra by Upagutta, and the decline of Buddhism, among other episodes.[47] By 1890, this version of the *Pathom Somphot* was further revised, with episodes such as Māra's binding and Buddhaghosa's prediction of Buddhism's disappearance after five thousand years regarded as too mythological and thus excised.[48] The revision was a response to King Chulalongkorn's decree that monks should not begin sermons with the prediction of the decline of Buddhism, which emphasizes fear of the future rather than ethical behavior in the present as motivation for following the Buddha's Dharma.[49]

Although Nangklao made some efforts to historicize Buddhism, they were not as progressive as the reforms of Mongkut and Chulalongkorn. Prior to becoming king, Mongkut was a Buddhist monk who founded the Thammayut nikai, a reformist school, which among other things refused to hold Thet Maha Chat ceremonies that center on the Vessantara Jātaka and Phra Malai texts because they were not recognized as part of the canon.[50]

Despite the efforts of three generations of kings to deemphasize annual festival ceremonies and texts long central to Thai Buddhist practice, they did not disappear. The Thet Maha Chat and Bun Phra Wet festivals with their illuminated manuscripts and dramatizations of the Vessantara Jātaka and Phra Malai narratives continue, though they may be less elaborate than in the past.[51] Modern hell parks like the one at Wat Saen Suk continue to draw visitors. Efforts to modernize Thai Buddhism in the nineteenth century focused on texts and images. However, as I argued at the beginning of this essay, neither texts nor images are most central to Buddhist practice in Thailand. Instead, it is participation in the moral economy of merit-making and the laws of cause and effect that allow Buddhists to see the Dharma, and thus to see the Buddha. It matters little whether he is standing or sitting.

Notes

1. Bhikkhu Bodhi 2003, 939.
2. Rotman 2009.
3. National Statistical Office 2020, iv and ix.
4. National Statistical Office 2020, iv and ix.
5. *Divyāvadāna* 7.28–8.2, in Rotman 2009, 24.
6. *Divyāvadāna* 7.28–8.2, in Rotman 2009, 24.
7. *Divyāvadāna* 10.21.29, in Rotman 2009, 25.
8. Bhikkhu Bodhi 2003, 164–65.
9. Gombrich 1978, 297.
10. For a detailed study of the Udayana image, drawn largely from Chinese sources, see Carter 1990.
11. Swearer 2004, 14–55.
12. Gombrich 1978, 296.
13. Swearer 2004, 15.
14. Gombrich 1978, 298.
15. Swearer 2004, 17.
16. Gombrich 1978, 300.
17. Gombrich 1978, 301.
18. Swearer 2004, 15.
19. Swearer 2004, 19.
20. Nattier 1991, 56–58.
21. Swearer 2004, 182.
22. Skilling and Pakdeekham 2007, 79.
23. Skilling and Pakdeekham 2007, 79.
24. According to the eighteenth-century account *Evidence Given by the Inhabitants of Ayutthaya*, King Narai (r. 1656–88) brought a sandalwood sculpture to Ayutthaya from Chiang Mai; however, this sculpture is described as a *naga*-protected buddha image, which are typically seated. See Woodward 2005, 52. It is not until the late Ayutthaya period that we see images of a standing buddha in a restraining posture emerge. Even so, this iconic type of buddha image does not appear to be readily adopted until the nineteenth century.
25. There is no conclusive opinion on the date and place of origin of the *Māleyyadevathera-vattu*. Eugène Denis and Saeng Monwithun have argued that the text has its origins in Sri Lanka, but Denis dates it to the eighth century, whereas Monwithun dates it to the twelfth century. Supaporn Makchang argues that it was written in Burma sometime between the tenth and the thirteenth centuries. Suphaphan na Bangchang believes that it was written in northern Thailand in the sixteenth century. For a thorough historiography of the *Māleyyadevathera-vattu*, see Brereton 1995, chap. 3. Justin McDaniel (2011) argues that the text is either from Sri Lanka or Thailand and dates to the fifteenth or sixteenth century (121).
26. Brereton 1995, 28, 67–68.

27. Brereton 1995, 28, 67–68. She notes that a vernacular recitation, rather than Pāli, makes it easy to understand and memorize, and contributes to the story's popularity. The annual three-day Vessantara Festival has traditionally been the greatest merit-making occasion of the year in Thailand, allowing for multiple days of conspicuous giving. The text is also recited during funerals as a form of making merit on behalf of the deceased.
28. Brereton 1995, 7–15. The summary that follows is adapted from Brereton's summary in chapter 1.
29. Other versions of the story, such as the *Phra Malai Kham Luang* ("royal version"), include only a minimal discussion on hell and hungry ghosts.
30. Brereton 1995, 112–13, 115.
31. Brereton 1995, 115.
32. Lefferts 2006–7, 151–54.
33. Jory 2016, 24.
34. Jory 2016, 25.
35. Bowie 2017, 125.
36. Bowie 2017, 130.
37. Lefferts 2006–7, 151–54.
38. National Statistical Office 2020, 67–71.
39. Brereton 1995, 110. For a study of these hell parks, see Anderson 2012.
40. Brereton 1995, 108–9.
41. This sculpture of the *Buddha Subduing the Sandalwood Image* comes from a set of thirty-seven sculptures commissioned by King Nangklao (1788–51) to commemorate the thirty-three kings of Ayutthaya, King Taksin of the Thonburi period (1767–82), and the Chakri kings. To access a photograph of this sculpture, see Hoskin 1994, 138.
42. Jory 2016, 10.
43. Jory 2016, 46.
44. HRH Damrong Rajanubhab 1982, 34–35.
45. Rod-ari 2017, 30.
46. A late Ayutthaya period sculpture of the Buddha subduing the sandalwood image, now in the royal collection at the Grand Palace in Bangkok, reflects an earlier tradition of images of this iconic type. However, after its reintroduction by King Nangklao, images of the Buddha subduing the sandalwood image become more readily adopted among elite patrons.
47. Swearer 2004, 125.
48. Swearer 2004, 125.
49. Reynolds 1972, 136.
50. Jory 2016, 109. In central Thailand the festival is referred to as Thet Maha Chat ("the great birth story"), whereas in northern Thailand and Lao it is referred to simply as Bun Phra Wet ("Vessantara Festival").
51. The festivals are still an important aspect of Thai Buddhist practice. This can be seen at all levels of society, including the royal family. King Bhumibol and Queen Sirikit

attended a Thet Maha Chat on the occasion of the king's eighty-fourth birthday in 2011. Similarly, Princess Sirindhorn has revived the recitation of the Vessantara Jātaka as a means of preserving Thai culture. The royal version of the text (*Maha Chat Kham Luang*) is chanted before the emerald Buddha annually. See Jory 2016, 12, 25.

Bibliography

Anderson, Benedict. 2012: *The Fate of Rural Hell: Asceticism and Desire in Buddhist Thailand*. London: Seagull Books.

Bhikkhu Bodhi, trans. 2003. *The Connected Discourses of the Buddha: A New Translation of the Saṃyutta Nikaya*. Boston: Wisdom Publications.

Bowie, Katherine A. 2017. *Of Beggars and Buddhas: The Politics of Humor in the Vessantara Jātaka in Thailand*. Madison: University of Wisconsin Press.

Brereton, Bonnie. 1995. *Thai Tellings of Phra Malai: Texts and Rituals concerning a Popular Buddhist Saint*. Tempe: Arizona State University Program for Southeast Asian Studies.

Damrong Rajanubhab, H. R. H. 1982. *Monuments of the Buddha in Siam*. Translated by Sulak Sivaraksa and A. B. Griswold. Bangkok: Siam Society.

Carter, Martha L. 1990. *The Mystery of the Udayana Buddha*. Naples: Istituto Universale Orientale.

Chiu, Angela. 2018. *The Buddha in Lanna: Art, Lineage, Power, and Place in Northern Thailand*. Honolulu: University of Hawai'i Press.

Gombrich, Richard. 1978. "Kosala-Bimba-Vaṇṇanā." In *Buddhism in Ceylon and Studies on Religious Syncretism in Buddhist Countries*, edited by Heinz Bechert, 281–303. Gottingen: Abhandlungen der Akademie der Wissenschaften.

Hoskin, John. 1994. *Buddha Images in the Grand Palace*. Bangkok: The Office of His Majesty's Principal Private Secretary.

Jory, Patrick. 2016. *Thailand's Theory of Monarchy: The Vessantara Jātaka and the Idea of the Perfect Man*. Albany: State University of New York Press.

Lefferts, Leedom. 2006–7. "'Bun Phra Wet': Painted Scrolls of Northeastern Thailand in the Walters Art Museum." *Journal of the Walters Art Museum* 64–65: 149–70.

McDaniel, Justin. 2011. *The Lovelorn Ghost and the Magical Monk*. New York: Columbia University Press.

National Statistical Office. 2020. *The 2018 Survey on Conditions of Society, Culture, and Mental Health*. Bangkok: Statistical Forecasting Division, National Statistical Office.

Nattier, Jan. 1991. *Once Upon a Future Time: Studies in a Buddhist Prophecy of Decline*. Berkeley, CA: Asian Humanities Press.

Reynolds, Craig J. 1972. *The Buddhist Monkhood in Nineteenth-Century Thailand*. Ann Arbor: University of Michigan Dissertation Services.

Rod-ari, Melody. 2017. "The Buddha as Sacred Siamese King: A Seated Buddha in the Walters Art Museum." *Journal of the Walters Art Museum* 73: 25–34.
Rotman, Andy. 2009. *Thus Have I Seen: Visualizing Faith in Early Indian Buddhism.* Oxford: Oxford University Press.
Skilling, Peter, and Santi Pakdeekham. 2007. "For Merit and Nirvana: The Production of Art in the Bangkok Period." *Arts Asiatiques* 62: 76–94.
Swearer, Donald K. 2004. *Becoming the Buddha: The Ritual of Image Consecration in Thailand.* Oxford: Oxford University Press.
Woodward, Hiram. 2005. "The Buddha Images of Ayutthaya." In *The Kingdom of Siam: The Art of Central Thailand, 1350–1800*, edited by Forrest McGill, 47–59. Ghent: Snoeck Publishers.

Bewildering Sounds of the Bardo

KURTIS R. SCHAEFFER

"Within those radiances, the natural sound of the Truth will reverberate like a thousand thunders. The sound will come with a rolling reverberation, [amidst which] will be heard, 'Slay! Slay!' and awe-inspiring mantras. Fear not. Flee not. Be not terrified."

—EVANS-WENTZ, *THE TIBETAN BOOK OF THE DEAD*, 1927.

INTRODUCTION

THE STORY OF EUROPEAN engagement with the *Tibetan Book of the Dead* begins in 1927, when Kazi Dawa Samdup's English translation was published by W. Y. Evans-Wentz with Oxford University Press. Donald Lopez has told that story brilliantly. His book, *The Tibetan Book of the Dead: A Biography*, explores the impact that this single strange book has had in Europe and America since the late 1920s. It is probably no exaggeration to say that throughout the mid-twentieth century, this translation was the most popular Tibetan Buddhist work in the English-speaking world. Lopez charted the path for anyone wishing to explore the cultural reception of the work (which I will refer to in this essay as Evans-Wentz's *Tibetan Book of the Dead*, or simply *The Book*). And once we walk down that path, we realize that the countryside is larger than it seems, with many ways and byways leading to multiple sites of meeting with this corpus of Tibetan Buddhist funerary literature, with its myth, ritual, theology, and emotional depth.

Here I follow one of these paths in search of a sound, the sound of that famed realm situated outside of physical human modes of existence, the *bardo*, the "in-between." "Bardo" (*bar do*) is a Tibetan term (a translation of the Sanskrit term *antarābhava*) that more literally means "between two" and is often translated as "intermediate state," referring primarily to the time-space between death and rebirth. More broadly, certain currents of Indian and Tibetan Buddhism speak of six intermediate states: (1) the present life, (2) meditative absorption, (3) dreams, (4) the moment of death, (5) reality, and (6) becoming (i.e., rebirth). The Nyingma tradition of Tibetan Buddhism elaborated extensively on this set of six states in compendia of funerary texts. A portion of this literature called "The Great Liberation through Hearing in the Intermediate State," dealing with states four through six—death, reality, and rebirth—is what Evans-Wentz published in 1927 as the *Tibetan Book of the Dead*.

While the bardo is a central point of doctrine in the theology of rebirth in Tibetan Buddhism, in the West it has tended to be treated as an imaginative vision of time and space that lies outside the material realm. This idea of the bardo has fascinated Western audiences for almost a century, a fascination that has prompted many creative adaptations throughout the arts, literature, film, and music. Even when we look just to ways in which musicians have interpreted, adapted, and refashioned *The Book*, the field is large and worthy of being fully mapped for those interested in the history of music and Asian religions in the Euro-American imagination. In this essay I focus on a single piece of music, *Le Voyage* by Pierre Henry, which is, I suggest, the most important[1] musical adaptation of Evans-Wentz's *Tibetan Book of the Dead*, as well as one of the most thoughtful Western interpretations of *The Book* in any medium. *Le Voyage* offers the possibility of attuning to the rich vocabulary of the senses in *The Book*. At first glance the primary sense that comes into play in the text, and that should occupy us as we read and interpret the text, is sight, for objects of sight are plentiful. But there is also a rich vocabulary of sound on nearly every page of *The Book*. The lama "calls" to the deceased. The deceased hears his loved ones "wail." Thunder "reverberates," and the breath "inspires" and "expires." Somewhat more abstractly, the numerous lights in the bardo are sources of sound, and "reality" itself manifests as sound. Finally, the deceased traveler in the bardo is almost as occupied with hearing the phenomena of the bardo as they are with seeing it. And while there are multiple sources and types of sound in the bardo, they are not value-neutral, and most sounds represent negative aspects of human experience. They represent the ordeals that the deceased person must undergo in the bardo. At least insofar as the deceased traveler experiences the sounds of the bardo, they are deeply troubling. They are "bad sounds."

But the bad sounds of the bardo are, from another perspective, not inherently bad. They are just misunderstood. For a sound in the bardo could be, as often as not, the sound of reality signaling to the traveler, offering directions toward enlightenment and away from negative rebirths. This is "good sound" by any measure. Unfortunately, the traveler fails at every turn to properly interpret this sound of reality, mistaking it instead for something terrifying that should be avoided at all costs. The traveler persists in this misrecognition because they are "bewildered"; they are incapable of accurately perceiving reality due to the bad habits of perception they have acquired through long lifetimes of equally bad karmic activity. In this sense, the bad sounds of the bardo are nothing more than the sounds of bewilderment. Pierre Henry's musical journey, *Le Voyage*, offers an imaginative experience of how this state of bewilderment in the bardo might feel for the deceased traveler. It does so by taking advantage of a novel form of acoustic experience that came into conceptual relief only when emerging techniques of twentieth-century electronic music could produce, to great effect, "acousmatic" sounds—sounds that you hear from an unknown source. In what follows we will listen to Henry's tale told in acousmatic sound in the hopes of better hearing the enigmatic and bewildering sounds of the bardo.

Le Voyage: A Brief History

Pierre Henry (1927–2017) was a French composer of, primarily, electronic music. He had a prolific career of seventy years, from his early work with *musique concrète* co-pioneer Pierre Schaeffer in the late 1940s and early 1950s until the end of his life. His published catalog includes scores of works, many of which are complex productions of an hour or more. He is best known for his contributions to electroacoustic music: instrumental music created by manipulating recordings of both traditional musical instruments and non-traditional sound sources, including, in principle, anything that can make a sound. In France, electroacoustic music was an outgrowth of innovations in *musique concrète* during the 1940s. Led by Schaeffer, *musique concrète* concentrated on using sound as both an object of philosophical inquiry and as a technique for phenomenological research. By contrast, electroacoustic music took advantage of the expanded repertoire of "instruments," the new range of timbres afforded by this exponential growth of potential sound sources, and the new recording and audio mixing technologies to push the boundaries of twentieth-century post-classical art music forward. Pierre Henry was at the forefront of this movement, and *Le Voyage* is a prime example from his early-middle period.[2]

Henry created *Le Voyage* as music for the choreographer Maurice Béjart's planned ballet of the same name. It was produced initially in his private studio, Studio Apsome, established in 1958.[3] He began recording the initial version of the piece in late December 1961 and completed it in late January of the following year. The work was, effectively, a live piece of electronic music produced in the studio; according to Michel Chion, who has written the most extensive analysis of the piece, recordings made throughout the prior decade were mixed from multiple sources onto a two-track tape. The main work of performance consisted of manipulating the recordings of the sound sources while simultaneously mixing them down into two tracks. This was by all accounts an active, intensive process; Chion recounts the words of one of Henry's assistants: "[Henry] clung to the knobs, perspired, writhed, and 'danced like an orchestra unto himself!'"[4] The piece had its debut several months after that, when it premiered in Béjart's ballet at the Cologne Opera House on April 15, 1962.

Henry performed the work live between 1962 and 1963; it is not known how many performances there were. A recording of a performance on June 25, 1963 was released on an album in 1963 in France on the Phillips label, and in 1968 in the United States on the Mercury Records imprint for experimental music, Limelight.[5] *Le Voyage* receives passing mention in histories of electronic music.[6] Its popular reception in the 1960s appears to have been more robust than histories might suggest. Upon its US release it was named in the weekly album release notes in *Billboard Magazine* in 1968 (placed in the Classical section between *Mozart: Quartets K 412 & K 575* and *Schumann: Fantasy in C/Symphonic Etudes*), with the following promotional copy: "Based on the Tibetan 'Book of the Dead,' Pierre Henry's 'Le Voyage' is an inventive electronic work that evokes the atmosphere from final breath ('Breath I') to rebirth ('Breath II'). The work, which has been choreographed, details the three stages between death and reincarnation and 'Le Voyage' follows this pattern with telling effect."[7] If, at the time of its release, *Le Voyage* was undertaken primarily by patrons of avant-garde art music, by the late 1960s it had entered into the realm of popular music, finding a home in both psychedelic and electronic subcultures, valued in each for its musical and technological innovation as well as its "spiritual" import. Which brings us back to Evans-Wentz's *Tibetan Book of the Dead*, enjoying its own counterculture success during that decade.

Narrating the Bardo in Le Voyage

Henry began reading *The Tibetan Book of the Dead* in 1960. It is likely, though not certain, that he read *The Book* in French translation. It had been translated into French by Marguerite La Fuente and published in 1933 with a preface by the Tibetologist Jacques Bacot. This translation went through several reprints, including one in 1958. Presumably it is La Fuente's translation that Henry read and adapted.[8] He appears to have already begun work on a musical adaptation of the work in 1960. When the choreographer Maurice Béjart approached him with an invitation to collaborate on a new ballet, Henry suggested his adaptation of *The Book* for the stage, a suggestion that Béjart took up.[9]

Le Voyage is just over forty-nine minutes long and is structured into seven separately titled sections, or perhaps "movements." Each of the seven movements treats a particular event in the central passage of Evans-Wentz's *Tibetan Book of the Dead*, the journey of the deceased from death to birth through the bardo. "Breath 1" (7 minutes, 7 seconds) takes the listener from the labored dying breaths of the traveler as they begin their journey to the in-between, and then on "through" the passage between life and death. "After Death 1" (9'44") portrays the first moments of awareness after death, a time when the traveler does not know where they are or even what has happened to them. At this crucial moment the traveler does have some chance of achieving liberation, if only they can recognize the light of reality. But they cannot. Their strength fails as darkness overcomes them. In "After Death 2" (7'33") the traveler hears and sees many people and things from the world yet is unable to make any substantial contact with them. "Peaceful Deities" (9'27") introduces the benevolent forces that the traveler encounters. They are nevertheless unable to recognize them as welcoming and see these beings as menacing threats. "Wrathful Deities" (3'14") offers the traveler one last chance to recognize the clear light of reality, yet these beings too are mistaken for true threats and the traveler flees in terror. In "The Coupling" (6'50") the traveler encounters would-be parents in the next physical realm. Witnessing those parents-to-be having sex, the traveler is forced from the immaterial to the material realm and is born again. "Breath 2" (5'02") finds the traveler arrived at their fated destination, back where they began, rasping the breath of life, forgetting all that they have just gone through, the memory fading of their fleeting chance to recognize the light of reality, to achieve liberation.

Henry's retelling of the story of passing from life to death and to life again was, first and foremost, musical. But he also adapted *The Book* into a brief prose version. This seven-paragraph précis of the events before, during, and after the voyage in the bardo was included in the album notes for both the French and US releases and in Henry's collected essays.[10]

Roughly, *Le Voyage* covers the events depicted over some one hundred pages of Evans-Wentz's *Tibetan Book of the Dead* (pages 89–193)—that is, the narrative that takes the traveler from the last moments of life through death to the first moments of birth as a human. This is a complex narrative, full of steps, missteps, retracings, possibilities, and inevitabilities, and *Le Voyage* and its accompanying brief text do not—cannot—treat each moment of the text in equal detail. What's more, the lengthy passage includes a great deal of theology, in which the phenomena that the traveler encounters are linked with more or less specificity to Buddhist doctrines mostly dealing with the nature of absolute reality. Henry's text barely alludes to these; it is a matter of interpretation whether the music "refers" to these ideas or not.

Here is a translation of Henry's text, along with the titles of each of the seven movements of *Le Voyage* and the roughly corresponding page numbers in the English version of Evans-Wentz's *The Tibetan Book of the Dead*:

1. Breath I (Evans-Wentz 89–95): "Hearing may be the last means of perception. Swollen in the ears of the dying, the last clamor of earthly life, a thousand whispered voices, a thousand cars, a thousand sea horns, rips of teeth, hands, the radio pushed to its climax. And a wind, a wind that comes closer, that he recognizes to be his breathing. Beside him is the lama, the priest, or the friend. Then it's the slow suck of the breath."

2. After Death I (Evans-Wentz 95–104): "At this moment appears the clear light which the *Tibetan Book of the Dead* says releases from the cycle of rebirths if it is recognized. Distressed, the being seeks to reach it. He leaps! He leaps, weakening as black clouds are rising, blinding him, slowly plunging him into darkness."

3. After Death II (Evans-Wentz 95–104): "Half-awake, and he sees his parents, his friends, his house. He rushes, shouts, begs, and breaks on a transparency. Around him are born sounds, rays. The other world is manifesting itself. Unknown vibrations strike him with terror. Disturbing forms seem to want to devour him. He is brushed by beings in a high voice. The wind of karma carries him, pushes him toward sudden abysses. Brutal gleaming lights make him lose his mind."

4. Peaceful Deities (Evans-Wentz 104–31): "Yet along this road, gods of light, gods of wisdom, smile at him, waiting for his coming. Locked in an abject terror, the being walks in a series of mirages born only of his imagination."

5. Wrathful Deities (Evans-Wentz 131–51): "Even the terrible angry goddesses hide behind their frightful cries a call for final liberation."

6. The Coupling (Evans-Wentz 153–83): "When he has become a total wreck, when he has refused all opportunities to escape the wheel of life and death, the being is doomed to be reborn. The wind of karma pushes him toward the gates of six matrices, each

color of which indicates a climate of spiritual life on Earth. Gigantic couplings arise. He gasps. A desirous matter is spreading. Male and female beings surround him. An invincible force attracts him. The atmosphere becomes hostile. Finally, he throws himself into the matrix that corresponds to his desire for life. The male and the female mate. The doors close again."

7. Breath II (Evans-Wentz 183–93): "Again the ear perceives the sharp wind of reality. Being finds a land hostile and hard. The breath takes possession of bones and flesh. The breathing agrees with the dementia wind. Memory disappears."

Henry's narrative adaptation of *The Book* in this brief précis of the seven movements provides the context in which we hear Henry's sounds of the bardo. Without the narrative, there is no reason for sound. Sound features in the opening moment of Henry's textual sound narrative. It also ends the story, and it plays a pivotal role in the central portion, the encounter with deities. Breath, the most human of sounds, both opens and closes *Le Voyage*. It is the sound of the breath that is modulated almost beyond recognition at the moment of death (Breath I, 4'20"), eventually becoming the "wind of karma," the winds of the bardo propelling the traveler forward. Sound is also a causal factor in the narrative, for it (along with imagery, of course) drives the narrative forward. In movements 3 and 4 the traveler comes upon a deity, experiences the sound and vision of the deity, is repelled (through their own misapprehension), and is propelled onward, toward the next encounter.

The sonic vocabulary of *The Book*, which we will explore below, is not extensively adapted in Henry's text narrative; this he leaves largely for the music itself. But it also is not entirely absent. Wind is here, as it is in *The Book*, though in Henry's telling wind is more prominent than in his source text (a single mention). Movement 4, when the deities "call" out to the traveler, is pivotal in Henry's text, and this "call" is the raw material of the two central movements. Henry himself left no record of how or if he annotated *The Book* as he adapted it. It seems to have been paramount to Henry to bring into relief the narrative of the deceased's journey—the "voyage"—against the densely packed amalgam of narrative, theology, ritual, and direct and indirect speech of this section of *The Book*. His goal in his text is to tell a tragic tale that binds together in reduced form all of the disparate elements in *The Book*. It is left to us to imagine precisely where—what chapter, line, and verse—Henry might have found his inspiration, beyond the narrative that he epitomizes in his own text.

And what was inspiring *musically* for Henry in Evans-Wentz's *Tibetan Book of the Dead*? Did Evans-Wentz's text suggest certain timbres, tonalities, or forms? And was it the vocabulary, style, progression of events, or ideas that captured Henry's imagination? In the next section we can attend to timbre and the "sonic vocabulary" of *The Book*. But first we can ask about form, for certainly the narrative itself, as Henry reconstructs it, provides a course for the flow of the seven movements, perhaps leading him in certain directions as he worked on the musical form of each individual movement. We can see something of this work if we listen more carefully to one of the movements: "Peaceful Deities."

Musical Form in Le Voyage as a Reading of the Tibetan Book of the Dead Narrative

"Peaceful Deities" (9'27" or 9'18", depending on the pressing) stands at the center of *Le Voyage* and could be considered its most compelling rendering of the imagery, narrative, and mythology of the *Tibetan Book of the Dead*. A close listening to the sounds and structure of this movement might, then, help us to interpret Henry's sonic vision of the in-between.

The structure of "Peaceful Deities" is ABA.[11] Part A1 lasts from approximately 0'00 to 4'20, B from 4'20" to 7'18", and A2 from there to the conclusion at 9'27". Part A1 begins quietly and softly, then rises in volume and intensity over its four minutes, suggesting perhaps a slow gathering of the traveler and the beings they encounter, the deities themselves. Long, drawn-out sounds with slow attack and quick decay dominate Part A, with horn-like (or foghorn, perhaps) squelches punctuating the languorous pace. Part B moves to a higher-pitched set of sounds with slow attack and relatively slow decay. Part A2 returns to horn-like sounds of A1, repeating them with increased frequency.

According to Chion, the two primary sound sources in "Peaceful Deities" are feedback and vibrating metal rods, with the latter dominating. For

Henry and his colleagues composing electroacoustic music, feedback was a significant sound source. Much experimental music of the period uses feedback as a sonic medium of great plasticity. New instruments using metallic rods rigged onto bespoke frames so that they could be played were also popular at the time. Finally, most sounds are fairly well drenched in reverb, lending a sense of space.

A third sound source, or "instrument," was the recording and playback studio itself. Audio playback and modulation systems—tape recorders and players, equalizers, amplifiers, filters, and so forth—were relatively novel forms of technology even in 1962. One of the key innovations of the *musique concrète* movement was to shift the horizon of possibility for what one can and should do with a recording studio. Formerly the studio was intended to capture live performances of music with as much fidelity as the technology allowed. Now the particularities of the electronic equipment were no longer simply passive recorders of sound but creators of sound, and the idiosyncrasies of available audio equipment were no longer liabilities but rather advantages in the search for new timbres and tonalities. This was, perhaps, an ideal creative medium for exploring the unknown space of the in-between.

If we attempt to describe the sounds of "Peaceful Deities" in more detail, we might say: Part A1 begins with a low ambient rumble (0:00) that slowly increases in volume until the introduction of a high, slow squeal (0:35). After another 25 seconds a new tone, a "bent" note that is microtonally related to the previous squeal, is introduced (0:55). By minute 2 the two "voices" are juxtaposed, weaving microtonally in and out of each other, toward and away from each other. A new voice, a high buzz, begins (01:20), followed by yet another new sound, a horn-like staccato tone (01:35). At 1:50 a more urgent howl and rumble emerges, and then (01:58) a vibrating bass leads into the most complex passage yet as four or five tones sound simultaneously (02:00). Throughout minute 3 (02:00–03:00) these multiple voices are juxtaposed with silence, until a deeper bass tone dominates (03:00), periodically set in relief by a contrasting higher-pitched buzz (03:00–04:15). Mid-range tones emerge as dominant as Part A fades into silence.

Part B begins (04:15) with a high ambient swirl, made to seem "distant" through volume and reverb. Two notes eventually emerge (04:45), both high and reedy. At slightly past the half-way point (05:00) percussive sounds are introduced for the first time, after which a distant whistle is interposed with a high reed (05:20). Some two-thirds of the way through the piece (06:10) a crescendo signals increased dramatic intensity, a climax of sorts, in which most of the sounds of Part B are brought together. By minute 7 (07:00) only reeds remain, the percussion subsides and becomes distant, leaving us in silent expectation of the final part.

The conclusion turns out to be a recapitulation: Part A2, the final movement of three in "Peaceful Deities," begins with the return of the horn-like sound of minute 1'35" (07:20). At 8'00" a long crescendo begins, repeating the howl and rumble of 1'50," this time with higher volume and greater frequency of recurrence. As the end nears (08:39), high, sharp descending tones dominate. Finally, the conclusion is signaled with a high, urgent descending tone (09:10) before receding into silence once again.

Form in experimental music, bereft of the innate structures of tonality and recognizable timbres that might be mapped onto traditional performance instrumentation, can be challenging to discern. Yet form lends structure to a set of sounds that appear, at first, to resist structuring. More important for our attempts to hear *Le Voyage* and *The Book* in relation to each other, the musical form of "Peaceful Deities" lends end-to-end narrative logic to a section of the book that is otherwise episodic, with no real beginning and end, only a series of more or less equal scenes. In *Le Voyage*, by contrast, the traveler follows a narrative arc that includes, at least, a journey toward adventure, the adventure itself, the—in this case—failure to succeed in the adventure, and the retreat from that central action. Emotionally, the piece moves from low intensity to high intensity, lingers there in an ambiguous state of action, and finally settles back again to low intensity. In other words, the traveler comes into the presence of the deities, remains there, and recedes. (Or is it that the deities move forward and back while the traveler remains stationary? The musical form does not make this explicit.) In *Le Voyage*, all of this happens once over the course of nine minutes. In *The Book*, the basic movement of coming-staying-going happens no less than seven times, or once per day for seven days. In *Le Voyage*, Henry compacts multiple encounters into a single, protracted, instance. Once is enough, perhaps. To work through how the sounds that make up the form of "Peaceful Deities" might relate to *The Book*'s themes and narrative elements in more detail, it will be useful to look more closely at the portrayal of sound in the text itself.

Connecting Sound and Music to the Bardo

Evans-Wentz's *Tibetan Book of the Dead* contains a rich vocabulary of sounds and sound sources. This vocabulary is central to the work's depiction of the in-between state. As such, the lexicon of sound used in Evans-Wentz (as well as, just as important, the French lexicon that Marguerite La Fuente employed to translate Evans-Wentz) presumably impacted Henry's interest in *The Book* as well as the specific narrative and musical choices he made in his adaptation of it. And because of the imaginative nature of the subject—a realm of time and space that occurs after death, before birth, and that is, significantly, immaterial—the exact nature of the sounds and their sources are not clear. What are the sounds? Deities' voices? Movement? Landscapes? Emotions? Visceral feeling? What are the sources of sound? Material objects? How does sound travel in the in-between? And by what sense does the traveler "hear" sounds? None of these questions have easy answers, a situation that adds to both the challenge and the allure of imagining an idea such as the in-between through sound.

The vocabulary of sound in Evans-Wentz's *Tibetan Book of the Dead* is extensive, especially if we consider that, on balance, light and visual imagery dominate the sections on peaceful and wrathful deities. The central sections treating the journey from death to birth provide a sense of the sonic world of the bardo; we find well over one hundred occurrences of some three dozen sound words, ranging from "crumbling" to "echo" to "voice." Each of these terms calls for analysis in the source language (Tibetan) and the target languages (English and French), for each term suggests a landscape of meaning and embodied experience situated within each of those three distinctive cultural worlds. Further, if we were to expand this list to potential sound sources, extending a category of terms that is best exemplified by "wind" that "blasts" or "seas" that "overflow," the list would double in size. The bardo is brimming with sound. Almost everything in it makes a sound. Even light can be a sound source (if perhaps indirect): "From the midst of that radiance . . . sound . . . will come."[12] The movements of the traveler, the landscapes (however abstract), the amorphous masses of the deities, the figures encountered by the traveler, the interiors, exteriors—each of these suggests a distinctive sound, a sound that is at least supportive of the visual imagination, often constitutive of the visual, and at times the sole source and product of a sonic rather than visual imagination.

A few examples make clear the extent to which sound is a leading phenomenon in *The Book*, and where aurality is at times a prevailing imaginative mode. It is in the passages dealing with deities that this vocabulary is perhaps used to best effect, both the peaceful deities (Evans-Wentz 104–31) and the wrathful deities (Evans-Wentz 131–51).

The section on peaceful deities comprises a seven-day itinerary through the in-between that formulaically moves through a series of encounters with deities. Each encounter provides the traveler with the chance to recognize the nature of reality "behind the veil" of the visions encountered. Predictably, our tragic hero fails to make this recognition each time. Along the way, the section associates six features with a given deity of the day. First, each deity is paired with a distinct color of "radiant" light and a distinct "dull light." These are the phenomena that the traveler "sees." Next, each deity is associated with an element and a psychophysical aggregate. Finally, each complex of deity/light/aggregate is tied to rebirth in one of the six realms of existence in the wheel of life, as well as a dominant emotion that provides a karmically causal link between the traveler and rebirth in one of the six realms. Schematically, the peaceful deities' system looks like this: (see tables on pp. 78–79).

The section on peaceful deities is dominated, on the surface at least, by visions of light. In what we might call theological terms, the system is constructed of visual ideas. Some of these are more closely associated with traditional Buddhist visual representations of divinity: the colors of the gods might suggest to some the images of deities found in paintings, though there is little detailed iconography in this section of *The Book*. Some of this imagery has less to do with formal Tibetan art, such as the orbs or the distinction between the bright lights and the "dull" lights. And the six realms may or may not conjure memories of the wheel of life in the mind's eye of the reader or listener. Vision is key here, of course.

Day	Element	Radiant Light	Deity
1	(Whole Heavens)	Blue	Vairocana (Blue)
2	Water	White	Vajrasattva (Blue)
3	Earth	Yellow	Ratnasambava
4	Fire	Red	Amitābha
5	Air	Green	Amoghasiddhi
6	All Four	All (as Orbs)	Forty-two
7	(Propensities)	Varicolored	Knowledge-Holders, Ḍākinīs, Ḍākas

But sound is never far away. It is implied throughout, for the entire "peaceful deities" section is bounded by several key passages featuring sound, and itself includes significant moments where sound comes to the fore. Two passages lead into the first of the seven days. The first occurs just after the newly deceased traveler has attempted to communicate across the divide between death and life to their weeping and wailing friends and relatives. The traveler is unable to make contact, and so leaves, frustrated. Where they go is not entirely clear, but then this is stated: "At that time, sounds, lights, and rays—all three—are experienced. These awe, frighten, and terrify, and cause much fatigue."[13] Lights, light rays, and sounds: these are the raw materials out of which the beings and phenomena are soon to be encountered—namely, that from which the deities and their "communications" are fashioned. These sounds, along with their attendant lights and rays, ultimately confound the traveler, for they fail, time after time, to recognize them for what they are: dispatches from reality, natural and pure, working to find a way through the traveler's karmically impeded senses.

Yet even when light is a dominant metaphor for the *appearance* of reality, *reality itself* is characterized by reference to sound: "From the midst of that radiance, the natural sound of Reality, reverberating like a thousand thunders simultaneously sounding, will come. That is the natural sound of thine own real self. Be not daunted thereby, nor terrified, nor awed."[14] If one can hear this sound, one is liberated. If not, one passes on to the next day in the

Aggregate	Dull Light	Six Realms	Emotions
Matter	White	Gods	(Bad Karma)
Consciousness	Smoke	Hell	Anger
Touch	Bluish-Yellow	Human	Egotism
Feeling	Red	Hungry Ghost	Attachment
Volition	Green	Demigod	Jealousy
—	All	All Six	—
—	Blue	Animal	Ignorance

in-between, the next deity, the next chance to hear it right, become liberated, and avoid rebirth in one of the six realms.

Toward the conclusion of the section, *The Book* returns to this particular sound, the sound of reality struggling, seemingly, to be correctly heard clearly through the karmic static, no matter how bad the connection is: "Within those radiances, the natural sound of the Truth will reverberate like a thousand thunders. The sound will come with a rolling reverberation, [amidst which] will be heard, 'Slay! Slay!' and awe-inspiring mantras. Fear not. Flee not. Be not terrified. Know them [i.e., these sounds] to be [of] the intellectual faculties of thine own [inner] light."[15]

It is the "rolling reverberation" that stands out here, as well as the hyperbole—not just one instance of thunder, but a thousand thunderclaps. And with reverb! The radiance that confronts the traveler may be seen, but the rolling thunder is *felt*. The light is visual; the sound is multisensorial. You hear it, you feel it, you see the lightning and clouds. It is all around you, and all the more awe-inspiring precisely because its sources are gleaned through vision yet not precisely located. It is everywhere. Rolling reverberation: Kazi Dawa Samdup and/or Evans-Wentz were, it appears, having fun with alliteration, the sounds of English, as they worked to capture something distinctive here in *The Book*'s sonic vocabulary. And the sound has emotional depth. A light might be startling, but thunder can be terrifying. With such cacophony cascading through whatever space the in-between might be, is it any wonder that the traveler failed to understand reality's message of liberation?

In central portions of the "peaceful deities" section sound features in the refrain that accompanies each day's encounter with a new deity. Sound is not specifically associated with a deity and its attendant colored light in each of the seven days (this is more frequent in the following section, on wrathful deities). Yet it is enough to establish a pattern. Here is day four: "[T]hough so often set face to face [with the deity in the bardo, KRS], there are classes of men who, having created much bad karma, or having failed in observance of vows, or, their lot [for higher development] being altogether lacking, prove unable to recognize [the deity, KRS]: their obscurations and evil karma from covetousness and miserliness produce awe of the sounds and radiances, and they flee."[16] On day five, "awe and terror [are] being produced by the sounds and radiances."[17]

In both of these passages, sounds and lights confront the person wandering the in-between. But it is not the phenomena themselves that are the cause of the traveler's reaction, it is the limitation of their perception. And this limitation is created through karma, through the long repetition of negative behaviors—covetousness, miserliness, jealousy. Terror ensues as the traveler escapes the presence of the deity and its enlightened display of sound and vision (it is implied in English that the deity is stationary while the traveler moves).

Sound is more deeply embedded within the scene of the seventh and final day of the encounters with peaceful deities. Strictly speaking, the traveler does not meet peaceful deities on day seven, but rather knowledge-holder deities and other celestial figures. These beings, who sit between the peaceful and wrathful deities in *The Book*, exhibit both peaceful and wrathful features, though on balance their features align them more closely with the wrathful deities who come in the next section. *Le Voyage* does not distinguish this category explicitly; the fact that they are grouped under the heading of "peaceful deities" in Evans-Wentz's *Tibetan Book of the Dead* would suggest that Henry included them within the purview of the fourth movement, "Peaceful Deities." Here *The Book* tells us that: ". . . heroes, heroines, celestial warriors, and faith-protecting deities, male and female, each bedecked with the six bone-ornaments, having drums and thigh-bone trumpets, skull-timbrels, banners of gigantic human[-like] hides, human-hide canopies, human-hide bannerettes, fumes of human-fat incense, and innumerable [other] kinds of musical instruments, filling [with music] the whole world-systems and causing them to vibrate, to quake and tremble with sounds so mighty as to daze one's brain, and dancing various measures, will come to receive the faithful and punish the unfaithful."[18]

In this passage sounds are more clearly linked to sound sources than in the previous examples. The host of beings still represent reality, and as such are the visceral front-end of an experience/place/entity that is, for the traveler, all but intangible. In contrast to the properly peaceful deities encountered in days one through six, these quasi-wrathful beings are more fully realized in their particulars, with much more detail drawn into their descriptions. And the sound here is not any sound; it is music. It comes from instruments that are, to a certain extent, recognizable as instruments—trumpets and various drums. The beings with these instruments are doing something recognizable: dancing and performing music. This is *The Book* in its, relatively speaking, "realist" mode, where a sensory phenomenon can be traced back to its cause (even if the cause is a drum made of human skin played by a dancing demon who, despite appearances to the contrary, has your best interests at heart, trying to talk to you through their drum and bass performance). And yet here the magnitude of sound's impact extends beyond this pseudo-realism into the realm of the hypertelescopic imagination in which one sees, in a single instance, oneself simultaneously located in the micro-landscape where one's body currently is and in the macro-landscape of the universe, its galaxies and stars.[19] The sound moves worlds. Galaxies shake. And the traveler is astonished and bewildered. It is sound that has causal force here, and especially where it counts, in the mind of the wandering being trying to make sense of what they are experiencing.

Throughout *The Book*'s section on peaceful deities, sound seems at first glance to play a secondary role. But upon second listen, even when there is no mention of sound or sounds at all, light and visual imagery in *The Book* possess a quality that is easily—and perhaps better—evoked by sound: movement. The deities and beings are in constant movement relative to our protagonist, whether it is the deities or the traveler who move. Henry captures the implicit movement at play in *The Book* with exquisite grace in *La*

Voyage. Variation in volume, timbre, stereo imaging, and reverb depth all evoke a sense of movement. And they do so with a level of indeterminacy that fits the subject well. For it is the indeterminacy of the visual—their actual shapes, their directionality, their *intentionality*—that the traveler routinely fails to correctly perceive or understand. Sound, shorn from its source, embodies this indeterminacy, and far more effectively than words.

Conclusions

I said at the beginning of this essay that I take Pierre Henry's *Le Voyage* to be not just a significant adaptation of *The Tibetan Book of the Dead* but a significant interpretation of *The Book*. That is, in my view, *Le Voyage* offers an analysis of *The Book* as well as an argument for what it means. It is thus comparable to the works on Buddhist ideas, texts, and practices that we more typically call interpretation—*textual* interpretation. Experimental music, or perhaps more broadly the creative use of sound, can turn our focus to the potential roles of sound in Buddhism itself. As interpretive modes, music and sound move us from visual and doctrinal modes of engagement to imagined experience, experience not predicated on statement or belief.

Take, for example, the idea of "bewilderment" (*'khrul pa*/*bhrānti*). *Le Voyage* might aid us in work on this key Buddhist concept, which has a long history in, especially, Yogācāra literature, and features critically in *The Tibetan Book of the Dead*. As Gyurme Dorje usefully summarizes in the context of *The Book*, "bewilderment" is "the confusion arising from the subject-object dichotomy and fundamental ignorance, on the basis of which rebirth in cyclic existence is perpetuated."[20] He goes on to point out that "the harsh and bewildering experiences related to past actions (*las kyi 'khrul snang*) are those manifestations of sound, lights and rays of light which appear during the intermediate state of reality (*chos nyid bar do*)."[21] In other words, the precise doctrinal reason that the deceased person tragically fails at every turn to recognize reality in the bardo when given the chance—multiple chances—is bewilderment. Over the centuries this term has expanded from a rather narrowly constrained notion of mistaking objects in the real world to what we find in the *The Tibetan Book of the Dead* and its larger Nyingma doctrinal context—namely, the fundamental reason for existence itself, with all of its pain and suffering, and the foremost impediment to liberation.

An intellectual history approach to bewilderment might track changes over the centuries as the term morphed from one to another meaning, or look at debates about the causes and scope of bewilderment among the various schools of Buddhist thought. But what if one asks, "What does it *feel* like to be existentially bewildered?" This is a reasonable question; Buddhists claim this state to be an all-encompassing malady that effects mind, body, and emotion. And what could such an experience possibly feel like *in the bardo*? If feeling is believing, what sorts of technologies do texts such as *The Book* employ in an attempt to inculcate such a feeling? How do we—how does anyone—possibly imagine the sort of human experience that the text speaks of as if it were an experience like any other? A classic text-based technique is to cite a visual example, such as the proverbial rope/snake. Does this work? Imagine looking at tree, smelling its fragrance, touching its bark, experiencing it viscerally, but not knowing its species—is that what bewilderment is like? No, words fail here. But sound . . . sound has something over word and text here. And specifically, because of a unique property that musicians and researchers in the *musique concréte* movement identified, named, and creatively explored: that something may be the acousmatic experience.

"Acousmatic" is a term coined in 1952 by Pierre Schaeffer—who here is better thought of as a phenomenologist rather than a sound researcher—to refer to an "auditory situation in which we hear sounds without seeing their cause or source."[22] This much is fairly rote today; such sounds occur constantly around us in our media environment. But Chion teases out the implications of this notion that are relevant to bewilderment: "This is one of the defining features of media such as the telephone and radio, but it often occurs . . . in countless auditory situations in everyday life when a sound reaches us without our seeing its cause." He continues, "The effects of acousmatic perception vary widely, depending on whether or not we have previously seen the source of the sound. If the source has been seen, the acousmatic sound carries along with it a mental visual representation; when the source has not been seen, the sound strikes us more abstractly and, in some cases, can become an enigma."[23]

Enigma. This is a good term to summarize the music of *Le Voyage*—"a mystery, puzzling or difficult to understand." And, as with Buddhist bewilderment, this enigma is frustrating. The frustration experienced by the traveler on their voyage through the in-between is the frustration experienced by the listener; we hear the sounds but we do not know their source. Sound may evoke images, but we have no way to ascertain how accurately or inaccurately the sounds relate to that imagery. The sound is inescapable, but we do not understand it in reference to anything else. We can hear the components out of which it is created, but we cannot put those pieces together in any easily meaningful fashion. We do not know how the sound was made. We do not *know what it is*.

An enigma. Sound as bewilderment. The experience of it undeniable—its source, its cause, and therefore its significance, unknown. *Le Voyage* is built entirely of acousmatic sound; at no point does the listener (even, for the most part, a listener with experience in electroacoustic music, I would wager) know where the sound comes from. The unique capacity of electroacoustic music to sever the bond between sound and its source, between the music and the "instrument," affords the chance to visualize, to "auralize," the unknown, the misrecognized. We are not even sure if the sounds in *The Book*'s extensive sound lexicon are communication or not. Is meaning intended in *The Book*'s portrayal of deities? Is its portrayal of ultimate reality "messaging" humanity? The music of *Le Voyage* offers experience, suggests meaning, hints at an immensity of cosmic dimensions. Yet it stops short of denoting the content of that meaning. Perhaps this is a good way to treat the language whirling around "reality" in *The Book*, to temper expectations that language should or even *can* explain this key theme of Tibetan Buddhist ontology and cosmology.

What better way to represent, to interpret, the sound of the gods, the sound of the radiance, the sound of reality pulsing through the in-between? *Le Voyage*'s sound is an enigma, as are the sounds the traveler encounters in the bardo. It is "bad sound" to the extent that it is the sound of bewilderment, a sound that, whatever its source, is inscrutable to the perceiver, to the traveler, who can only run from it in fright. Perhaps, then, listening to *Le*

Voyage can help us to imagine the bewilderment of encountering the voice of reality only to fail—endlessly—to recognize the liberating immensity that exists just beyond our grasp on the journey through the in-between.

Notes

1. Other major works include R. Murray Schafer's *From the Tibetan Book of the Dead* (1973), Éliane Radigue's *Trilogie de la Mort* (1988), Hans Zender's *Bardo* (2000), and Jonathan Harvey's *Wagner Dream* (2007), to name some of the several dozen works that engage the *Tibetan Book of the Dead* in electronic, experimental, contemporary classical, and rock music.
2. Refer to Manning 2013, chap. 1, and references therein for a brief history of *musique concrète*, and to Chion and Riebel 1976 for an earlier, less streamlined account of electroacoustic music in Europe, authored by two practitioner-scholars who were part of the electroacoustic movement.
3. Holmes 2004, 72.
4. Chion 2003, 86.
5. This is according to the liner notes of the Phillips album: "Création á Paris le 25 juin 1963 en l'Eglise Saint-Julien-le-Pauvre, dans la version concert qui est celle de ce disque." However, according to Chion (2003, 89), it was a stereo version recorded on December 21, 1962 that was published on disc. Whichever the case, it appears that only a single version has been issued on album in multiple pressings. The French pressing of 1963 and the US pressing of 1968 are listed in the recordings section of the bibliography.
6. For example, Manning 2013, 144.
7. "Pierre Henry, Le Voyage," *Billboard*, March 16, 1968, 74.
8. Evans-Wentz 2000. References to *The Tibetan Book of the Dead* in this essay follow the English of Evans-Wentz 2000. Those who may wish to follow along with the more contemporary translation can compare Dorje 2005, 205–303.
9. Chion 2003, 84.
10. Henry 2004, 73–76.
11. Chion 2003, 94.
12. Evans-Wentz 2000, 102.
13. Evans-Wentz 2000, 102.
14. Evans-Wentz 2000, 104.
15. Evans-Wentz 2000, 129.
16. Evans-Wentz 2000, 112–13.
17. Evans-Wentz 2000, 115.
18. Evans-Wentz 2000, 128.
19. Stapledon 1972, 16.
20. Gyurme Dorje 2005, 448.

21. Gyurme Dorje 2005, 426n30.
22. Chion 2009, 465.
23. Chion 2009, 465.

Bibliography

Recordings

Pierre Henry. 1963. *Le Voyage: D'après le Livre des Morts Tibétain*. France: Series Prospective 21e Siècle, Phillips 836.899 DSY, LP, album.

Pierre Henry. 1968. *Le Voyage: The Fantastic Journey from Death to Life, An Electronic Score Based on the Tibetan Book of the Dead*. USA: Limelight/Mercury LS 86049/SR90482, LP, stereo.

Radigue, Eliane. 1998. *Trilogie de la mort*. USA: Experimental Intermedia Foundation, series XI 119, 3 compact discs.

Zender, Hans. 2007. *Schumann–Phantasie: Bardo for Cello and Orchestra*. USA: Hännsler Classic 93.128, compact disc.

Books

Augoyard, Jean-François, and Henry Torgue. 2005. *Sonic Experience: A Guide to Everyday Sounds*. Montreal: McGill-Queens University Press.

Chion, Michel. 2003. *Pierre Henry*. Paris: Fayard.

———. 2009. *Film, a Sound Art*. New York: Columbia University Press.

———. 2019. *Kubrick's Cinema Odyssey*. New York: Bloomsbury Publishing.

Chion, Michel, and Guy Reibel. 1976. *Les musiques électroacoustiques*. Aix-en-Provence: Edisud.

Evans-Wentz, W. Y. 1933. *Le Livre des Morts Tibétain: Ou les expériences d'après la mort dans le plan du Bardo*. Translated by Marguerite La Fuente. Paris: Adrien Maissoneuve.

———. 2000. *The Tibetan Book of the Dead. With a New Foreword and Afterword by Donald S. Lopez, Jr.* New York: Oxford University Press.

Gyurme Dorje, trans. 2005. *The Tibetan Book of the Dead*. New York: Penguin Books.

Harvey, Jonathan. 2012 [2007]. *Wagner Dream*. Belgium: Cypress.

Henry, Pierre. 2004. *Journal de mes sons: Suivi de préfaces et manifestes*. Paris: Actes Sud.

Holmes, Thomas. 2004. *Electronic and Experimental Music: Technology, Music, and Culture*. New York: Routledge.

Lopez, Donald. 2011. *The Tibetan Book of the Dead: A Biography*. Princeton, NJ: Princeton University Press.

Manning, Peter. 2013. *Electronic and Computer Music*. 4th ed. New York: Oxford University Press.

Pinch, T. J., and Frank Trocco. 2002. *Analog Days: The Invention of the Moog Synthesizer*. Cambridge, MA: Harvard University Press.
Schafer, R. Murray. 1973. *From the Tibetan Book of the Dead*. Universal Edition.
Stapledon, Olaf. 1972 [1937]. *Star Maker*. New York: Penguin.

The Sound of Music

DONALD S. LOPEZ JR.

For eloquence the soul, song charms the sense
—MILTON, *PARADISE LOST*

SO MUCH comes to mind when we think of sound in Buddhism, even when we limit the topic to the Buddha himself. There is his "lion's roar" (*siṃhanāda*) that silences all the lesser animals in the jungle: the various *tīrthika* teachers, who are compared to jackals and other ignoble beasts. There is the fact that orthodoxy is based on whether or not a statement is *buddhavacana*, the voice or speech of the Buddha, a term that provided the Buddhists with their own parallel to the eternal Veda while distinguishing the words of the Buddha from it, solving some hermeneutical problems but raising many more, problems that Buddhists and Buddhologists struggle with to the present day.[1] This essay will deal with only two of the many topics that fall under the category of "sound" in Buddhism. The first is the Buddha's voice, the second is music.

Voice

There are times when the Buddha made no sound, remaining silent. People seem to have learned that when he was asked a question three times and did not respond, that meant "yes." But sometimes it meant "I refuse to answer," as when he was asked a series of questions to which he famously responded with silence, questions called "the ten (or fourteen) undetermined" (*avyākṛta*) questions, like "Is the world eternal?" "Are the soul and body the same?" "Does the Tathāgata exist after death?"[2] His noble silence in response to what the nineteenth-century American translator Henry Clarke Warren called "questions that tend not to edification" constitute a philosophical form of "taking the fifth." And sometimes the Buddha after refusing three times would relent when asked a fourth time, as when he grudgingly acceded to his widowed stepmother's request, conveyed by Ānanda, to allow women to become nuns.[3]

The beauty of the Buddha's voice and the quality of his speech are repeatedly extolled, for example, in lists like the relatively uninteresting "sixty qualities of melodious speech," which contain such adjectives as gentle, soft, appealing, attractive, pure, flawless, distinct, captivating, worthy, indomitable, pleasant, melodious, and clear. The Buddha is said to know all languages and to be able to speak them simultaneously, so that in a single setting all the members of his audience hear the Dharma in their native tongue. The huge compendium of philosophy called the *Great Exegesis* (*Mahāvibhāṣa*) declares that in fact the Buddha speaks only a single syllable and yet each member of the audience hears a full discourse, intended just for them, and in their own language.[4] Although we tend to associate the tongue with the sense of taste, it is obviously also key to speech. Among the thirty-two major marks of a buddha, the tongue is alluded to twice: a buddha has an excellent sense of taste and his tongue is long and broad. How long? The Buddha was able to lick behind his ears. How broad? The Buddha was able to cover his entire face with his tongue. He covers his face on numerous occasions, often saying after doing so, "What do you think, brahman, would a person who can stick out his tongue from his mouth and cover the entire sphere of his face knowingly tell lies?"[5]

On the rock edict of the Emperor Aśoka at Bhairāt, we find these words carved: "All that the bhagavan Buddha has spoken is well spoken." This statement receives a twist in a Mahāyāna sūtra called *Inspiring Determination* (*Adhyāśayasañcodana Sūtra*) as well as in the Pāli Aṅguttara Nikāya, where we read, "All which is well spoken is spoken by the Buddha."[6] At first sight, this would seem to remove all restrictions to what can be considered the word of the Buddha. Fortunately, the sūtra quickly explains what is meant by "well spoken." All inspired speech should be known to be the word of the Buddha if it is meaningful and not meaningless, if it is principled and not unprincipled, if it brings about the extinction and not the increase of the afflictions, and if it sets forth the qualities and benefits of nirvāṇa and not the qualities and benefits of saṃsāra.[7] In both Pāli and Sanskrit sources, we often find the statement called "the sūtra of the two nights," which declares that from the night when the Tathāgata awakens into unsurpassed perfect complete enlightenment until the night when he passes into the final nirvāṇa without remainder, everything that he states, speaks, and explains is just so and not otherwise. In a Mahāyāna text called the *Sūtra Setting Forth the Inconceivable Secrets of the Tathāgata* (*Tathāgatācintyaguhyanirdeśa Sūtra*), we find the statement that from the night when the Tathāgata awakens into unsurpassed, perfect, complete enlightenment until the night when he passes into the final nirvāṇa without remainder, he does not declare or speak a single syllable.[8]

The description of the Buddha's speech as always pleasant did not go unchallenged. Having been told by the monk Nāgasena that the Buddha's speech is always courteous, the Greek king Milinda reminds him of the time that the Buddha spoke rather unpleasantly to the monk Sudinna, upbraiding him for having sex with his wife at his mother's request, the act that led the Buddha to impose the rule of celibacy. The Buddha said to Sudinna, "Worthless man, it would be better that your penis be stuck into the mouth of a poisonous snake than into a woman's vagina."[9] The king notes that this rebuke was so harsh that it prevented Sudinna from achieving the first stage of enlightenment. In the Buddha's defense, Nāgāsena says that those words were not abusive because they were not motivated by anger and because they were truthful.[10]

When we think of sound in Buddhism, we think of the famous figures who have the word "voice" (*ghoṣa*) as part of their name, from Buddhaghosa ("voice of the Buddha"), the greatest of the Pāli authors, to Mañjughoṣa ("sweet voice"), the bodhisattva of wisdom, to Aśvaghoṣa, the Buddha's biographer, one of the most esteemed of the Sanskrit poets, despite the fact that his name means "horse voice." This suggests that in ancient India, the neighing of a horse might have been a good sound.

As mentioned in the introduction to this volume, only two of the five senses—sight and sound—can be raised to the level of super knowledge (*abhijñā*), powers that are generally said to be the byproduct of advanced states of meditation and that can also be achieved by non-Buddhists. But, as also mentioned in the introduction, these two supernatural abilities are available to certain devotees of the Dharma without needing to meditate at all. In chapter 19 of the *Lotus Sūtra*, the chapter on the benefits obtained by the expounder of the Dharma, the Buddha declares that sons or daughters of a virtuous family who preserve, recite, explain, or copy the *Lotus Sūtra* will attain the twelve hundred qualities of the ear. Thankfully, he does not list them, but he does describe them—first in prose, then in verse—for three pages.

As in the case of sight, that chapter wants to make clear that the devotees of the *Lotus Sūtra* have not achieved the *abhijñā* of the divine eye and the divine ear, but rather that they hear all the sounds of the universe and the abodes of rebirth using their natural ear. Thus, the text says, "although they do not have the divine faculty of hearing, they will always hear and know everything both within and beyond the great manifold cosmos, through the purified, natural bodily ears given by their parents. They distinguish all these various sounds and yet their faculty of hearing remains unharmed."[11]

Although sound is typically described as a hindrance to meditation, there is at least one famous instance in which sound is seen as a means to silent illumination. In Chinese, the name of the bodhisattva Avalokiteśvara is Guanshiyin, a translation of Avalokitaśvara (an alternate version of his Sanskrit name), meaning "Perceiver of the Sounds of the World." In the Chinese apocryphon called the *Śūraṅgama Sūtra*, the bodhisattva says that he achieved enlightenment when a previous buddha taught him to turn the hearing of sound back upon itself, thereby causing both the sound and the hearing of sound—that is, the object and the subject—to vanish, dissolving into emptiness. He goes on to say that beings achieve liberation not by hearing his teachings, as one might expect, but by his hearing their cries.[12]

Before turning to the category of "good sound," we must briefly mention what is considered the most potent form of Buddhist speech: mantras, especially when we expand this term to include not only the mantras found in so many tantric texts but the *dhāraṇī* found at the end of so many Mahāyāna sūtras and the *paritta* ("protection") of the Pāli tradition. These are words said to have special powers, functioning almost as magic spells, able to bring about what the speaker wishes, whether the aim be mundane or transcendent. We note that when works containing mantras were translated into other languages, the mantras, even those that have semantic meaning, were not translated but instead were phoneticized in an effort to retain their power as sound. That power is said to have thereby been preserved, even though the rendering of Indian mantras into Chinese and Tibetan often bear little sonic resemblance to the original Sanskrit or Prakrit.

The fact that in tantric Buddhism mantras tend to be classified based on their capacity to pacify, increase, control, or exorcize suggests that, depending on one's perspective, they are not always "good sound." Less ambiguous is the form of speech called the "statement of truth" (*satyavacana*), where simply saying something that is truthful has a magical effect. We find such statements throughout Buddhist literature, especially in the Jātaka and Avadāna collections when a body part that has been amputated to save the life of another is magically restored through the power of an honest proclamation.[13]

Music

And now to good sound. Again, there is much to say. There are all of the bird songs that we hear, or hear about, in the sūtras, bird songs both in this world and the next. How, for example, the songs of the birds in Sukhāvatī, the pure land of the buddha Amitābha, convey the Dharma, despite the fact the birds that sing them are not real birds, but magically created birds; according to the vow of Dharmākara, the bodhisattva who became Amitābha, there are no animals, ghosts, or denizens of hell in his buddha field. Eleven species of birds are mentioned just in this one sūtra, each said to be "singing with the voice of the Buddha."[14]

As always, one of the most fruitful domains for the exploration of the senses is the monastic code, for a variety of reasons. First, it provides us with at least a glimpse of Buddhism in a social setting, with so many of the minor rules meant to distinguish Buddhist monks and nuns from the other religious groups, whether they be sacrifice-performing brahmins or naked Jains—with whom they competed for alms and patronage. One of the ways that the Buddhist clergy distinguished itself was in how the Dharma was recited.

It is important to recall that Buddhism was an entirely oral tradition for the first few centuries of its history, with the standard word for a disciple of the Buddha being "one who hears" (*śrāvaka*), and the standard term for a learned person, what we would call "well read," being "one who has heard much" (*bahuśruta*). One of the primary duties of a monk was to memorize and chant the sūtras. Unfortunately, we do not know what that sounded like, whether those who heard it would categorize the chanting as good sound or bad sound, with the answer likely depending on one's religious affiliation.

After two monks, both from the brahman caste, had set the Buddha's teachings in metered verse, he famously told them not to, saying that the Dharma should be taught in the local dialect, with much debate about what he meant.[15] This decision is sometimes cited as one of the reasons that his teachings came to be translated, allowing the Dharma to spread beyond India and eventually around the world. Still, there are specific instructions on how the Dharma should be taught, with the Buddha also prohibiting monks from singing the Dharma, in whatever language, because it causes the singing monk to become enamored with his own voice, because it will be displeasing to the laity, because it hinders his concentration, and, interestingly, because people will come to expect it. And yet the Vinaya does allow a kind of chanting called *sarabhañña* in Pāli, sometimes translated as "vowel reciting" or "vowel intoning," thirty-two varieties of which are permitted, so long as the monk does not get carried away, losing the meaning and distorting the consonants, whatever that might mean.[16] And we recall that the Sanskrit word for the gathering of monks to redact the canon, translated into English as "council" (as if it were a conclave of the Church Fathers), is *saṅgīti*, literally "sing together."[17]

This is one of many cases in which the doctrine of impermanence, so often emphasized in teachings about sense experience, also hinders our research. We know what sandalwood smells like, we know what ghee tastes like, but we cannot easily imagine how drawn-out vowels, which are not allowed, differ from intoned vowels, which are allowed. Like the echo that is given as an example in so many perfection of wisdom sūtras, those sounds have long ago disappeared into space. There is surely something here intended to distinguish the chanting of the Dharma from the chanting of the Veda, but it is not clear what that is.

What was the Buddhist attitude to one the most important forms of sound: music? As is well known, beginning with the rules for novices and carrying over to the rules for the fully ordained, dancing, singing, playing music, as well as attending their performance is prohibited for monks and nuns; apparently even watching a peacock dance is not allowed. Doing so is said to make a monk a corrupter of families.[18]

This chapter is supposed to be devoted to the topic of "good sound," but the point here is that there seems to be a rather vague and shifting boundary between good and bad. To explore this borderline further, the remainder of this chapter will be devoted to three sūtras, one more mystical, two more mundane. In each, sound, and what for the moment we might consider "good sound," plays a key role.

The Sound of Music

In the Tibetan canon, we find a sūtra called the *paripṛcchā*, or the *Questions of the Kinnara King Druma*. A *kinnara* is one of the "eight types of non-humans" often mentioned in the sūtras.[19] The word *kinnara* literally means "how human," in the sense of "How could that possibly be a human?" Sometimes they are depicted with a human body and the head of a horse; in Buddhist iconography they typically have a human head and the body of a bird, as we see so often depicted in Buddhist temples in Southeast Asia. Regardless, they are renowned as musicians, playing a lute (*vīṇā*), and their king, Druma (who is listed among the audience of the *Lotus Sūtra*) is particularly renowned for his musical skill, often performing an offering of music to the Buddha, who, unlike his monks, is apparently allowed to listen to music. He even sometimes allows monks to do so. In a text from the Mūlasarvāstivāda Vinaya, Anāthapiṇḍada, the Buddha's wealthy patron, suggests that a festival be held to celebrate the anniversary of the Buddha's enlightenment, with a procession of monks carrying a statue of the youthful Prince Siddhārtha meditating under a tree, complete with music. When Upāli, upholder of the Vinaya, objects, asking the Buddha if it is permissible to make music, the Buddha says that it is not, but makes an exception in this case.[20]

Returning to King Druma, the sūtra deals with topics familiar from other Mahāyāna sūtras, discussing emptiness (*śūnyatā*) and the six perfections (*pāramitā*) in some detail. Toward the end, the Buddha provides lengthy instructions on what women should do to be reborn as men. Before all this, however, celestial music is heard. The Buddha announces that this means that King Druma is on his way. Druma arrives with his beautiful lute and begins to play for the Buddha and the august assembly. Suddenly, with the exception of the Buddha and the bodhisattvas, "the dispassionate monks, nuns, male lay practitioners, and female lay practitioners, as well as the gods . . . humans, nonhumans, worthy ones absorbed in the eight liberations [*vimokṣa*; eight levels of deep meditation], and the entire retinue became overwhelmed upon hearing the tunes emitted by that lute. They stood up and started to shake, shiver, and tremble; they bent, bowed, and twisted; and they danced, swayed, and whirled. Even all the great śrāvakas could not remain in their seats. They trembled, shook, acted wildly, and danced around like small children."[21]

Here, in one of the more improbable scenes in Buddhist literature, the dancers include such august and intimidating arhats as Mahākāśyapa himself. Of course, one of the bodhisattvas, named Divyamauli, cannot resist asking him about this, rather rudely saying, "You have reached old age and are frail, you are content and have few desires, you uphold the ascetic practices, and you are the focus of worship for the world with its gods, humans, and demigods. Why can you no longer control your body? You are an elder, but you dance around like a small child."[22] The famously severe monk does not have a good answer, simply saying that when a hurricane begins to blow, even the mountains move. There is much to be said about the dance scene and what it suggests about the ambivalent Buddhist attitude toward the senses and toward sound. First, however, it is important to note the identities of the dancers and to place the scene in a larger setting.

Despite its name, the Mahāyāna seems to have remained in the minority during its history in India. In an effort to defend the Mahāyāna, the authors of its sūtras went on the literary offensive, belittling what they regarded as the low vehicle (*hīnayāna*), the earlier tradition and its adherents, who denied that the Mahāyāna sūtras were the teachings of the Buddha.[23] One form of condemnation was to have the famous arhats of the early tradition play the fool in the Mahāyāna sūtras. Thus, in the *Lotus Sūtra*, Śāriputra, the wisest of the Buddha's disciples, one who has achieved the stage in which there is nothing left to learn, is baffled by the Buddha's use of the term *upāya*, skillful means. Later, when the Buddha reluctantly agrees to explain what it means, five thousand haughty monks and nuns walk out. In the *Diamond Sūtra*, the Buddha's interlocutor is the arhat Subhūti, to whom the Buddha explains the true nature of reality. In the *Vimalakīrti Sūtra*, the most famous arhats demur at the Buddha's request to visit the ailing Vimalakīrti, each monk recounting the time he had been humiliated by the insights of the Mahāyāna layman.

We should also note two moments of silence in this sūtra, each with a very different meaning. In the first, a goddess asks Śāriputra how long he has been liberated. The arhat does not answer, and when challenged by the goddess, adopts a Mahāyāna trope, explaining that he is silent because liberation is inexpressible. The goddess, however, challenges this, saying that silence and speech equally have the nature of liberation, that syllables are neither internal nor external: "Therefore, reverend Śāriputra, do not define liberation by excluding words."[24] In the eighth chapter, Vimalakīrti asks thirty-two bodhisattvas who have gathered at his house to explain the meaning of non-duality. After each gives his answer, Mañjuśrī asks Vimalakīrti to do so. He remains silent. Rather than chastising him, the bodhisattva of wisdom praises the layman's answer, saying, "There is no use of syllables, words, and utterances to make anything known."[25] After he says this, five thousand bodhisattvas enter the door of non-duality. Although silence is notoriously difficult to interpret, the silence of Śāriputra and the silence of Vimalakīrti are often compared—the first criticized, the second exalted. The philosophical implications of these moments of silence are complex. What is clear, however, is that they are another example of sound, or the lack of sound, as a means to demean an arhat.

Here in the *Questions of the Kinnara King Druma*, the arhat is Mahākāśyapa, renowned for his practice of ascetism. He is one of the most important disciples of the Buddha and members of the monastic order, early on exchanging robes with the Buddha, foreshadowing his later leadership.

In the Chan tradition, Mahākāśyapa is identified as the first recipient of the "mind to mind transmission" when he understands what the Buddha means when he silently holds up a flower. Mahākāśyapa was not present at the death of the Buddha but was considered so important that the gods prevented the Buddha's funeral pyre from igniting until he arrived. His final homage at the foot of the bier of his teacher is one of the more moving scenes in the canon. Although the Buddha famously did not appoint a successor, Mahākāśyapa seems to have served as one, calling what is known as the First Council a few months after the Buddha's death, where the teachings of the Buddha were collected and recited. At the end of his life, rather than pass into nirvāṇa, he is said to have entered a state of suspended animation inside a mountain. He will reemerge billions of years in the future upon the advent of the next buddha, Maitreya, presenting him with the robe of Śākyamuni. In brief, this austere and severe arhat is not a monk to meddle with.

And yet the Mahāyāna sūtras do. Thus, in the *Vimalakīrti Sūtra*, he, like other arhats, politely protests when the Buddha instructs him to visit the ailing Vimalakīrti. In the case of Mahākāśyapa, his reluctance comes from the time the wealthy layman deigned to instruct the master of asceticism in one of his specialties, how to beg for alms, providing him with an instruction on the five senses: "You should accept alms without accepting; see shapes just the same as someone blind from birth; hear sounds as if they were echoes; smell scents as if they were mere air; taste flavors without registering them; touch tangible things with your awareness remaining untouched; you should be aware of all objects of thought with the awareness of an illusory man."[26] Mahākāśyapa, often haughty in other settings, admits to the Buddha that he had never thought of this before and says that it converted him to the Mahāyāna.

When Mahākāśyapa hears the beautiful strains of Druma's music, what happens to this most dignified of monks is much more demeaning. He rises from his seat against his will and seems to do the Hippy Hippy Shake, a dance described in a song written by Chan Romero and recorded by the Beatles in 1963. The song begins, "For goodness sake, I got the hippy hippy shake. Well, I got the shake; I got the hippy hippy shake. I can't stand still with the hippy hippy shake." In doing so, he both listens to music and dances, two violations of his vows. That he does so against his will makes it all the more consequential.

As an arhat, Mahākāśyapa is supposed to have purified his mind of the myriad forms of pollution enumerated in Buddhist texts, with names like afflictions (*kleśa*), oozings (*āsrava*), proclivities (*anuśaya*, of which ninety-eight are mentioned), obstructions (*āvaraṇa*), fetters (*saṃyojana*), and floods (*ogha*), this last of which includes something called *kāmarāga*, literally a rage or passion for desirable things—that is, for the objects of the senses. As an arhat, Mahākāśyapa is supposed to have destroyed all of these and be in complete control of his mind and body, having achieved what is called "the knowledge of the destruction of the afflictions" (*kṣayajñāna*) and "the knowledge that they will not arise again" (*anutpādajñāna*).

There are doctrinal reasons that might explain Mahākāśyapa's dance. In the Abhidharma, there is the category of the "latencies of the afflictions" or "impregnations of the passions" (*kleśavāsanā*), as the great Belgian scholar Étienne Lamotte rendered the term. The category seems to have been used to explain odd, and what appears to be unconscious, behavior by the arhats. That behavior is said to be the karmic residue from previous lives. Thus, Mahāmaudgalyāyana, renowned for his magical powers, jumps around when he hears music because he was a monkey in his past lives. Gavāṃpati, one of the earliest disciples of the Buddha to become an arhat, would chew his food, spit it out, and eat it again because he had spent five hundred lifetimes as a cow. This may be why his name means "Lord of Cows."[27]

Yet the *Questions of the Kinnara King Druma* is likely not concerned with those fine points of doctrine. When Mahākaśyapa hears Druma's lute, he rises against his will and begins to dance, as if he had donned Hans Christian Andersen's red shoes. The scene is meant to suggest, in the most embarrassing way, that the arhats, those who are called *aśaikṣa*—that is, with nothing more to learn—cannot even keep the vows of a novice. Divyamauli rather rudely points out that none of the bodhisattvas, presumably also monks, were compelled to dance when Druma played his lute, clear evidence of the superiority of the Mahāyāna.

The doctrinal point is that the arhats have not understood the nature of reality, emptiness (*śūnyatā*), which the Buddha has revealed in the Mahāyāna sūtras. To make this clear, when Druma begins to play again, the notes of his lute become eloquent verses of the Dharma. After his performance, the king of the *kinnaras* gives a brief discourse about how all sounds come from space and the nature of space is sound, going on to expound on the meaning of emptiness. This is a point, and a metaphor, very familiar to those who have read the Mahāyāna sūtras. Perhaps the more important point is how a beautiful piece of music, what would be considered "good sound," is used to humiliate an old monk, making it "bad sound," at least for him. Perhaps no sound is inherently good or bad; it is instead how it is heard, and what effect that hearing has on the mind. This is an obvious point. What might be more important here is the story that is told in order to make it, with the authors of this particular Mahāyāna sūtra adding beautiful music to their arsenal of weapons against the venerable heroes of the early tradition.

Before leaving King Druma and Mahākāśyapa and turning to two other sūtras, we should mention another case of music being weaponized to advance the Dharma. In this case, the musician is the Buddha himself. In an odd scene in the account of his last days, also related in the Vinaya, he rises from his deathbed, or at least creates an emanation of himself, in order to convert a king of the *gandharvas*, another class of celestial musicians ranked above the *kinnaras*. This particular *gandharva* is named Sunanda. The Buddha picks up his instrument, a thousand-stringed lute made of beryl, and challenges the *gandharva* to a Vedic-period version of a 1960s guitar duel, trading solos while removing one string each time. This obviously took some time. When they each got down to one string, neither would concede defeat. Finally, the Buddha cut the last string and played a beautiful solo, humiliating Sunanda. The Buddha then assumed his true form and Sunanda knelt before him, asking to become his disciple. In Tibetan literature, this is the story often told to illustrate the kind of emanation body or *nirmāṇakāya* called a *śilpanirmāṇakāya*, or "artist emanation body."[28]

But all this is the wondrous realm of fantasy, where so many of the Mahāyāna sūtras take place. When we seek to understand what sound has meant in Buddhism, we must also consider what Buddhism might have sounded like. What were the sounds that monks and nuns produced? What sounds were they encouraged to produce? What sounds did they like to hear? Among the senses, sound is the most difficult to recover. As noted above, we have images that were seen centuries ago that we can still see today. We have the names of flowers whose fragrance we know. We have the names of foods that were eaten in ancient India, many of which continue to be eaten in one form or another to the present day. And our bodies are still covered by the largest of the sense organs that can feel the heat of the sun, the rain of the monsoon, and the north wind. But sound disappears into space, as King Druma reminds us. Still, we can at least try to imagine something that is impossible to recover: what Buddhism might have sounded like in India. Let me close by focusing on two short and presumably insignificant sūtras found in the Tibetan canon. The first is about a piece of wood called a *gaṇḍī*.[29]

The *Gaṇḍī Sūtra* deals with the glories of the *gaṇḍī*, a wooden beam that is struck with a hammer. In English it would apparently be called a *semanterion* or a *phonoxyle* (as opposed to a xylophone). In the sūtra, King Prasenajit comes to the Buddha and tells him that in the future beings will be overcome by the afflictions, causing them to abandon the Dharma. He asks the Buddha how to counter this and how to encourage beings to seek enlightenment. Versions of this question provide the occasion for many sūtras. As he so often does, the Buddha praises the question, and as he so often does, he goes into *samādhi*. When he comes out, he extols the perfection of wisdom as the subduer of all evil. Again, nothing new here. But then he says that the perfection of wisdom takes the form of the *gaṇḍī*. King Prasenajit immediately asks for the specifications. The Buddha obliges, describing what kind of wood to use—aloe, walnut, mango, and aśoka are all fine—as well as the horrors that will result from using the wrong wood, what size the *gaṇḍī* should be (eighty-four fingers long, six fingers wide, and two fingers high, or about ten feet by nine inches by three inches), going on to explain how to make the striker, where to place the *gaṇḍī* in the monastery, how to wash it with flower-petal water, how to consecrate it, and so forth. He then explains:

> O King, when throughout the land
> that *gaṇḍī* resounds,
> the year will be good there,
> with splendor, fame, and all desirable things.

> There will be no fear of foreign armies,
> and the crops will never fail.
> With the wealth of the Buddha's blessings,
> māras will be tamed there.
>
> The Dharma drum will thunder everywhere,
> right up to the summit of existence.
> The worlds of hell and ghosts
> will undoubtedly be destroyed.[30]

In addition to these remarkable powers, the Buddha explains that anyone who hears the *gaṇḍī* four times a day will be enlightened. Despite all the specificity about wood selections and dimensions, perhaps we still remain in the realm of fantasy. Still, this sūtra provides us with a glimpse of the quotidian. The *gaṇḍī* seems to be a standard feature of the Indian monastery, used primarily to mark the important moments of the monastic day. If we regard this text as *buddhavacana*, the word of the Buddha, it seems yet another catalog of the wonders of this or that text or practice. But if we consider the text to be the work of a *gaṇḍī* maker, or of a monk who was particularly proud of his monastery's *gaṇḍī*, we receive a fascinating insight into Indian monastic life, where those things that seem most banal, the sound made by hitting a board with a hammer, become infused with deep meaning.

The second short sūtra contains a bit more of the quotidian. It deals with what is called the "ringing staff" or the "rattling staff," the *khakkhara* in Sanskrit, familiar to us today primarily through images of the bald bodhisattva Jizō (Kṣitigarha in Sanskrit, Dizang in Chinese). However, it is listed as one of the requisites of a fully ordained monk and, according to the Mūlasarvāstivāda Vinaya, the fully ordained nun as well. There are two texts about the *khakkhara* in the Tibetan Kangyur, one more interesting for our purposes than the other. In the less interesting text about the *khakkhara*, the Buddha praises the staff as something carried by all the buddhas, before describing a range of symbolic meanings for it. For example, "those who hold it will distance themselves from the five sense objects." He then provides homologies for its four rings and twelve prongs. The four rings cause the monk to recall the four truths, the twelve prongs cause the monk to recall the twelve links of dependent origination, and so on.

The more interesting text is called *The Rite for the Protocols Associated with Carrying the Khakkhara*.[31] It is less concerned with the symbolic and more concerned with the real. Here we read, for example, that the *khakkhara* can be used to distance oneself from a snake. Whether this would be considered different from distancing oneself from the five sense objects is a question to ponder. The *khakkhara* seems to be something that was carried only outside the monastery; it was not to be carried among the saṅgha, taken to the toilet, or carried after twelve noon, presumably since that was a traditional nap time. It seems to have been something of a badge of honor for a *bhikṣu*, not to be held by novices or laypeople. But what about the sound? Since it had rings, it must have made some sound as one walked, but when would it have been actively rattled? Among the twenty-five rules for the use of the *khakkhara*, only two mention rattling it. The first is when one sees an image of the Buddha when entering or exiting, which presumably means when entering or exiting the monastery. This seems a nice homage to the Buddha, or perhaps a greeting to his animated image. Yet in the Chinese version of the text, it says that when seeing an image of the Buddha, the *khakkhara* should not be rattled. The other rule about rattling has to do with the daily begging round and reads as follows: "Go to the door of a patron and rattle the staff three times. If no one responds, you should rattle it five times. If no one responds when you rattle it five times, you should rattle it seven times. If no one responds when you rattle it seven times, you should proceed to another household and rattle the staff there." There is much to consider here, but for the purposes of this volume, one might ask: From the point of view of the patron, is that a good sound or a bad sound?

NOTES

1. See Lamotte 1988a, 11–28; Lopez 1988a, 47–70; Lopez 1996, 19–46; Davidson 1990. Despite the fact that the Buddhists' greatest philosophical opponent in India was the Mīmāṃsā, the school of the Vedic ritualists, we find one of the Buddhist schools, the Vaibhāṣika, describing the speech of the Buddha as *apauruṣeya*—that is, "not human," in the sense that it has no author, either human or divine. Here the

Buddhists borrow one of the most famous adjectives used to describe the Hindu Vedas, which are said to be eternal sound. See Jaini 1959, 107.

2. For the list of ten see, for example, the *Aggivacchagotta Sutta* in Bhikkhu Bodhi 1995, 590–91.
3. Horner 2001, 352–54.
4. See Lamotte 1988b, 551.
5. Rotman 2008, 141. On the other miraculous qualities of the Buddha's tongue, see Skilling 2013.
6. See Snellgrove 1958, 621. For the Aṅguttara Nikāya passage, see Collins 1990, 94–95.
7. See Davidson 1990, 310.
8. For references to this statement in Pāli canon, see Lamotte 1962, 109n52.
9. See Thanissaro Bhikkhu 2013a, 13.
10. See Horner 2015, 240–41.
11. Kubo and Yuyama 2007, 252.
12. I am grateful to Robert Buswell for pointing out this passage. For the Korean monk Chinul's description of this meditation practice of turning sound back on itself, see Buswell 1991, 104–5.
13. For a study of the "gift of the body" (*dehadāna*) and the role of the statement of truth in its restoration, see Ohnuma 2007.
14. See Gómez 1996, 104.
15. See Lamotte 1988b, 552–58.
16. See Thanissaro Bhikkhu 2013b, 89.
17. Buddhist monks continue to "sing" scriptures until the present day. One thinks, for example, of the chord-singing Gyutö monks of Tibetan Buddhism. Their 1989 CD, *Freedom Chants from the Roof of the World*, was produced by Mickey Hart of the Grateful Dead. For a study of ritual chanting in Zen Buddhism, see Mross 2022.
18. Thanissaro Bhikkhu 2013b, 118.
19. The other seven are *deva*, *nāga*, *yakṣa*, *asura*, *gandharva*, *garuḍa*, and *mahorāga*.
20. Schopen 2005, 134.
21. *The Questions of the Kinnara King Druma*, 1.68.
22. *The Questions of the Kinnara King Druma*, 1.71.
23. One of the most detailed discussions of the mainstream, or *śrāvaka*, critique of the Mahāyāna is found in a Mahāyāna treatise, the *Blaze of Reasoning* (*Tarkajvālā*), by the sixth-century Madhyamaka author Bhāviveka. For a translation of the relevant section, see Eckel 2008, 110–13 and 126–31.
24. Gómez and Harrison 2022, 75.
25. Gómez and Harrison 2022, 99.
26. Gómez and Harrison 2022, 26.
27. See Lamotte 1974. On the larger question of whether arhats realize the most profound emptiness, see Lopez 1988b.
28. See Obermiller 1931, 59–60.
29. On the *gaṇḍī*, see Sobkovyak 2015.

30. *The Gaṇḍī Sūtra*, 1.29–1.31.
31. For a discussion of the Tibetan and Chinese versions of this text, see the Introduction to *The Rite for the Protocols Associated with Carrying the Ringing Staff*.

Bibliography

Bodhi, Bhikkhu, trans. 1995. *The Middle Length Discourses of the Buddha: A New Translation of the Majjhima Nikāya*. Somerville, MA: Wisdom Publications, 1995.

Buswell, Robert E., Jr. 1991. *Tracing Back the Radiance: Chinul's Korean Way of Zen*. Honolulu: University of Hawai'i Press, 1991.

Collins, Steven. 1990. "On the Very Idea of the Pali Canon." *Journal of the Pali Text Society* 15: 89–126.

Davidson, Ronald M. 1990. "An Introduction to the Standards of Scriptural Authenticity on Indian Buddhism." In *Chinese Buddhist Apocrypha*, edited by Robert E. Buswell Jr., 291–325. Honolulu: University of Hawai'i Press, 1990.

Eckel, Malcolm David. 2008. *Bhāviveka and His Buddhist Opponents*. Cambridge: Harvard University Press.

The Gaṇḍī Sūtra. 84000: Translating the Words of the Buddha. Toh 298, K71, mdo sde, *sha*, 301.b–303.b. Translated by Annie Bien. https://read.84000.co/translation/toh298.html.

Gómez, Luis O. 1996. *The Land of Bliss: The Paradise of the Buddha of Measureless Light*. Honolulu: University of Hawai'i Press.

Gómez, Luis, and Paul Harrison, trans. 2022. *Vimalakīrtinirdeśa: The Teaching of Vimalakīrti*. Berkeley, CA: Mangalam Press.

Horner, I. B., trans. 2001 [1952]. *The Book of Discipline (Vinaya Piṭaka), vol. 5 (Cullavagga)*. Oxford: The Pali Text Society.

———, trans. 2015 [1963]. *Milinda's Questions*, vol. 1. Bristol: The Pali Text Society.

Jaini, Padmanabh S. 1959. "The Vaibhāśika Theory of Words and Meanings." *Bulletin of the School of Oriental and African Studies* 22: 95–107.

Kubo, Tsugunari, and Akira Yuyama, trans. 2007. *The Lotus Sūtra*. 2nd rev. ed. Berkeley, CA: Numata Center for Buddhist Translation and Research.

Lamotte, Étienne. 1962. *L'Enseignemente de Vimalakīrti*. Louvain: Université de Louvain Institut Orientaliste.

———. 1974. "Passions and Impregnations of the Passions in Buddhism." In *Buddhist Studies in Honour of I. B. Horner*, edited by L. Cousins, A. Kunst, and K. R. Norman, 91–104. Dordrecht: D. Reidel.

———1988a. "Assessment of Textual Interpretation in Buddhism." In Lopez, *Buddhist Hermeneutics*, 11–28.

———. 1988b. *History of Indian Buddhism*. Translated by Sara Webb-Boin. Louvain: Peters Press.

Lopez, Donald S., Jr. 1988a. "On the Interpretation of the Mahāyāna Sūtras." In

Buddhist Hermeneutics, edited by Donald S. Lopez Jr., 47–70. Honolulu: University of Hawai'i Press.

_____. 1988b. "Do Śrāvakas Understand Emptiness?" *Journal of Indian Philosophy* 16.1: 65–105.

———. 1996. *Elaborations on Emptiness: Uses of the Heart Sūtra*. Princeton, NJ: Princeton University Press.

Mross, Michaela. 2022. *Memory, Music, Manuscripts: The Ritual Dynamics of Kōshiki in Japanese Sōtō Zen*. Honolulu: University of Hawai'i Press.

Obermiller, Eugene, 1931. *History of Buddhism by Bu-ston*, vol. 2. Heidelberg: Harrassowitz.

Ohnuma, Reiko. 2007. *Head, Eyes, Flesh, and Blood: Giving Away the Body in Indian Buddhist Literature*. New York: Columbia University Press.

The Questions of the Kinnara King Druma. 84000: Translating the Words of the Buddha. Toh 157, K58, mdo sde, *pha*, 254.a–319.a. Translated by the Dharmachakra Translation Committee. https://read.84000.co/translation/UT22084-058-006.html.

The Rite for the Protocols Associated with Carrying the Ringing Staff. 84000: Translating the Words of the Buddha. Toh 336, K72, mdo sde, *sa*, 274.a–275.a. Translated by the Sarasvatī Translation Team. https://read.84000.co/translation/toh336.html.

Rotman, Andy. 2008. *Divine Stories: Divyāvadāna, Part 1*. Boston: Wisdom Publications.

Schopen, Gregory. 2005. *Figments and Fragments of Mahāyāna Buddhism in India: More Collected Papers*. Honolulu: University of Hawai'i Press.

Skilling, Peter. 2013. "The Tathāgata and the Long Tongue of Truth: The Authority of the Buddha in Sūtra and Narrrative Literature." In *Scriptural Authority, Reason, and Action: Proceedings of a Panel at the 14th World Sanskrit Conference, Kyoto, September 1–5, 2009*, edited by Vincent Eltschinger and Helmut Krasser, 1–47. Vienna: Austrian Academy of Sciences Press.

Snellgrove, David. 1958. "Note on the *Adhyāśayasaṃcodanasūtra*." *Bulletin of the School of Oriental and African Studies* 21: 620–23.

Sobkovyak, Ekaterina. 2015. "Religious History of the *Gaṇḍī* Beam: Testimonies of Texts, Images and Ritual Practices." *ASIA* 69.3: 685–722.

Thanissaro Bhikkhu. 2013a. *The Buddhist Monastic Code I*. 2nd rev. ed. Valley Center, CA: Metta Forest Monastery.

———. 2013b. *The Buddhist Monastic Code II*. 2nd rev. ed. Valley Center, CA: Metta Forest Monastery.

What Is *Bad* about Bad Smell? Relativity, Relationship, and Revelation in the Buddhist Olfactory Imagination

LINA VERCHERY

If you examine thoroughly, you will not avoid the smell of shit.
—CASE 62, *BIYAN LU* 碧巖錄 (*THE BLUE CLIFF RECORD*)[1]

SMELLS PERMEATE the Buddhist *imaginaire*. This is true in the literary world—where miracles are presaged by sweet aromas, the baby Śākyamuni is gestated in a "perfume womb" (*gandhakūṭāgāra*), and the Pure Land is suffused by ten thousand kinds of delicate fragrance—and in the world of everyday practice—where incense wafts through temple halls, altars are adorned with fragrant foods and flowers, and a typical morning in a Chinese Buddhist monastery begins with the *Baoding zan* 寶鼎讚 (Jeweled Censor Praise), a chanted invocation of a cosmic smellscape.

But the salience of olfaction in Buddhism is not limited to pleasant smells such as these. Indeed, many claim the atavistic power of smell is at its most potent in the case of *bad* smells. Evolutionary psychologists argue that our aversion to foul odors is a universal adaptive response, designed to protect us from infection by avoiding substances likely to contain parasites or pathogens, like bodily fluids, excrement, open wounds, dead or decomposing bodies, worms, bugs, and so on.[2] Yet this overlooks the fact that the way we ascribe meaning to smells is highly subjective and contextual. Those, for instance, who complain that fine cheeses smell like stinky feet are not wrong. The ammoniac odor characteristic of fetid feet comes from the digestive waste of *Brevibacterium linens*—bacteria that feed on sweat and dead skin cells between the toes—and these very same bacteria create the mouth-watering aromas of celebrated cheeses like Époisses, Münster, and Brie. An odor that is repulsive in one context is relished in another. This raises the question: What exactly is *bad* about bad smell?

The Buddhist sources on smell have much to say about this question, and they lead us directly to the interstitial space where mind meets body, culture meets biology, and the symbolic meets the material. Indeed, we might describe smell as constituted by this very liminality. Smell reveals who we are and shapes our relations with others. More than anything, smell is a window into reality. Like a permeating stench—seeping through cracks and under doors, invisibly defying efforts at containment—smell reveals the inescapable truth of our existential situation. This can make bad smell dangerous, but, as we shall see in the ethnographic case study with which this chapter concludes, this is also the source of smell's revelatory potential.

Morality and Materiality

The *School Sayings of Confucius* contains the following verse about the power of smell:

> Being in the company of virtuous people is like entering a room
> full of orchids.
> After a while, you no longer notice the fragrance because you have
> been immersed it in.
> Being in the company of bad people is like entering a fish shop.
> After a while, you no longer notice the stench because you have
> been immersed in it.[3]

Smell, as this passage illustrates, is more than skin-deep. Unlike sight or even touch, which settle on surfaces, smell can access interiors and essences, revealing that which often goes unnoticed by the other senses.[4] In an oft-quoted line from the Zen kōan commentarial collection the *Blue Cliff Record*, the monk Yuanwu Keqin 圓悟克勤 exclaims that Master Xuedou Chongxian 雪竇重顯 "doesn't notice the smell of his own shit!"[5] Whether in its literal or figurative interpretation (to wit, Xuedou does not realize his own buddha nature), smell can reveal aspects of a person that even they themselves fail to notice, as also related in the Confucian epigraph above.

Because of this revelatory capacity, smell operates as a powerful moral diagnostic in the Buddhist *imaginaire*. As Śāntideva tells us, beings can literally "stink with sin" or be "perfumed . . . with virtues."[6] In a contemporary commentary on the *Avataṃsaka Sūtra,* the Chinese monk Hsüan Hua 宣化 writes that people who uphold precepts always smell good, "no matter how many days they go without bathing, they still do not stink . . . Their bodies naturally emit a pleasant odor."[7] Conversely, punning on the Chinese word for arrogance, 自大 (*zida*)—which if arranged vertically resembles the character for stench, 臭 (*chou* or *xiu*)—he adds, "What is a 'stench' (臭)? It is arrogance (自大) if you add a dot! To regard oneself (自) as very grand (大), now *that* is what I call 'stench' (臭)."[8] In other words, moral failings and character flaws—like arrogance and attachment to self—quite literally *stink*.

Buddhist literature is also full of poetic parallels between karma and smell. Like karma, which usually has obvious effects but unknown causes (at least to the unenlightened), smells can be perceived even when their source is concealed.[9] Habituated karmic patterns from past lives (*vāsanā*, Ch. *xiqi* 習氣) are said to "perfume" (*vāsana*) one's present dispositions, in the same way that odorant molecules pass from one medium to another—for example, from flower petals to oil—in the fabrication of perfume.[10] No petals remain in the oil; only their fragrance crosses over. Likewise, smell acts as a bridge between past and present, explaining how karma unfolds through time without the presupposition of a reified or enduring self. As we shall see, this metaphor rests on one of smell's most unique and intriguing properties: its ambivalent materiality.

Smell sits at the cusp of several salient conceptual boundaries: past and present, contact and distance, matter and immateriality. The latter pair is especially important for the role of smell in the Buddhist imagination. Although the pre-modern Indian sources classify odors as decidedly material, their particles are considered so minute that they can be carried on the wind.[11] Thus, unlike grosser forms of matter, smells can move *as though* they were immaterial: invisibly, ethereally, uninhibitedly. This liminality, located at the very cusp of the material and immaterial, makes smell a quintessential boundary crosser. As Vasubandhu elaborates in the *Abhidharmakośa*, this enables smell to bridge the so-called contact and distance senses: while the materiality of olfaction places it in the category of contact senses, like taste and touch, olfaction can also operate from afar, like vision and hearing. As James McHugh notes, smell is the "only sense that allows one to partake of an object's particles at a distance."[12] This gives smell a special mediatory power.

Consider, for instance, how smell mediates between worlds, enabling offerings from the human realm to reach the faraway celestial abodes of ancestors, buddhas, and bodhisattvas. In Buddhism, as in Vedic religion, smell is believed to invisibly carry the material particles of offerings from the human realm to higher ones, often in the form of fragrant steam or smoke, where the particles can be enjoyed at a distance. It should thus come as no surprise that the items typically selected for religious offerings—food, incense, and flowers—are all noted for their fragrant qualities. To cite but one ethnographic example of this logic at work, one day I assisted a Chinese Buddhist nun as she made her daily offering rounds (*gongfo* 供佛), placing rice, fruit, packages of gourmet cookies, crackers sealed in plastic, and bags of chips before the buddhas on the monastery's many altars. Before delivering each of the wrapped items, she instructed me to carefully cut a small slit in each package lest the smell remain trapped inside the bag, preventing the offering from reaching its intended recipients.

This propensity for crossing boundaries gives smell a unique mediatory power. But if, as the anthropologist Mary Douglas famously argued, we should understand "dirt as matter out of place," then this propensity also carries the risk of contamination.[13] Because smell is decidedly *material*, to inhale a scent is to physically bring particles of the odorant into one's body. Whereas sight, sound, and even touch can keep the sense object outside the self, smell—like taste—brings it *inside*. As such, smell blurs the boundary of inside and outside, self and other. Whether one smells of orchids or fish, to recall the pithy Confucian aphorism, the influence of others, like their scent, leaves an imprint on us. In this respect, smell becomes a metaphor for the inescapability of relationship. Indeed, this principle is not merely metaphorical but also pragmatic, since managing smell is part of managing community, a fact amply illustrated in the Buddhist Vinaya.

The Odors of Others: Smell and Sociality

Relationships are regulated through smell, whether we realize it or not. The scientific study of pheromones, still in its infancy, is beginning to uncover forms of olfactory communication that arguably inform everything from one's choice of mate to success in job interviews. The authors and compilers of the Vinaya and the Chinese *Qinggui* 清規 (Monastic Purity Rules) were also acutely aware of the social dimensions of smell. Though today we might frame these concerns in terms of public health or hygiene, the monastic rules saliently frame smell-management explicitly in terms of *sociality*, emphasizing the collective and institutional importance of smell control.[14] Managing one's smell, we learn, is not something one does for oneself alone; it is something one does for others. Conforming to collective conventions of how one should or should not smell thus becomes a performative affirmation of one's belonging to the group. To veer away from these olfactory expectations—that is, to smell *bad*—is not merely a personal choice but a symbolic rejection of the social order.

In practical terms, the Buddhist monastic rules evince concern about all the usual suspects—urine, feces, flatulence[15]—as well as with foul breath, body odor, and even the stench of the body after death. The rules dictate that monastics may not urinate, defecate, or fart near a stūpa, lest the smell defile the monument.[16] All human and animal excrement should be dutifully swept up each day to avoid assailing people's nostrils.[17] Latrines are to be built according to particular specifications to prevent their stench from wafting through the monastery grounds.[18] We find instructions about chewing "tooth wood" (*chimu* 齒木) to reduce bad breath and using fragrant mud to deodorize the body.[19] Body odor becomes an even graver concern when the bodies in question are no longer alive: cremations are forbidden in the vicinity of stūpas, lest the foul-smelling odor penetrate the sacred space.[20] Even monks who practice austerities at cremation grounds—though sometimes lauded for their asceticism—are shunned for their smell. Because of the stench of the funerary shrouds they wear as robes, the Mūlasarvāstivāda Vinaya forbids such monks from approaching a stūpa, preaching to laypeople, participating in ceremonies, or entering monastic dorms. (Because of their rank odor, they are instructed to "stand outside the door.") Foul-smelling monks may return to collective life only after they have become free of odor by bathing, fumigating themselves with incense, and sunning their freshly washed robes in the forest for seven to eight days until the stench has fully dissipated.[21]

Keeping bad smells at bay is essential not only for harmony among monastery residents, it is also crucial for upholding the dignified public image of the saṅgha, especially in the eyes of the lay patrons upon whom the community's livelihood depends.[22] We repeatedly read that bad smell damages the saṅgha's reputation and drives people away. The Mahāyāna *Mahāparinirvāṇa Sūtra* warns, for instance, that garlic breath produces a dirty smell that is "unbearable" and causes others to "leave that person and go away."[23] Such smells repel not only potential economic benefactors but spiritual benefactors as well. Since buddhas and bodhisattvas are repulsed by the foul breath of humans, sūtra recitations often begin with a *dhāraṇī* to purify the mouth.[24] According to the *Da biqiu sanqian weiyi* 大比丘三千威儀 (*Three Thousand Regulations for Great Bhikṣus*),[25] foul-smelling monastics are not allowed to worship the Triple Jewel, participate in rituals, or approach the abbot. Should they do so anyway, their otherwise meritorious actions will accrue no merit on account of their bad smell.[26]

The repulsive effect of foul odor once again illustrates the social significance of smell. What is *bad* about bad smell, in other words, is that it thwarts beneficial relationships. Indeed, the converse is also true: bad smell *attracts* undesirable relations. Writings on garlic and the pungent vegetables (*wuxin* 五辛) make this especially clear. Hungry ghosts, for example, do not just stink, but are also attracted to bad smells, such as urine, feces, and garlic breath. In his commentary on the Dharmaguptaka Vinaya, the *Sifenlü xingshi chao zichi ji* 四分律行事鈔資持記, the Song-dynasty Vinaya scholar Yuanzhao 元照 warns that if a person eats garlic, hungry ghosts will be attracted by the stench and linger at their lips.[27] The person's merit will erode daily and their actions will never bring benefit. To this already grim prognosis, he adds the lecherous detail that ghosts will not merely hover *near* the mouths of such stinky people; rather, they find garlic breath so irresistible that they will passionately lick and kiss the person's lips and mouth.

This illuminates another facet of what makes bad smell *bad*: it acts as a gateway to graver forms of immorality. In the prior example, we might say bad breath is doubly transgressive. Not only does it attract unsavory relations, thereby constituting a social transgression, but the very *nature* of those relations is problematic, as it turns a social transgression into a sexual one. The Vinaya includes other examples of bad smell as a gateway to—or correlate of—broader moral transgression. The five pungent-smelling vegetables, for instance, are so closely associated with loss of control that the formidable seventh-century Vinaya commentators Daoxuan 道宣 and Daoshi 道世 routinely include them in the same category as alcohol.[28] Similarly, in the first *Pācittiya* section of the *Bhikkhunīvibhaṅga* of the Pāli Vinaya, we meet the nun Thullanandā who, in a frenzy of gustatory mania, led her fellow nuns to steal all the garlic from a nearby lay donor's field, thereby violating the core precept against theft.[29] We might also detect sexualized undertones in this story, insofar as the Vinaya implies that this obsession with garlic—widely considered an aphrodisiac in both South and East Asia[30]—is primarily a *female* vulnerability. Whereas garlic consumption by monks is a mere *dukkaṭa*, a "light or minor" offense, the same act by nuns is punished as a *pācittika*, a "violation requiring confession." The Vinaya justifies the more severe punishment for women on the basis of their "insatiable longing" for the foul-smelling plant, leading us to wonder whether the nuns' insatiability for garlic might insinuate other sorts of insatiabilities as well.[31]

Indeed, the connection between smell and sex is not as far flung as it may seem.[32] Sex, after all, is the crossing of a boundary between self and other; so is smell. Insofar as the goal of the Vinaya is the clear elucidation of the boundary between the permitted and the forbidden, it stands to reason that smell—a boundary-crosser by nature—can be dangerous. This danger is perhaps nowhere more acute than in the most extreme form of interpersonal boundary crossing: the physical act of eating another's body.

The Stench of Death: Meat and the Semiotics of Smell

Although eating meat is not technically forbidden in the Vinaya nor in several branches of Buddhism, we have evidence that in China vegetarianism became *de rigueur* for Buddhist clergy as early as the third century CE.[33] It is both salient and surprising that the arguments in the East Asian Buddhist sources against eating meat are so frequently framed in terms of smell rather than taste. And the smells in question are rarely those of the meat, but those of the meat eater. The *Laṅkāvatāra Sūtra*, for instance, characterizes meat eaters as "ill-smelling, contemptuous, born deprived of intelligence."[34] According to the Mahāyāna *Mahāparinirvāṇa Sūtra*, their stench is so foul that any being who smells them "will become afraid and be filled with the fear of death."[35] The smell of meat eaters clearly inspires terror, but what precisely is the nature of this terror? Most obviously, it is the smell of death. But on a deeper level, we might describe it as the violation of proper relations. The fact that the horror of eating meat is so prevalently framed in terms of smell rather than taste, I suggest, tells us something significant about relationality and the unique semiotics of smell.

As we have seen, the hallmark of olfaction is that it crosses boundaries: between distance and contact, materiality and immateriality, inside and outside, self and other. Meat eating is perhaps the most extreme form of boundary crossing, whereby two subjects do not merely come into temporary contact, but one completely subsumes the other. The horror of meat, in other words, arises not just from the violence of killing but from an act of relational violence.

Consider, for instance, the popular verse about the famous Liang dynasty Buddhist monk Zhigong 誌公, recounted in a sūtra commentary by Hsüan Hua. Zhigong was attending a wedding, when he suddenly exclaimed: "How strange! How bizarre! The grandson marries the grandmother and the daughter eats the mother's flesh. The drum the son beats is stretched with the father's skin. Pigs and sheep are on the seat and the six close kin cook in the brazier. The people gather to celebrate; I see all this as a form of suffering (古古怪，怪怪古；孫孫娶祖母，女食母之肉；子打父皮鼓；豬羊炕上坐，六親鍋裏煮；眾人來賀喜；我看真是苦)!"[36] In a flash of insight, Zhigong saw that the groom's deceased grandmother had so loved her grandson that she was reborn as his wife-to-be. The bride's father had been reborn as the deer whose hide was used for the wedding drum. The pig being feasted upon was the bride's own mother, and the animals boiling in pots on the fire had been members of this family in their past lives. Saliently, the horror of this scene is not framed in terms of violence or killing but rather dwells on the horror of perverse family relationships. Here the consumption of meat is exposed as more than just an act of killing (a violent transgression); it is an act of matricide (both a violent transgression and a relational transgression).

The consumption of meat, we might add, is more than just turning another subject into an object; it is turning another subject into *oneself*. This erasure of the other's *otherness* is perhaps the most dumbfounding aspect of eating meat, and throughout the Chinese Buddhist sources, we see efforts to recall the erased subjectivity of those who have been eaten. Smell, it turns out, is often the last lingering trace of that subject, and can thus function as a window through which to recover them. Consider, for example, the following commentarial passage:

> People smell like the food they eat. If they eat onions, they smell like onions. If they eat garlic, they reek of garlic. If they eat fish, they smell fishy. If they eat pork, they smell like pork. If they eat mutton, they smell like mutton. Whatever type of food you eat, you'll become incorporated with that food.[37]

Here we have a Buddhist spin on the familiar maxim "you are what you eat"—namely, you *smell* like what you eat! When one subject eats another, the consumed being vanishes in *almost* every way. They can no longer be seen, heard, tasted, or touched. But, it turns out, they can still be smelled through the body of the one who has consumed them. This points to the unique semiotics of smell: because smell, as we have seen, is a material particle, an odor is an actual physical fragment of the odorant. A smell, in other words, does not *represent* the odorant; it *is* the odorant itself. One does not, then, merely smell *like* what or whom one has eaten; more accurately, one smells *of* whom one has eaten.

This illuminates a further dimension of what is *bad* about bad smell. In the case of meat eating in Chinese Buddhism, the horror revealed by the bad smell goes beyond the violence of killing to the violence of relational subjugation. The smell is horrific not simply because it represents or stands for that subjugation, but because the smell is an instantiation of the subjugation itself. This is why smell presents an acute risk of pollution: a bad smell does not merely symbolize impurity; rather, smelling itself constitutes an act of contamination. And yet the same propensity for boundary crossing that can make smells materially polluting is also what gives them their relational potential, which is at work, as we have seen, whenever a fragrant offering is placed on an altar. Indeed, it may be that "bad" smells—those of contamination and improper relations—and "good" smells—those of connection and beneficial relations—are two sides of a single coin. Perhaps we cannot have the possibility of one without the risk of the other.

So Bad It's Good: The Smell of Reality

Perhaps smells are not good or bad in themselves. After all, artisanal cheese and stinky feet do not merely smell *similar*; bacterially-speaking, their scent is materially *identical*. What makes one good and the other bad has less to do with their chemical composition than with matters of context and perspective. The same holds true in the Buddhist sources, which are full of examples of the relativity of smell. The *Dīrghāgama* reminds us that just as we humans regard feces-eating ghosts as smelly and unclean, from the perspective of the fine-nosed beings in the heavenly realms, our human world is "stinky, filthy, and unclean," and we humans stink like a latrine.[38]

The relativity of smell suggests not just that what smells good to one might reek to another, but also that a single smell might be both bad and good at the same time. Take, for instance, the famous *aśubha* meditations (Ch. *bujing xiang* 不淨想 or *bujing guan* 不淨觀) on the foulness of the body, which instruct the practitioner to contemplate a rotting corpse "completely reeking with stench and impurity" as a means to gain insight.[39] In this case, a bad smell can become a vehicle for liberation. Our question, then, might shift from asking "what is *bad* about bad smell" to asking what might be *good* about it. It would seem bad smell is good insofar as it helps one realize the truth about the way things really are. A festering corpse might thus be a "better" smell than a sweet perfume that hides the truth about the body and its impermanence.

The *aśubha* contemplations, in which bad smells become a vehicle for spiritual revelation, are emblematic of the larger Buddhist conviction that it is only by first realizing the foulness of saṃsāra that one can embark on the path toward liberation. Thus, to recognize bad smells *as bad* is itself a *good* thing. It is, in other words, to see reality as it really is. In his essay about cleaning the family outhouse, John Berger says the stench of shit "nags teleologically."[40] Shit, to be sure, is a kind of *telos* or "end point" in the literal sense. Indeed, all the smells we conventionally characterize as "bad" seem to be the smell of endings of one form or another: digestion, decay, disease, death. What is discomfiting about such smells is that they confront us so directly with the reality of mortality and impermanence, facts we usually prefer to ignore. Yet if unflinching recognition of these very facts constitutes the first step toward liberation, then maybe bad smell isn't so bad after all.

Mahāyāna antinomian discourse takes this principle to an extreme, expressing liberation as immersion into vileness itself. "What is Buddha?" a student asked. "Dried Shitstick!" the Zen master Yunmen famously replied.[41] What are the five sacred ambrosias (*pañcāmṛta*) extolled in some tantric traditions? Urine, feces, blood, semen, and flesh.[42] As the *Heart Sūtra*, chanted daily in every Chinese Buddhist monastery, insists with its relentless beat: "There is no purity and no impurity."[43] In the Mahāyāna vision, breaking down false notions of pure and impure, good and bad, enlightenment and delusion makes everything a potential gateway to liberation, even—and sometimes especially—that which is conventionally considered "bad." I encountered a powerful real-life example of this during my ethnographic fieldwork at a Buddhist temple in Taiwan, where bad smell led to profound spiritual transformation.

From Repulsion to Revelation

Wanglei[44] was a middle-aged temple attendee I met during my fieldwork at the Taibei Fajie 台北法界 Buddhist monastery in Taiwan. On the last day of the Chinese New Year, a group of us gathered for a celebratory dinner at a small Buddhist vegetarian restaurant. Wanglei was there with his wife and two teenage sons. As we slurped our sweet tapioca and coconut-milk desserts, I asked Wanglei what led him to become such a devout Buddhist. Gesturing to his two teenage sons across the table, he told me, "they used to be three."

Wanglei went on to recount the story of his infant son, who died suddenly and without warning. "One day he was a very happy baby," he explained, "and then very suddenly he was gone." In the weeks and months following their son's death, Wanglei and his wife were awash with grief. At first they refused an autopsy, but because this was a case of child death from unknown causes, an autopsy was legally mandated. Wanglei attended the procedure but was unable to watch. "I was in the room," he said, "but turned my back. At one point, though, I glanced over." As he spoke, Wanglei covered his eyes with his hands, leaving a thin sliver of space between his fingers through which he gazed at me. "And out of the corner of my eye, I saw my son cut open like this." Recreating the path of the surgical saw, he traced his fingers down his body, as though slicing himself in half, from between his eyes through the middle of his chest and down to his waist. The sight of his son cut in half clearly shook him, but it was what came next that was most harrowing. Shifting his tone to a grave whisper, he continued, "You know, there is a kind of smell." He paused. "The moment I smelled that smell, I became vegetarian."

On the surface, Wanglei's story might recall standard Chinese Buddhist arguments for the virtues of vegetarianism, which prevents the generation of "killing karma" (*shaye* 殺業) and creates karmic merit. But I suggest this interpretation of Wanglei's story overlooks its most salient feature, the fulcrum of which is smell. Wanglei's moment of moral transformation—the instant he committed to never again eat animals—was not occasioned by the sight of his son's disfigured body, horrific as it must have been, but by its *smell*. What precisely was that smell? It was the smell of animal meat. Wanglei continued, "Years later, I worked across the street from a food stall where they barbecued meat. And every day that smell would waft into my workplace. And I always thought of my son."

In Wanglei's story, a repulsive smell became a gateway for moral transformation. In everyday life, we tend to value human lives over those of non-human animals. Indeed, Buddhism itself is not infrequently accused of anthropocentrism, given the doctrinal insistence that human rebirth is the most advantageous form of life. Yet the teaching of rebirth also emphasizes that all beings continually cycle through the various realms of saṃsāra, such that every living being has at one time been one's mother, father, sister, brother, son, or daughter.[45] This vision of radical interconnection might ordinarily seem distant and abstract, but Wanglei's olfactory revelation enabled him to experience it in a tangible way. When he realized the smell of his son's corpse to be the same smell as animal meat, Wanglei caught a glimpse of something akin to what Gananath Obeyesekere calls the "homology of species sentience"—that is, the idea that despite superficial differences of appearance, all living creatures belong to a common order of life.[46] The smell revealed—not intellectually, but *materially* and *sensorially*—that the bodies of the animals we kill to eat are not different from those of the family members we love and cherish. By uncovering the commonality that underlies superficial physical differences, bad smell enlarged the scope of Wanglei's connection with living beings, and this radically expanded the moral purview of his world.

What Is Bad about Bad Smell?

What can we learn from how bad smell is presented in Buddhism? A first set of lessons has to do with the nature of smell. Smell, the sources suggest, is not just something you *have* or something you *do*, it points to something you *are*. Contrary to the truism about sight—that you can't judge a book by its cover—it turns out you *can* judge a person by their smell. This is evinced throughout the Buddhist sources: not only by the myriad accounts of the Buddha's extraordinary fragrance, but even more by the stubborn insistence that he never smelled bad. The tradition ties itself in knots to assert that, unlike regular human bodies, the Buddha's body never produced an unpleasant odor.[47] Even the *Lalitavistara Sūtra* account of Queen Māyā's perfume-womb can be read as evidence of anxieties about the Buddha's proximity to the polluting smells of reproduction. That Buddhist authors went to such lengths to sanitize the Buddha's olfactory existence demonstrates the profound connection between one's smell and one's spiritual and moral standing in the Buddhist *imaginaire*.

By virtue of its unique ability to carry particles across a distance, smell—perhaps more than any of the other senses—is a boundary-crosser *par excellence*. Whether we like it or not, smells bridge self and other and shape the nature of relationships (a fact foregrounded, as we have seen, in the Vinaya). Smells can also bridge temporal, geographic, and even cosmological boundaries, as when odors carry offerings from human to celestial realms, or when Wanglei, through olfaction, glimpsed the permeability of human-animal boundaries. In all of these cases, smell functions as both the vehicle and the evidence of our relational entanglements. The boundary-crossing nature of olfaction reveals the inescapability of sociality, which carries both a risk of contamination and the potential for meaningful connection. According to the Buddhist sources, it would appear we cannot have the one without the other.

A final lesson we might learn from bad smell has less to do with smell than it does with *badness*. While the difference between good smell and bad smell initially seems self-evident, this binary begins to dissolve upon further examination. Even the baddest of bad smells—like the universally repulsive smells of disease, decay, and death—can, in their very badness, reveal something arguably *more* true than what any good smell can show. This is the truth of impermanence, of saṃsāra, of reality. To drench a fetid corpse in perfume is not only futile, it is a dangerous denial of the way things are. Insofar as bad smells can unflinchingly reveal the reality of our existential situation, they can become—as we saw in the story of Wanglei—a powerful source of insight.

The Buddhist scriptures, too, blur the line between "good" and "bad." The *Avataṃsaka Sūtra* tells us: When bodhisattvas "smell putrid objects they do not consider them stench; when they smell fragrant aromas they do not consider them fragrant. When they smell both together, their minds remain equal, perceiving neither fragrance nor stench."[48] If bad smell can lead one closer to reality, then *bad* becomes *good*. And when, as the *Avataṃsaka* suggests, both good and bad are transcended, one is simply left with the smell of reality itself. This may be another sense in which, to recall Berger's phrase, bad smell "nags teleologically." Perhaps the "end" to which bad smell points is not just the inevitable end of decay and death. Perhaps bad smell also points to an end in the more ultimate sense. Insofar as the Buddhist sources suggest that bad smell can be a path toward insight, perhaps it can draw us toward not merely a *terminus* but—in the true sense of *telos*—toward a kind of aim or aspiration.

Notes

1. Cleary and Cleary 2005, 352.
2. Curtis, de Barra, and Aunger 2011; Oaten, Stevenson, and Case 2009.
3. *Kongzi Jiayu* 孔子家語 (*The School Sayings of Confucius*). My translation.
4. Classen, Howes, and Synnott 1994, 4.
5. Cleary and Cleary 2005, 426.
6. Mrozik 2007, 1.
7. Hua 1979. All translations from foreign-language sources are my own unless otherwise noted.
8. Hua 1968.
9. On the notion of the opacity of karma, see Hallisey and Hansen 1996; and Crosby 2008.
10. McHugh 2012, 141.
11. McHugh 2012, 6.
12. McHugh 2012, 230.
13. Douglas 2003, 36.
14. Heirman and Torck 2012, 7.
15. Some entertaining examples include Schopen 2015, 20; Bareau 1960, 254; and Heirman and Torck 2012, 96.
16. Bareau 1960, 254.
17. *Gaomin si guiyue* 高旻寺規約 (*The Rules of Gaomin Monastery*), B18.98.333a, 8–17.
18. Heirman and Torck 2012, 96.
19. Heirman and Torck 2012, 31 and 111.
20. Bareau 1960, 254.
21. Taishō 1451.24.282c23–283a3.
22. See Heirman and De Rauw 2006, 71 and 79; and Heirman and Torck 2012, 110.
23. Yamamoto 1973, 52.
24. This is the "*dhāraṇī* to purify the mouth karma," or *jing kouye zhenyan* 淨口業真言.
25. Taishō 1470.24.912.
26. Heirman and Torck 2012, 74.
27. Taishō 1805.40.378b, 21–24.
28. Heirman and De Rauw 2006, 70.
29. Horner 2014, 1144.

30. See Wujastyk 2003, 196; and Kieschnick 2005, 202.
31. Heirman and De Rauw 2006, 62.
32. On the psychosexual analysis of smell, see Wolfe and Mitchell 2003; Howes 2003; and Verchery 2019.
33. Greene 2016, 2.
34. Suzuki 1999, 221.
35. Blum 2013, 112.
36. Hua 1980b, 35.
37. Hua 1980a, 127.
38. Taishō 1.1.43c, 2–3.
39. Taishō 1.1.77b15.
40. Berger 1989, 61.
41. Aitken and Huikai 1990, 137.
42. Garrett 2010, 301.
43. Taishō 251.8.848c9.
44. Although the man I am calling Wanglei explicitly requested that I share his story, I have changed his name in this essay in keeping with the conventions of ethnographic writing.
45. This ubiquitous trope can be found, among other sources, in the *Mātā Sutta* (Thanissaro Bhikkhu 1997).
46. Obeyesekere 2002, 43–44.
47. See, for example, Schopen 2015, 14.
48. Taishō 279.10.303a, 8–9.

Bibliography

Aitken, Robert, and Huikai. 1990. *The Gateless Barrier: The Wu-Men Kuan (Mumonkan).* San Francisco: North Point Press.

Bareau, André. 1960. "La construction et le culte des *stūpa* d'après les *Vinayapiṭaka*." *Bulletin de l'École française d'Extrême-Orient* 50: 227–74.

Berger, John. 1989. "Muck and Its Entanglements: Cleaning the Outhouse." *Harper's Magazine*, May, 60–61.

Blum, Mark L. 2013. *The Nirvāṇa Sūtra (Mahāparnirvāṇa-sūtra).* Moraga: Bukkyo Dendo Kyokai and BDK America.

Classen, Constance, David Howes, and Anthony Synnott. 1994. *Aroma: The Cultural History of Smell.* London: Routledge.

Cleary, Thomas F., and J. C. Cleary. 2005. *The Blue Cliff Record.* Boston: Shambhala Publications.

Crosby, Kate. 2008. "Kamma, Social Collapse or Geophysics? Interpretations of Suffering Among Sri Lankan Buddhists in the Immediate Aftermath of the 2004 Asian Tsunami." *Contemporary Buddhism* 9.1: 53–76.

Curtis, Valerie, Mícheál de Barra, and Robert Aunger. 2011. "Disgust as an Adaptive System for Disease Avoidance Behaviour." *The Royal Society* 366.1563: 389–401.

Douglas, Mary. 2003 [1966]. *Purity and Danger: An Analysis of Concepts of Pollution and Taboo.* London: Routledge.

Garrett, Frances. 2010. "Tapping the Body's Nectar: Gastronomy and Incorporation in Tibetan Literature." *History of Religions* 49.3: 300–326.

Gaomin si guiyue 高旻寺規約 (*The Rules of Gaomin Monastery*). *Dazangjing Bubian* 大藏經補編 (Supplement to the Tripiṭaka). Chinese Buddhist Electronic Text Association. CBETA, B18.98.

Greene, Eric M. 2016. "A Reassessment of the Early History of Chinese Buddhist Vegetarianism." *Asia Major* 29.1: 1–43.

Hallisey, Charles, and Anne Hansen. 1996. "Narrative, Sub-Ethics, and the Moral Life: Some Evidence from Theravāda Buddhism." *The Journal of Religious Ethics* 24.2: 305–27.

Heirman, Ann, and Tom De Rauw. 2006. "Offenders, Sinners and Criminals: The Consumption of Forbidden Food." *Acta Orientalia Academiae Scientiarum Hungaricae* 59.1: 57–83.

Heirman, Ann, and Mathieu Torck. 2012. *A Pure Mind in a Clean Body: Bodily Care in the Buddhist Monasteries of Ancient India and China*. Gent: Ginkgo Academia Press.

Horner, I. B., trans. 2014 [1942]. *The Book of the Discipline: Vinayapiṭaka.* London: Pali Text Society and SuttaCentral.

Howes, David. 2003. *Sensual Relations: Engaging the Senses in Culture and Social Theory.* Ann Arbor: University of Michigan Press.

Hua, Hsüan. 1968. *Da foding shoulengyan jing qianshi.* 大佛頂首楞嚴經淺釋. http://www.drbachinese.org/online_reading/sutra_explanation/Shu/volume4.htm.

———. 1979. *Dafangguang fo huayan jing qianshi.* 大方廣佛華嚴經淺釋. http://www.drbachinese.org/online_reading/sutra_explanation/Ava/Ava_Vol39-4.htm.

———. 1980a. *Flower Adornment Sutra: Chapter 39, Part V, Entering the Dharma Realm*. Talmage, CA: Dharma Realm Buddhist University, Buddhist Text Translation Society.

_____. 1980b. *The Śūraṅgama Sūtra, Volume 4: Commentary by Tripiṭaka Master Hsüan Hua*. Translated by Heng Chih and the Buddhist Text Translation Society. Talmage, CA: Sino-American Buddhist Association and Dharma Realm Buddhist University.

Kieschnick, John. 2005. "Buddhist Vegetarianism in China." In *Of Tripod and Palate: Food, Politics and Religion in Traditional China*, edited by Roel Sterckx, 186–212. New York: Palgrave Macmillan.

Kongzi Jiayu. 孔子家語 (*The School Sayings of Confucius*). Chinese Text Project. https://ctext.org/kongzi-jiayu/liu-ben.

McHugh, James. 2012. *Sandalwood and Carrion: Smell in Premodern Indian Religion and Culture*. Oxford: Oxford University Press.

Mrozik, Susanne. 2007. *Virtuous Bodies: The Physical Dimensions of Morality in Buddhist Ethics*. Oxford: Oxford University Press.

Oaten, Megan, Richard J. Stevenson, and Trevor I. Case. 2009. "Disgust as a Disease-Avoidance Mechanism." *Psychological Bulletin* 135.2: 303–21.

Obeyesekere, Gananath. 2002. *Imagining Karma: Ethical Transformation in Amerindian, Buddhist, and Greek Rebirth*. Berkeley: University of California Press.

Schopen, Gregory. 2015. "The Fragrance of the Buddha, the Scent of Monuments, and the Odor of Images in Early India." *Bulletin de l'École Française d'Extrême-Orient* 101.1: 11–30.

Suzuki, Daisetz Teitaro. 1999. *The Laṅkāvatāra Sūtra: A Mahāyāna Text*. Delhi: Motilal Barnarsidass Publishers.

Taishō shinshū daizōkyō. 大正新脩大藏經 (Taishō Tripiṭaka). Chinese Buddhist Electronic Text Association, CBETA. https://www.cbeta.org.

Thanissaro Bhikkhu, trans. 1997. "Mata Sutta: Mother" Saṃyutta Nikāya 15.14–19. Last revised for Access to Insight (BCBS edition), November 30, 2013. https://www.accesstoinsight.org/tipitaka/sn/sn15/sn15.014.than.html.

Verchery, Lina. 2019. "Both Like and Unlike: Rebirth, Olfaction, and the Transspecies Imagination in Modern Chinese Buddhism." *Religions* 10.6: 364–80.

Wolfe, Cary, and W. J. T. Mitchell. 2003. *Animal Rites: American Culture, the Discourse of Species, and Posthumanist Theory*. Chicago: University of Chicago Press.

Wujastyk, Dominik. 2003. *The Roots of Ayurveda: Selections from Sanskrit Medical Writings*. London: Penguin Books.

Yamamoto, Kōshō. 1973. *The Mahāyāna Mahāparinirvāṇa-Sūtra*. Ube: The Karinbunko.

Thus Have I Smelled

John S. Strong

IN 1907 Reginald Farrer, an English botanist on a visit to what was then called Ceylon, got permission to view the Buddha's tooth relic in Kandy. Along with a few other privileged guests, he was ushered into the inner chamber of the temple in which the sacred tooth is kept. At first, as his eyes were adjusting to the dim light, he could see nothing except "a ghostly shape of gold" that turned out to be the outermost dagoba of the relic. It was rather his nose that gave him the first sense of the holiness of the place, for, in his memoirs, he mentions that a "pungent sweetness fill[ed] that tiny vault of darkness with an almost overpowering ecstasy."[1] Forty years earlier in the 1870s, William Gregory, the then governor of Ceylon, had a quite different reaction. After viewing the Kandyan tooth, he complained that the odor of the relic chamber was "detestable" and that he was "heartily glad to get out of the heat and smell" for a cup of tea in the old palace, which was quite close by.[2]

We know from physiologists and philosophers that experiences of smells can vary from individual to individual, something I like to call "the durian effect," after the Southeast Asian fruit whose odor evokes ecstatic addictive desire in some and utter repugnance in others.[3] We know from anthropologists and historians that such experiences are also, to an extent, culturally determined and may evolve or devolve over time.[4] We know too that odors tend to reflect and determine classificatory schemes by which particular smellers distinguish and define "self" from "others," whether those "others" be animals, humans of different classes or ethnicities, or, more relevantly for this essay, supernatural beings.[5] Simply put, one's own gods or saints are odorized differently than someone else's, and within one's own tradition, good spirits almost always smell better than evil ones. Thus it comes as no surprise that to Farrer, a recent lay convert to Buddhism, the Buddha (or at least his relic chamber) smelled sweet, but to Gregory, whose feelings about Buddhism were much less sympathetic and scented by his own Roman Catholic background, its odor was nauseating.

In this essay, I wish to look at good smells in Buddhism from the perspective of the Buddhist tradition. More specifically, I shall focus on ways in which Buddhists recalled and experienced the fragrance of the Buddha. I will primarily use Indic sources, although I believe my findings may be applicable to Buddhism in other parts of Asia as well. By and large this is a topic that has been rather neglected by Buddhologists.[6] This may be due to the fact that, at first glance, the tradition seems to privilege other senses. For instance, virtually every sūtra begins with the well-known words "Thus have I heard" (*evaṃ mayā śrutam*), said to have been spoken by Ānanda when he recited from memory the Blessed One's teachings at the first Buddhist council. The phrase suggests that primacy should be accorded to the auditory sense. More recently scholars have pointed to the importance of visual (in contradistinction to aural) encounters with the Buddha, resulting in books such as Andy Rotman's *Thus Have I Seen*.[7] Indeed, when the person of the Buddha is described in Buddhist sources, what is usually featured is his shining body "adorned with the thirty-two marks of a great man [*mahāpuruṣa*], and the eighty secondary marks[8] . . . , arrayed with light a fathom-wide, radiant in excess of a thousand suns, like a living mountain of jewels, handsome in its entirety."[9]

Though the Buddha's fragrance may not be emphasized in all stock portrayals of his person, there can be no doubt that he smells good to Buddhists. Like certain Christian saints, he has an "odor of sanctity."[10] He is, to borrow from the title of a recently published Newari biography of the Blessed One, "sweetly fragrant" (*saurabha*).[11] He is said to exude the scent of sandalwood,[12] and his breath is said to have a heavenly smell as though it were suffused with various perfumes.[13] According to some Buddhists, even his excrement smelled good, although this was disputed by others.[14]

A Life of Fragrant Moments

In researching the good smell of the Buddha in biographical materials, one of the first things to do is to see when and where it is brought to the fore. Basing himself on Rodney Needham's insights into the ritual role and effect of percussive sounds (drums, bells, etc.), David Howes has theorized that "there is [also] a connection between olfaction and transition," and that "smell is [actually] the liminal sense par excellence."[15] In other words, scents are most prominently featured at times when beings of different kinds (for instance, humans and supernaturals) interact, or when individuals undergo rites of passage or change states (whether psychological, sociological, emotional, or biographical). It comes as no surprise, then, to find in traditional life stories of the Buddha that good smells are particularly noted at important moments of transition in his career, such as his birth, his great departure, his awakening, and his death and *parinirvāṇa*.

Thus, in one Sanskrit biography, at the moment of his birth, the bodhisattva is "pure and devoid of any disagreeable odor."[16] Actually, this is true even before his birth, since, within his mother's womb, he resides in a kind of fragrant placental palace implanted there by the god Brahmā to shelter him from any fetidness. This is described as having three nesting chambers (*kūṭāgāra*), the outermost of which is made of sweet-smelling sandalwood while the innermost is "made of perfume" (*gandhamaya*).[17]

Another moment of transition in the Buddha's life—his great departure from the palace—is also marked by scents, this time due to the testimonial offerings of myriads of deities. According to a Pali biography, as the bodhisattva leaves home to embark on his quest for enlightenment, gods, *nāgas*, and *garuḍas* fill the world with perfumes, garlands, aromatic powders, and incense, until the sky is clouded over with flowers and the ground so covered with a tangled mass of perfumes and garlands that his horse Kaṇṭhaka has difficulty making his way through them.[18]

The flowers and aromatic powders can be smelled again at the time of the Buddha's awakening in Bodhgaya, but on this occasion they result from his own transformations of the weapons hurled at him by Māra. Wishing to impede the enlightenment process, Māra and his horde send forth successive showers of flaming boulders, swords, daggers, darts, and burning coals, but by the time they reach the bodhisattva seated at the foot of the bodhi tree, they are all transformed into wreaths of heavenly garlands. A blizzard of red-hot ashes is then changed into a sprinkle of sandalwood powder, and a storm of smoking mud is transformed into sweet-smelling ointments.[19]

Flowers and fragrances are also featured in the final moment of transition in the Buddha's life: his death and *parinirvāṇa*. Unlike ordinary Indian funerals, the Buddha's cremation is a sweet-smelling affair. Even before his actual death, the twin *śāla* trees under which he is lying flower out of season and drop their aromatic blossoms on his body as he rests there talking to Ānanda.[20] In East Asia, this becomes an important harbinger of impermanence,[21] but in the context of the *Mahāparinibbāna Sutta* and its commentary, it is part of a grander scenario that features the gods and good smells. For along with the *śāla* trees, the heavenly deities get into the act. Standing on the rim of the Cakravāḍa Mountains that surround our world-system, they rain down blossoms, perfumes, and divine sandalwood powder of various sorts, which they strew from gold and silver boxes, until the Buddha's body is completely covered.[22] These odors are then reinforced by the Buddha's funeral pyre, which in the Sanskrit tradition is said to be made of all sorts of fragrant wood,[23] and in the Pali text, to be made of all kinds of perfumes.[24]

The whole of the Buddha's life, then, is punctuated by good smells that serve to highlight important moments of transition. During these times his own fragrance comes to the fore, and it is evoked and amplified by the aromatic offerings of flowers, incense, etc., made to him by gods and humans and other devotees. This is a theme to which I shall return. First, however, a bit more needs to be said about how the Buddha got his good smell.

Fragrance and Karma

Generally speaking, the body odor of the Buddha—and indeed of all beings—appears to be related to karma. Simply put, good deeds result in sweet smells and bad deeds in foul smells. Sometimes this happens instantaneously. For instance, the Cetiya Jātaka recounts how habitual truth-telling can, among other things, give rise to breath with a blue lotus fragrance (*uppalagandha*) and a body exuding the odor of sandalwood (*candana-gandha*). Lying, however, can immediately result in the mouth becoming fetid, like a rotten egg, and the body foul, like an open latrine.[25] At other times, a fragrant body is the result of a transformative act of offering to a buddha or a stūpa in a past life. According to the karmic principle that like actions beget like results, "fragrant acts" can be seen to ripen into "fragrant rewards," even when done in the distant past. Consider, for example, the case of the arhat Sugandhi ("good odor"). Ninety-one eons ago, in a former life, he smeared the stūpa of the previous buddha, Vipaśyi, with aromatic unguents and made an offering of flowers and incense to it. As a result of this act, we are told, when Sugandhi was eventually reborn in Kapilavastu in the time of Gautama Buddha, his mouth exuded the scent of blue lotus and his body smelled of sandalwood, the fragrance of which pervaded the whole city.[26]

Similar acts of aromatic offerings are said to have been performed by Gautama Buddha himself in some of his former lives as a bodhisattva when he periodically renewed his vow for future buddhahood in the presence of various past buddhas. For instance, when, over four incalculable (*asaṃ-khyeya*) ages ago, as a brahman youth named Sumati, he first embarked on the bodhisattva path, he offered five lotuses to the past buddha Dīpaṃ-kara that magically rose into the air and formed a scented canopy of flowers over that buddha's head.[27] Then, over two incalculable ages ago, when Gautama had been born as a brahman, he made a gift of perfumes and garlands to the past buddha Maṅgala; and, over one incalculable age ago, when he was an ascetic, he made a gift of sandalwood to the past buddha Nārada; and 1,800 eons (*kalpa*) ago, again as an ascetic, he presented some heavenly flowers to the past buddha Atthadassi.[28] We are not told explicitly that such acts eventually resulted in his good fragrance when he finally attained buddhahood, nor that they ever resulted in his getting a name evocative of a sweet smell (e.g., Sugandhi), but this *is* the case with a number of other buddhas and buddhas-to-be. Thus, the future buddhas Gandhahastin ("perfume hands"), Gandhatejas ("perfume power"), and Gandhābha ("perfume splendor"), three of the one thousand buddhas of the present eon (*bhadrakalpa*) whose lives are summarized in the Mahāyāna

Bhadrakalpika Sūtra, are all named in recognition of some aromatic offering they made when they started, eons ago, on their bodhisattva path.[29] More famously, perhaps, in the *Lotus Sūtra*, the Buddha's disciple Maudgalyāyana, because he venerated the stūpas of 28,000 buddhas in the past with "flowers, incense, perfumed wreaths, and scented ointments and powders," will in the future become the buddha named Tamālapatracandanagandha (lit., "having the fragrance of tamāla leaves and sandalwood").[30]

It is clear from these examples that good smells can be transmitted over many lifetimes, a point that is reinforced by the fact that the intermediary beings that effectuate the karmic transition from one life to the next are commonly called "odor eaters" (*gandharvas*).[31] According to Vasubandhu, low-ranked unmeritorious *gandharvas* are defined by the bad odors (*durgandha*) they "eat," while high-ranked meritorious *gandharvas* are known by their good odors (*sugandha*), and they variously transmit these scents from one lifetime to the next.[32] Smell thus plays a key adjunct role in the transmission of karma, and so in the memory of past lives. Indeed, as David Shulman reminds us, in Indian tradition generally, recollections that emerge from previous existences (or memories that suddenly come out of the unconscious) are called *vāsanā*, literally "odors" or "perfumes."[33]

Fragrance, the Buddha, and the Gods

Since odors, good or bad, can be reflections and evocations of karmic status, it is possible to place beings on an olfactory spectrum of sorts running from the sweet smelling to foul smelling. At one end of this spectrum are the gods, and toward the other end are humans, who, from the gods' perspective at least, smell bad.[34] What is interesting here is to see where and how (and indeed whether) the Buddha fits on this spectrum. Generally speaking, Western Buddhologists have come to view the Buddha as a human being, but *olfactorily speaking*, he is much more akin to the gods, for like them he is redolent of the same smell of fine perfumes, fresh blossoms, or sandalwood. There are, however, some important differences. First, the Buddha may smell like the gods but his *sense of smell* (like his senses of seeing and hearing) is better than theirs. Simply put, he has a more sensitive nose, something the gods themselves are said to recognize.[35]

Second, unlike the Buddha's good fragrance, that of the gods is not permanent. It may last for most of their very long lives, but it disappears in the final week of their existence as deities, when, famously, five omens appear to signal their imminent fall from divinity and rebirth elsewhere. Significantly, three of these omens have to do with the sense of smell: the garlands around the deities' necks that had remained fresh and fragrant for eons begin to wither, sweat starts pouring from their armpits, and "a bad smell emerges from their bodies."[36] The Buddha, however, even when he takes on the form of the gods (for instance, in his penultimate life in Tuṣita Heaven) does not appear to lose his fragrance when he transitions to his next life.

Third, the Buddha is not affected by bad smells the way the gods are. Buddhist divinities seem to be allergic to rank odors; more specifically, they cannot stand the stench of humans. Thus, when the future Buddha is about to leave Tuṣita Heaven for his descent into his mother's womb, his fellow gods are shocked that he would choose to reside for ten months in what they think of as a stinking place of human female fetidness, and they are worried he will not be able to stand it. Accordingly, as mentioned above, they implant into Māyā a uterine chamber made of perfumes, which, in their ignorance, they think the bodhisattva will need and want to have.[37] In fact, they need not have bothered, for, unlike the gods, not only has the Buddha-to-be transcended attachment to good smells and repugnance toward bad ones, but his own fragrance is sweet smelling and powerful enough to mask out lesser odors. Thus, in the Mūlasarvāstivāda Vinaya's account of the Buddha's descent from Trāyastriṃśa Heaven (after teaching the Dharma to his mother, who had been reborn there),[38] some of the deities are said to have been reluctant to accompany him down to Earth because "the filth of humans could be smelled up to twelve miles (*yojana*) and [they were worried] they could not bear . . . it." However, they soon discovered that "the Blessed One emanated [such a strong] scent of *gośīrṣa* sandalwood [that] they could not smell that foul [human] odor."[39] In this way, the Buddha serves as a kind of living air freshener who can kill bad smells and so allow the gods to be present. An offshoot of this is that the good odor of the Buddha makes possible an actual commingling of gods and humans in which they can meet on the same plane.[40]

The Good Smell of Relics

I have so far been dealing with the fragrance of the living Buddha. In some ways, however, his good smell becomes more important after his passing, for it makes him aromatically present even after his cremation. As Schopen points out, the Buddha's funeral is productive not only of bodily relics but of a "pure, incorporeal fragrance" as well.[41] To take this one step further, it may be useful to think of this post-mortem smell of the Buddha as a kind of olfactory relic—a "body of fragrance" or "*gandhakāya*" (to coin a new Sanskrit term)—to go along with the visible relics of his physical body (*rūpakāya*) and the audible relics of the body of his teachings (*dharmakāya*).

Schopen has elsewhere shown how, in inscriptions and in texts, relics are often said to be "infused" or "saturated" or "imbued" (*paribhāvita*) with Buddhist virtues such as wisdom and morality, in the same way that the living Buddha is.[42] Robert L. Brown has suggested that the term *paribhāvita* may be seen as a "metaphorical link with perfumed scents," implying that relics were also imbued with perfumes.[43] He goes on to speculate, on the basis of Gandhāran bas-reliefs, that when the brahman Droṇa divided up the Buddha's relics following his cremation, he molded the ashes into balls, perhaps mixing them with "water, sandalwood powder, cosmetics or clay."[44] Further evidence of this scenting of the relics may be seen in the remains of perfume balls that archaeologists have found in relic deposits in stūpas, perhaps placed there to evoke and reinforce the Buddha's fragrance.[45] One might also speculate that the gold flowers that are so profusely found in Buddhist reliquaries were intended not only as votive jewelry but also symbolically as permanent flower offerings whose freshness (and so scent) would never fade.[46] Finally, all this is further reinforced by the fact that, in Gandhāra at least, reliquaries were often made in the shape of perfume bottles or actual perfume bottles were repurposed as reliquaries.[47] Indeed, we know from the Kharoṣṭhī inscription on one of the most famous Gandhāran relic containers—the so-called Kaniṣka Reliquary (second century CE) presently in the Peshawar Museum—that it was originally a "perfume [or incense] box" (*gadhakaraṃḍa*).[48]

Ritually Reinforcing the Buddha's Fragrance

As mentioned, the Buddha and his relics not only smell good themselves, but their good smell is constantly being reinforced by the odoriferous offerings of his disciples—whether made during or after his life. In Sri Lanka, for example, it is customary for devotees paying their respects to buddha images to offer flowers (which are described as having color and scent) and then incense to the Buddha. Each of these offerings is supposed to be accompanied by a Pali verse. The one for the incense may be translated as follows: "To the Tathāgata, whose body and face are fragrant, who is fragrant with infinite virtues, I pay homage with these fragrant perfumes."[49]

From this verse we can say that devotees recognize that the Buddha is inherently sweet smelling, but with the same aroma as their own fragrant offerings. At the same time, these devotees are perfumed themselves by those very offerings. Indeed, after presenting incense to an image, they may waft the sweet-smelling smoke back onto themselves with their open hand, or rub some incense powder on themselves.[50] This allows them to enter into the Buddha's "arena of fragrance" (see below), and to make scent contact with him, in the same way, perhaps, that *darśana* (seeing) allows a devotee to make eye-contact with a divinity.[51] Another way of putting this is that by smelling like the Buddha by virtue of their fragrant offerings, devotees are becoming a little more buddha-like. In this sense, aromatic offerings to the Buddha are as much for the devotees themselves as they are for the Buddha.

The general importance of good smells as a link between worshippers and their object of devotion is, of course, found in other religious traditions.[52] As Mark Smith put it in his discussion of fragrance in ancient Greco-Roman religions, "incense, traveling through the air, was believed to attract and unite humans and gods, while the absence of odour, or unpleasant odours, had the opposite effect."[53] The same thing was true in India, where, as early as the *Rig Veda*, it was the *smell* of the burnt sacrificial offerings carried by the smoke of the fire that brought the gods down to earth and ultimately ensured their interaction with humans.[54] In Buddhism, however, there was opposition to the Brahmanical fire sacrifice and a different conception of the recipient of devotion, and things developed accordingly. The scented offerings of Buddhist monastics and laypersons—

flowers, unguents, perfumes, incense—do not really "summon" the Buddha to their presence. Rather, they serve to amplify an aromatic arena redolent and evocative of him—to the extent that these odoriferous offerings are sometimes said to make the Buddha seem to be even more present, in both the temporal and the spatial sense.

Aromatic Arenas: The Gandhakuṭī and the Stūpa

In Buddhist practice in India, two of these aromatic arenas have been emphasized and cultically maintained in monasteries. The first of these is the *gandhakuṭī*, or perfumed chamber, of the Buddha. In legends, it is variously described as a sandalwood structure or a flowery pavilion, a kind of bower made of blossoms and perfumes—more in line perhaps with the original meaning of *kuṭī* as "hut."[55] As its name implies, what is important about it is its good smell. Eugène Burnouf calls the *gandhakuṭī* "the hall of perfumes," and adds that when the Buddha was living, it was the room in which he took his lodging, but after his death it was a room containing his statue, in front of which perfumes were burned.[56] The most famous *gandhakuṭī* was the one in the Jetavana monastery in Śrāvastī, but it seems (from archaeological and textual evidence) that many monasteries had a *gandhakuṭī*. It was "the room that was permanently reserved for the Buddha himself"—a place for him to be "present," whether he was actually there or not—somewhat like the bishop's chair in Christian cathedrals.[57]

Building and maintaining a *gandhakuṭī* was thus a way to affirm the presence of the Buddha in one's place. In a story found both in the *Divyāvadāna* and the *Commentary on the Saṃyutta Nikāya*, the Buddha's disciple Pūrṇa, far away in the land of Śroṇāparānta, builds a sandalwood *gandhakuṭī* in order to invite the Blessed One for a visit. He then climbs to the roof of this structure, burns incense, and throws flowers in the direction of distant Śrāvastī. Magically, the blossoms remain suspended in midair and take the shape of a pavilion of flowers that flies off to the Jetavana to fetch the Buddha. The incense smoke does the same in the form of a cloud. Significantly, at that very moment the Buddha is sitting in his own *gandhakuṭī* in the Jetavana, and it is from there that he steps into Pūrṇa's flying pavilion and goes off to Śroṇāparānta to enter the structure Pūrṇa has built for him. Sweet-smelling himself, he thus, at all times, also remains surrounded by the scents and sights of offerings.[58] In certain Mahāyāna texts, this scenario is expanded and the gods and humans together offer the Buddha flowers, unguents, perfumes, and aromatic powders, which rise in the air and transform the whole universe (the trichiliomegachiliocosm) into a perfumed pavilion for the Tathāgata.[59]

The *gandhakuṭī* was not the only fragrant part of the monastery. Another aromatic arena was the stūpa, which was also marked by the good smell of the Buddha. This fragrance was ritually and regularly renewed by devotees who variously smeared the monuments with unguents or sandalwood paste (as we saw in the past-life story of Sugandhi). This was, in fact, obligatory. As Schopen points out, the Mūlasarvāstivāda Vinaya contains a rule forbidding monks from decorating monastic buildings with paintings of living human beings but enjoining them to "smear and bathe the stūpa with scents."[60] One exception to this rule, though, was apparently allowed: the injunction against the portrayal of bodies did not extend to the marking of stūpas with perfumed palm prints, variously called "perfumed hands" (*gandhahasta*) or "five-fingered marks" (*pañcāngula*).[61] Such devotional markings on stūpas are mentioned in a number of texts and are in fact represented on depictions of stūpas at Bharhut.[62] I like to think of these scented handprints (quite apart from their apotropaic function) as having two significances: renewing the scent of the Buddha on the stūpa and bringing one's own personal aromatized scent to the stūpa—a sort of votive offering that can be left *ad sanctos*. At the same time, making such palm prints was karmically effective: the Buddha's handsome cousin Nanda, who had thirty of the thirty-two marks of the great man, is said to have earned those marks (so to speak) by, in a previous life, making thirty perfumed palm prints on the stūpa of a pratyekabuddha.[63]

But if monks were allowed to perfume the Buddha's stūpas, and in so doing to perfume themselves, outside of this ritual context, they were generally not permitted to use scented things on their own bodies and in their own dwellings. In this regard, Schopen further recounts an interesting story of a problem that arises when a monk smears unguents on the door to his monastic cell: the laypeople passing by are confused and start venerating the monk's room, thinking it must be the Buddha's *gandhakuṭī*.[64] Clearly, the scent of perfume was thought to be indicative of the presence of the Buddha and not that of an ordinary monk. Here we can see another dimension of the general Vinaya rule forbidding monks from adorning themselves with "garlands, scents, and unguents": it was not just to combat personal vanity, but also to keep them from making claims to being buddha-like.[65]

Concluding Thoughts

I started this essay with a basic assumption that, in addition to hearing and seeing, smell was and is another way for Buddhists to encounter the Buddha, whether alive or departed. In exploring this topic, a number of points about the importance of good smells came to the fore, which it may be helpful to summarize here. First, though the Buddha's fragrance is always assumed, it is not constantly emphasized in Buddhist sources; instead, it is highlighted at certain important moments of transition in his life story. Some of these (such as his time in utero, his birth, and his funeral) are occasions that ordinarily might be considered to be impure or foul-smelling; good smells at those moments thus serve to show the extraordinariness of the Buddha. Others (such as his great departure and his defeat of Māra) are transitions of a different sort in which the smells signal freedom from the traps of worldliness and death itself. Second, his fragrance, like his physical appearance, is the product of karma acquired while on the path to buddhahood. It thus serves to extend the scope of his biography by giving it an aromatic thread that ties together many lifetimes. The same is true of other buddhas and buddhas-to-be, some of whom actually began their bodhisattva career with an offering of sweet smells. Third, olfactorily speaking, the Buddha is more akin to the gods than he is to ordinary humans, although some special qualities (such as the permanence of his fragrance) make him even more distinguished than the deities. Fourth, his fragrance, because it overpowers all lesser odors, is able to bring together beings (e.g., gods and humans) who might otherwise stay apart from each other on account of olfactory prejudices. Fifth, his fragrance becomes most important after his *parinirvāṇa*, since it lingers on as a kind of olfactory relic that *smells the same* after his death as his body did before it. In this, it differs, perhaps, from visual and aural relics. Finally, his fragrance is ritually renewed and reinforced by the sweet-smelling offerings of devotees, thus allowing them to maintain and share in the Buddha's arena of fragrance and make olfactory contact with him there, whether that be in his *gandhakuṭī* or his stūpa.

Taken together, then, these findings make clear the importance of paying attention to the olfactory dimensions of the Buddhist tradition, for such an approach can give us new perspectives on aspects of the Buddha's life, as well as his ongoing ritual veneration. Indeed, it can be argued that for the ordinary worshipper today, the Buddha is just as accessible through scent as he is through sight or sound. Thus have I smelled.

Notes

1. Farrer 1908, 72. For a biography of Reginald Farrer, see Charlesworth 2018.
2. Gregory 1894, 281–82.
3. See the entry "Durian, Dorian" in Yule and Burnell 1903, 331–33. On the philosophical side, see Immanuel Kant's comments (1991, 136) about the inconstancy of smell, which was one of the reasons he chose to omit it from his study of aesthetics.
4. See, for example, Corbin 1986.
5. See Classen 1993, 79–105; Detienne 1994; and, with regard to Indian religions, McHugh 2012.
6. An important exception is Schopen 2015, from whose article I have gained much. It is worth noting that Buddhist studies in the West grew up in the eighteenth and nineteenth centuries at the same time as the supposed "olfactive revolution" that saw a "demotion" of the sense of smell was taking place in Europe. On this see Howes 1991, 145, and, more generally, Corbin 1986. For a critique of this view, see Smith 2007, 2–11.
7. Rotman 2008.
8. For lists of these, see Buswell and Lopez 2014, 1094–95 and 1096–98. It should be noted that none of the thirty-two marks has anything to do with smells, although one of the eighty secondary marks (#79) does refer to the Buddha's hair as fragrant (*surabhikeśa*).
9. This stock description is repeated over thirty times in the *Avadānaśataka*. See, for one instance, Appleton 2020, 68 (Skt. text in Avś, 297). See also Feer 1891, 8.
10. For examples of Christian saints noted for the fragrance of their bodies, see Classen 1998, 36–47, and, more generally, Albert 1990. On the importance of smells among early Christians, see Harvey 2006.
11. Lewis and Tuladhar 2010, iii. For a discussion of this term, see Schopen 2015, 11.

12. Ja, 3: 454; English translation, Cowell, 3: 272.
13. Ja, 1: 96; Cowell, 1: 2.
14. The view that the Buddha's feces smelled wonderful was maintained by the proto-Mahāyānist Andhakās and the Uttarāpathakas, but the Theravādins disagreed, saying that the Buddha did not feed on perfumes but ate rice and gruel like everyone else. As a consequence, his excreta smelled the same as other peoples'. On this Abhidharma debate, see Aung and Davids 1915, 326; Law 1969, 213; Bareau 2013, 356; and Schopen 2015, 14–15. The Theravādins, however, were hardly consistent in this view. Thus, in Dhp-a, 3: 270 (English translation, Burlingame 1921, 3: 79), when the Buddha is sick with diarrhea at Beluva, the contents of his chamber pot are likened to a bowl full of perfumes, which the god Sakka reverentially carries off, placing it on his head. See also Masefield and Revire 2021, 62.
15. Needham 1967, 606–14; and Howes 1991, 142–43.
16. Lal 60; French translation, Foucaux 1884, 59.
17. Lal 63; Foucaux 1884, 62. See also Schopen 2015, 13. More generally on the Buddha's life in utero, see Sasson 2009.
18. Ja, 1: 64; English translation, Jayawickrama 1990, 85.
19. Ja, 1: 73–74; Jayawickrama 1990, 96–97.
20. DN, 2: 137; English translation, Walshe 1987, 262. In the *Avadānaśataka* (260–63; French translation, Feer 2010, 430–36), the *śāla* trees shed their blossoms on the Buddha's body after his passing. For an interpretation of this, see Vaudeville 1964, 84–85.
21. See, for instance, the first line of the *Heike Monogatari*, in McCullough 1988, 23. See also Buswell and Lopez 2014, 821, s.v. "siku."
22. Sv, 2: 575–76; English translation, An 2003, 139–40.
23. Skt. *sarvagandhakāṣṭha*; see Waldschmidt 1949–50, 424.
24. Skt. *sabbagandhānaṃ citaka*; see DN, 2: 142; Walshe 1987, 263.
25. Ja, 3: 456–57; Cowell 1895–1907, 3: 273.
26. Avś, 157–58; French translation, Feer 1891, 238–39. It should be said that Sugandhi's original act of merit was accompanied by a vow (*praṇidhāna*) to eventually become the disciple of a master like Vipaśyi (i.e., another buddha) and to attain enlightenment under him. It is this vow that explains Sugandhi's arhatship, but it is his physical offering that results in his good smell. For an analysis of such deeds, see Strong 1979.
27. Div, 251; English translation, Rotman 2017, 31.
28. For these three stories, see Bv, 29–31, 47–49, and 62–64; English translation, Horner 1975, 32–35, 49–51, and 63–65. The *Mahāvastu* (Mtu, 1: 37–42; English translation, Jones, 1: 31–36) features instead the story of the bodhisattva who, as the monk Abhiya, buys one hundred thousand *kārṣāpaṇa*s worth of "*keśara* essence" (a perfume made of *keśara* blossoms) and sprinkles it on the past buddha Sarvābhibhū and the members of his saṅgha while renewing his vow to attain buddhahood.
29. Tibetan text and English translation in Yeshe De Project 1986, 1501, 1643, and 1699.
30. Sdmp, 5.29; English translation, Kern 1884, 149–50.

31. *Gandharvas* are also identified as "celestial musicians," one of the eight classes of deities in the Buddhist pantheon. See Buswell and Lopez 2014, 311–12, s.v. "gandharva."
32. Kośa, 125; French translation, La Vallée Poussin 1980, 47–48.
33. Shulman 1987, 220. See also O'Flaherty 1984, 220. The phenomenon is often dubbed "the Proust effect," after the scene in *À la recherche du temps perdu* in which the main character is flooded with memories when tasting and smelling a petite madeleine cake. See van Campen 2014.
34. Since this chapter deals with *good* smells, I am not considering here the extension of this spectrum to the animal, hungry-ghost, and hell-being realms, who smell even worse. See Avś 253 (Rotman 2021, 90).
35. See Lal. 60 (Foucaux 1884, 59); and Mtu, 1: 337 (Jones 1949–56, 1: 284).
36. Div 193 (English translation, Rotman 2008, 325). See also La Vallée Poussin 1980, 2:136. The other two omens are that the garments that remained crisp and clean for their entire lives become soiled and the throne they have been seated on suddenly becomes uncomfortable.
37. Lal, 60 (Foucaux 1884, 59–60). At the same time, another purpose of this uterine perfumed pavilion may have been to create an acceptably fragrant place for the gods when they came to venerate (and receive teachings from) the embryonic Buddha in his mother's womb.
38. On this episode in the Buddha's life, see the sources cited in Strong 2010.
39. Tibetan text and translation in Schopen 2015, 13.
40. On this theme, see Strong 2012.
41. Schopen 2015, 15.
42. Schopen 1997, 126–28.
43. Brown 2006, 201.
44. Brown 2006, 185. Brown's point is reinforced, perhaps, by the fact that in the Sanskrit *Mahāparinirvāṇa Sūtra*, Droṇa's name is given as Dhūmrasagotra, one possible meaning of which is "of the incense [or smoke] clan." See Waldschmidt 1949–50, 442.
45. Jongeward et al. 2002, 46; Brown 2006, 200.
46. Strong 2021, 196; see also Brown 2006, figs. 8.7 and 8.8.
47. Jongeward et. al. 2002, 46; Brown 2006, 200.
48. Jongeward et al. 2002, 81–82, 246. Space does not allow me to examine here the connections between fragrance and another type of relic—the Buddha image. Suffice it to say that it may be significant that in the Buddhist tradition the very first image of the Buddha is said to have been completely carved out of the most fragrant kind of sandalwood. See Strong 2022, 138–39.
49. Pali text and translation in Gombrich 1971, 116. The same verse is repeated when sandalwood water is offered to the Buddha's tooth relic in Kandy (see Seneviratne 1978, 45).
50. In East Asia, this ritual gesture is called *tuxiang* (Jpn., *zukō*). See online *Digital Dictionary of Buddhism* (http://www.buddhism-dict.net/ddb/), s.v. 塗香.
51. Eck 2005.

52. See Howes 1991.
53. Smith 2007, 61.
54. McHugh 2012, 230–31.
55. See Strong 1977, 394–95.
56. Burnouf 2010, 269n32. See also Norman 1908. So close was the relationship between the Buddha and *gandhakuṭī* that, according to a footnote in Yijing's Chinese translation of the Mūlasarvāstivāda Vinaya (Taishō 1451.24.331b), in India the Buddha was sometimes referred to as "the Perfumed Chamber," just as in China the emperor was sometimes referred to as "the Jade Steps." See Strong 1977, 391n4.
57. Schopen 2015, 15.
58. Div. 43–46 (Rotman 2008, 98–103); Spk, 2: 374–80 (French translation, Duroiselle 1905, 161–66). See also Strong 1977, 397.
59. Like the sweet-smelling embryonic palace in Māyā's womb, this is called a *kūṭāgāra*, but it is here given cosmic dimensions. See the passage in the *Large Sutra on Perfect Wisdom* in Zacchetti 2005, 159–60 (text), 267–68 (English translation).
60. Schopen 2015, 17–18.
61. Schopen 2015, 18. See also Vogel 1919.
62. Cunningham 1879, plate XXXI.4.
63. See Schopen 2015, 19. On the flip side of this, bad smells were to be kept away from the stūpa.
64. Schopen 2015, 18.
65. Vin, 1: 82; English translation, Horner 1938–52, 4:105.

Bibliography

Albert, Jean-Pierre. 1990. *Odeurs de sainteté: La mythologie chrétienne des aromates.* Paris: Éditions de l'École des Hautes Études en Sciences Sociales.

An, Yang-Gyu. 2003. *The Buddha's Last Days: Buddhaghosa's Commentary on the Mahāparinibbāna Sutta.* Oxford: Pali Text Society.

Appleton, Naomi. 2020. *Many Buddhas, One Buddha: A Study and Translation of Avadānaśataka 1–40.* Sheffield: Equinox.

Aung, Shwe Zan, and C. A. F. Rhys Davids. 1915. *Points of Controversy or Subjects of Discourse.* London: Pali Text Society.

Avś = *Avadāna-śataka.* 1958. Edited by P. L. Vaidya. Darbhanga: Mithila Institute.

Bareau, André. 2013. *The Buddhist Schools of the Small Vehicle.* Translated by Sara Boin-Webb. Honolulu: University of Hawai'i Press.

Brown, Robert L. 2006. "The Nature and Use of the Bodily Relics of the Buddha in Gandhāra." In *Gandhāran Buddhism: Archaeology, Art, and Texts,* edited by Pia Brancaccio and Kurt Behrendt, 183–209. Vancouver: University of British Columbia press.

Burlingame, E. W. 1921. *Buddhist Legends.* 3 vols. Cambridge, MA: Harvard University Press.

Burnouf, Eugène. 2010. *Introduction to the History of Indian Buddhism.* Translated by Katia Buffetrille and Donald S. Lopez Jr. Chicago: University of Chicago Press.
Buswell, Robert E., Jr., and Donald S. Lopez Jr. 2014. *The Princeton Dictionary of Buddhism.* Princeton, NJ: Princeton University Press.
Bv = *Buddhavaṃsa.* In *Buddhavaṃsa and Cariyāpiṭaka.* 1974. Edited by N. A Jayawickrama. London: Pali Text Society.
Charlesworth, Michael. 2018. *The Modern Culture of Reginald Farrer: Landscape, Literature and Buddhism.* Cambridge: Legenda.
Classen, Constance. 1993. *Worlds of Sense: Exploring the Senses in History and across Cultures.* London: Routledge.
———. 1998. *The Color of Angels: Cosmology, Gender and the Aesthetic Imagination.* London: Routledge.
Corbin, Alain. 1986. *The Foul and the Fragrant: Odor and the French Social Imagination.* Cambridge, MA: Harvard University Press.
Cowell, E. B., trans. 1895–1907. *The Jātaka, or Stories of the Buddha's Former Births.* 6 vols. London: Pali Text Society.
Cunningham, Alexander. 1879. *The Stūpa of Bharhut: A Buddhist Monument Ornamented with Numerous Sculptures.* London: W. H. Allen and Co.
Detienne, Marcel. 1994. *The Gardens of Adonis: Spices in Greek Mythology.* Translated by Janet Lloyd. Princeton, NJ: Princeton University Press.
Dhp-a = *The Commentary on the Dhammapada.* 1906–15. 5 vols. Edited by H. Smith and H. C. Norman. London: Pali Text Society.
Div = *Divyāvadāna.* 1886. Edited by E. B. Cowell and R. A. Neil. Cambridge: Cambridge University Press.
Duroiselle, Charles. 1905. "Notes sur la géographie apocryphe de la Birmanie." *Bulletin de l'École française d'Extrême-Orient* 5: 146–67.
Eck, Diana. 2005. *Darśan: Seeing the Divine Image in India.* New York: Columbia University Press.
Farrer, Reginald. 1908. *In Old Ceylon.* London: Edwin Arnold.
Feer, Léon. 1891. *Avadāna-çataka: Cent légendes bouddhiques.* Annales du Musée Guimet 18. Paris: Ernest Leroux.
Foucaux, Philippe Edouard. 1884. *Le Lalita Vistara: Développement des jeux.* Paris: Ernest Leroux.
Gombrich, Richard. 1971. *Precept and Practice: Traditional Buddhism in the Rural Highlands of Ceylon.* Oxford: The Clarendon Press.
Gregory, William. 1894. *An Autobiography.* London: John Murray.
Harvey, Susan Ashbrook. 2006. *Scenting Salvation: Ancient Christianity and the Olfactory Imagination.* Berkeley: University of California Press.
Horner, I. B., trans. 1938–52. *The Book of the Discipline.* 6 vols. London: Pali Text Society.
———, trans. 1975. *The Minor Anthologies of the Pali Canon, Part III.* London: Pali Text Society.

Howes, David. 1991. "Olfaction and Transition." In *The Varieties of Sensory Experience*, edited by David Howes, 128–47. Toronto: University of Toronto Press.

Ja = *Jātaka Together with Its Commentary.* 1877–96. 6 vols. Edited by V. Fausboll. London: Pali Text Society.

Jayawickrama, N. A., trans. 1990. *The Story of Gotama Buddha (Jātaka-nidāna).* London: Pali Text Society.

Jones, J. J., trans. 1949–56. *The Mahāvastu.* 3 vols. London: Pali Text Society.

Jongeward, David, Elizabeth Errington, Richard Salomon, and Stefan Baums. 2002. *Gandharan Buddhist Reliquaries.* Seattle: University of Washington Press.

Kant, Immanuel. 1991. *The Critique of Judgement.* Translated by James Creed Meredith. Oxford: Oxford University Press.

Kern, Hendrik, trans. 1884. *Saddharma-Puṇḍarīka, or the Lotus of the True Law.* Oxford: Clarendon Press.

Kośa = *Abhidharmakośabhāṣyam of Vasubandhu.* 1975. Edited by Prahlad Pradan. Patna: K. P. Jayaswal Research Institute.

La Vallée Poussin, Louis de, trans. 1980. *L'Abhidharmakośa de Vasubandhu.* 6 vols. Brussels: Institut Belge des Hautes Études Chinoises.

Lal = *Lalitavistara.* 1902. Edited by Salomon Lefmann. Halle: Verlag der Buchhandlung des Waisenhauses.

Law, Bimala Churn. 1969. *The Debates Commentary.* London: Pali Text Society.

Lewis, Todd, and Subarna Man Tuladhar. 2010. *Sugata Saurabha: An Epic Poem from Nepal on the Life of the Buddha by Chittadhar Hṛdaya.* Oxford: Oxford University Press.

Masefield, Peter, and Nicolas Revire. 2021. "On the Buddha's 'Karmic Fluff': The Last Meal Revisited." *Journal of the Oxford Centre for Buddhist Studies* 20: 51–82.

McCullough, Helen Craig, trans. 1988. *The Tale of the Heike.* Stanford, CA: Stanford University Press.

McHugh, James. 2012. *Sandalwood and Carrion: Smell in Indian Religion and Culture.* Oxford: Oxford University Press.

Mtu = *Mahāvastu.* 1882–97. 3 vols. Edited by Emile Sénart. Paris: Imprimerie Nationale.

Needham, Rodney. 1967. "Percussion and Transition." *Man* 2: 606–14.

Norman, H. C. 1908. "Gandhakuṭī—the Buddha's Private Abode." *Journal of the Proceedings of the Asiatic Society of Bengal* 4: 1–5.

O'Flaherty, Wendy [Doniger]. 1984. *Dreams, Illusion, and Other Realities.* Chicago: University of Chicago Press.

Rotman, Andy, trans. 2008. *Divine Stories, Divyāvadāna, Part 1.* Boston: Wisdom Publications.

———. 2015. *Thus Have I Seen: Visualizing Faith in Early Indian Buddhism.* Oxford: Oxford University Press.

———, trans. 2017. *Divine Stories, Divyāvadāna, Part 2.* Boston: Wisdom Publications.

———. 2021. *Hungry Ghosts.* Somerville, MA: Wisdom Publications.

Sasson, Vanessa R. 2009. "A Womb with a View: The Buddha's Final Fetal Experience."

In *Imagining the Fetus*, edited by Vanessa R. Sasson and Jane Marie Law, 55–72. Oxford: Oxford University Press.

Schopen, Gregory. 1997. *Bones, Stones, and Buddhist Monks: Collected Papers on the Archaeology, Epigraphy, and Texts of Monastic Buddhism in India.* Honolulu: University of Hawai'i Press.

———. 2015. "The Fragrance of the Buddha, the Scent of Monuments, and the Odor of Images in Early India." *Bulletin de l'École française d'Extrême-Orient* 101: 11–30.

Sdmp = *Saddharmapuṇḍarīka Sūtra*. 1912. Edited by Hendrik Kern and Bunyo Nanjo. Saint Petersburg: Imprimerie de l'Académie Impériale des Sciences.

Seneviratne, H. L. 1978. *Rituals of the Kandyan State.* Cambridge: Cambridge University Press.

Shulman, David. 1987. "The Scent of Memory in Hindu South India." *RES: Anthropology and Aesthetics* 13: 122–33.

Smith, Mark M. 2007. *Sensing the Past: Seeing, Hearing, Smelling, Tasting and Touching in History.* Berkeley: University of California Press.

Spk = *Sāratthappakāsinī: Buddhaghosa's Commentary on the Saṃyutta Nikāya.* 1929–37. 3 vols. Edited by F. L. Woodward. London: Pali Text Society.

Strong, John S. 1977. "*Gandhakuṭī*: The Perfumed Chamber of the Buddha." *History of Religions* 16: 390–406.

———. 1979. "The Transforming Gift: An Analysis of Devotional Acts of Offering in Buddhist Avadāna Literature." *History of Religions* 18: 221–37.

———. 2010. "The Triple Ladder at Saṃkāśya: Traditions about the Buddha's Descent from Trayastriṃśa Heaven." In *From Turfan to Ajanta: Festschrift for Dieter Schlingloff on the Occasion of His Eightieth Birthday,* edited by Eli Franco and Monika Zin, 967–78. Lumbini: LIRI, 2010.

———. 2012. "The Commingling of Gods and Humans, the Unveiling of the World, and the Descent from Trayastriṃśa Heaven: An Exegetical Exploration of Minor Rock Edict I." In *Reimagining Aśoka*, edited by Patrick Olivelle, 342–55. New Delhi: Oxford University Press.

———. 2021. "Beads and Bones: The Case of the Piprahwa Gems." In *Jewels, Jewelry, and Other Shiny Things in the Buddhist Imaginary,* edited by Vanessa R. Sasson, 185–207. Honolulu: University of Hawai'i Press.

———. 2022. "Relics and Images." In *Oxford Handbook of Buddhist Practice,* edited by Paula K. Arai and Kevin Trainor, 132–48. New York: Oxford University Press, 2022.

Sv = *Sumangalavilāsinī: Buddhaghosa's Commentary on the Dīgha Nikāya.* 1971. 2nd ed. 3 vols. Edited by William Stede. London: Pali Text Society.

Taishō shinshu daizōkyō. 大正新脩大藏經 [Taishō Tripiṭaka]. 1924–35. Edited by Takakusu Junjirō 高順次郎 et al. Tokyo: Taishō issaikyō kankōkai.

Van Campen, Crétien. 2014. *The Proust Effect: The Senses as Doorways to Lost Memories.* Translated by Julian Ross. Oxford: Oxford University Press.

Vaudeville, Charlotte. 1964. "La légende de Sundara et les funérailles du Buddha." *Bulletin de l'École française d'Extrême-Orient* 52: 73–91.

Vin = *Vinaya piṭakam.* 1969–84 [1879–83]. 5 vols. Edited by Hermann Oldenberg. London: Pali Text Society.

Vogel, J. Ph. 1919. "The Sign of the Spread Hand or 'Five-Finger Token' (*pañcāṅgulika*) in Pali Literature." *Verslagen en mededeelingen der Koninklijke Akademie van Wetenschappen* (Netherlands) 4: 218–36.

Waldschmidt, Ernst. 1949–50. *Das Mahāparinirvāṇasūtra.* Abhandlungen der deutschen Akademie der Wissenschaften zu Berlin, Philosophisch-historische Klasse. Berlin: Akademie Verlag.

Walshe, Maurice, trans. 1987. *Thus Have I Heard: The Long Discourses of the Buddha.* London: Wisdom Publications.

Yeshe De Project. 1986. *The Fortunate Aeon: How the Thousand Buddhas Become Enlightened.* 4 vols. Berkeley, CA: Dharma Publishing.

Yule, Henry, and A. C. Burnell. 1903. *Hobson-Jobson: A Glossary of Colloquial Anglo-Indian Words and Phrases.* Edited by William Crooke. London: John Murray.

Zacchetti, Stefano. 2005. *In Praise of the Light.* Tokyo: The International Research Institute for Advanced Buddhology.

Bad Taste: The Case of the Five Pungent Vegetables

JAMES ROBSON

IN CLASSICAL European studies of human perception, the five senses (vision, hearing, touch, smell, and taste) are often ranked. Vision always comes out on top, followed by hearing. Taste (sweet, salty, sour, bitter, and umami) gets situated at the bottom along with smell and touch. Vision and hearing are classified as the "higher" senses since they are related to the types of sensory input necessary for knowledge and communication. Touch, smell, and taste are senses connected with intimate bodily experiences and are therefore considered the least noble of the senses. Vision and hearing are often referred to as the "distant" senses, while smell, touch, and taste are referred to as "bodily" senses. Plato, in one of his enumerations of the senses, does not even include taste among them. For Plato the body is something that should be transcended in the apprehension of the truth, accomplished by knowledge acquired through vision and hearing. From one perspective, then, all taste is bad since it engages the body so potently and is mired in appetite and the dangers of indulgence and gluttony. Émile Durkheim went so far as to proclaim that "the act of eating is profane in itself."[1]

Eating is of course necessary for nourishment, but unlike animals, food for humans is more than just about nutrition, and taste is deeply imbricated in culture and values. As Martin Jay has noted, "sense, we have come increasingly to appreciate, refers not only to the natural corporeal endowments that provide access to the world, but also to the meanings we attribute to the results."[2] Taste can be either good or bad, pleasure or poison, delighting or disgusting, but taste, beyond the gustatory sense, is a term that came to be used for aesthetic judgments, especially since David Hume's "Of the Standard of Taste" (1757) and Edmund Burke's *On Taste: An Introductory Discourse* (1767), which each moved taste out of the realm of the body and into the mind.[3] Pierre Bourdieu, in his classic work *Distinction: A Social Critique of the Judgement of Taste* (1984), on the other hand, moved considerations of taste away from the body and into economy, society, and cultural production.[4]

Food and drink—the objects that stimulate taste—are often thought of and described by sociologists and anthropologists as that which brings people together for a period of convivial commensality to share in good taste. Yet food is also that which establishes boundaries, differences, and divisions with others. Foods considered unclean, disgusting, or bad tasting by some create distinctions between ethnicities, genders, and socio-economic classes. As is now well known from the work of Mary Douglas and Claudine Fabre-Vassas, alimentary prohibitions are central to the distinctions drawn between religious traditions, a well-known example being the Jewish and Muslim refusal to eat pork, as opposed to Christians who consume it.[5] Similar distinctions are drawn between Hindus, who forbid the eating of beef, and Muslims, who include it in their diet. Buddhists are also distinguished by what foods they eat and avoid, how and when they should eat, how much food should be consumed, and how food should be prepared. As we proceed it will become increasingly clear how difficult it is to treat the social and gustatory senses of taste in isolation, but let us begin with the latter sense of taste.

Taste is perhaps the most inscrutable of all the senses since it is a personal and hidden sense that registers internally. Taste is deeply ambiguous—*De gustibus non est disputandum*, or "There is no accounting for taste." The taste of foods is usually categorized as an opposition between what is good (usually sweet things) and what is bad (usually bitter things), but what specific foods are situated in those categories varies greatly across cultures and among individuals. Good-tasting food is one of life's pleasures, but at the other end of the spectrum is the disgust associated with bad-tasting food, which is the primary topic of this essay.

The word "disgust" in English means "bad taste." It came into English from French and Latin (*dis* being a negative prefix and *gustus* meaning taste). Disgust originated as a response to distasteful food. As William Ian Miller has noted, the "modern psychological interest in disgust starts with [Charles] Darwin, who centers it in the rejection of food and the sense of taste" in his *The Expression of the Emotions in Man and Animals*, published in 1872.[6] There was little subsequent theorization of disgust until the publications of the Hungarians Aurel Kolnai and Andras Angyal. Kolnai, whose work "Disgust" ("Der Ekel") was written in German and published in 1927 by Edmund Husserl, situated disgust in the context of things that decay and putrefy, like rotting food and a decaying corpse.[7] Angyal's "Disgust and Related Aversions," published in 1941, stimulated interest in disgust, which he described as "a specific reaction toward the waste products of the human and animal body," but he also noted that it is "a general experience that the strongest disgust reactions can be elicited during eating."[8] Angyal related the strength of disgust to the degree of intimacy of contact, with the mouth as the most sensitive orifice and taste as a trigger for the emotion of disgust. Angyal's work was extended significantly by Paul Rozin, the father of disgust studies, who drew the most explicit connections between food and disgust.[9] The linkage between food and disgust, which we will see is central to the Buddha's life story, is particularly strong due to the vulnerabilities associated with what enters our mouth and activates our sense of taste.

Much has been written on food and taste by scholars of Christianity and by anthropologists of South Asia interested in food and food prohibitions.[10] We may no longer be in the lamentable situation once described by Caroline Bynum whereby "modern scholars have ignored a religious symbol that had tremendous force in the lives of medieval Christians. They have ignored the religious significance of food."[11] But despite a surfeit of scholarship on the perennial topic of Buddhism and vegetarianism, there remains a paucity of studies on food and taste in the Buddhist tradition.[12] Most scholarship on Buddhism has been tasteless, but Buddhist studies is slowly coming to its senses and acknowledging that food and taste were more significant topics in Buddhism than scholars have recognized. Nonetheless, we still lack a robust alimentary history of Buddhism and know next to nothing of monastic cuisine despite the fact that the story of the development of Buddhism—from the Buddha's life story to Buddhist philosophy—is one in which food and taste mattered a great deal.

• • •

The first time the future Buddha, Prince Siddhārtha, experienced bad-tasting food was when he departed from his luxurious life in the palace and learned that as a mendicant he should beg for his food. The *Nidānakathā* describes how he took his bowl and "collected a mixed meal, and when he knew that it was sufficient for his sustenance, he left the city by the gate through which he had entered it; and seating himself with his face towards the East, in the shadow of the mountain Pandava, began to eat his food. Then his intestines began to turn and were about to come out of his mouth. Being disgusted with that loathsome food the like of which he had never set his eyes on before, he then began to admonish himself." Disgust has a particular ability to trigger philosophical reflection, and the young prince reflected on his feeling of abjection and that he had grown up in a house where food was plentiful, being "accustomed to eating food prepared from perfumed *sāli* rice kept in storage for three years, and . . . various delicacies," but that he had long wondered when he would leave that life to "collect scraps of food and eat them like a mendicant dressed in robes made of rags."[13] In the face of the revulsion experienced from eating his first begged meal he chastised himself, overcame his disgust, and ate his food. This remarkable scene sets up a vivid opposition between the tasteful delicacies of the palace and the disgust-inducing food that he collected in his begging bowl outside the palace.

The Buddha's life story is marked by experiences with food at every critical juncture. The *Nidānakathā* narrative works so dramatically precisely due to what preceded it. The early parts of his biography are filled with references to exquisite-tasting food and drink that are part of the king's efforts to have the prince only enjoy pleasure. Food and taste are central motifs in biographies of the Buddha, where one can palpably sense their importance. The scene of the Great Departure in the *Lalitavistara* famously depicts Prince Siddhārtha being reminded of all the sensuous delights that he will be giving up when he leaves. Those passages are structured by appeals to the five senses, including vision (beautiful women in the harem), hearing (music), smell (incense and flower garlands), touch (unguents and fine cloth), and taste (delicious foods and sweet drinks). "For uncountable and endless eons have I, Chandaka, enjoyed these sensuous objects of beauty, sound, odour, flavour, and taction, of all the various kinds known to man; but I have not been gratified thereby."[14] The *Mahāvastu* also says: "I was delicately, most delicately brought up, monks. And while I was being thus delicately brought up, my Śakyan father provided me with a varied diet, namely rice from which the black grain had been sifted and curry of various flavours, that I might divert, enjoy, and amuse myself."[15] Good food and bad food are described in equally sensory detail, and an opposition is set up between exquisite and wretched food.

After experiencing disgust upon consuming his first bowl of begged food, Siddhārtha embarked on an abstemious period of decreasing food and drink consumption. Disgust, in other words, led to abstinence, and during this period we learn that Siddhārtha subsisted on a single jujube per day or a single grain of rice and a drop of water. The rejection of food led him to waste away, as depicted in the famous Gāndhāran statues of the emaciated prince.[16] But extreme forms of abstention are not tenable, and in Siddhārtha's life story it leads to his physical deterioration. Good food then reappears in the story when he vows to regain his strength and Sujātā provides him with a rice-milk pudding on the day of his enlightenment (no wonder there are many Indian restaurants named Sujātā). It is this meal that sustains Siddhārtha through the enlightenment process that immediately follows.

Bad food, of course, returns in narratives about the end of the Buddha's life and his infamous last supper. The well-known account of the "fine meal" that the Buddha's lay follower Cunda wanted to serve him includes reference to the much-debated meal of "pig's delight" that is recounted in the *Mahāparinibbāna Sutta*.[17] After eating some of the food, the Buddha knew others would not be able to digest it, and so he ordered the rest of the dish to be buried in a hole. He thus both honored the layman by accepting the food and protected his monks by having the remainder discarded. Shortly thereafter he became violently ill and died.[18]

Taste is not only significant in Buddhist narrative literature but is also discussed in doctrinal texts. Buddhist thinkers were deeply interested in the functioning of the senses and perception. The twelve sources (*āyatana*)—six sense organs and the six objects of those senses—and the eighteen constituents (*dhātu*)—six sense organs, the six objects of those senses, and the six consciousnesses that arise from them—explain the various relationships between physical and mental events connected with the objects of the senses. There is a rich and complicated body of philosophical reflection on the senses in Buddhism that—as in Western philosophy—separates vision and hearing as "distant" senses that do not require contact with their object, while taste, smell, and touch are more "proximate" senses that are particularly susceptible to the arising of greed and desire.[19] The connection between food and desire is an important issue raised in the *Āhāra Patikūlasaññā*: "In material food there is the danger of desire (for taste); in contact there is the danger of approach (or attraction to the object)."[20] The *Milindapañha* (*Questions of King Milinda*) also says that "he who has passion and he who is free from passion have the same wish, that his food, whether hard or soft, should be good; neither wishes for what is bad . . . he that is not free from passions experiences both the taste of that food, and also passion due to that taste; while he who is free from passion experiences the taste of that food, but no passion due to that taste."[21] The taste of good food presents an ever-present danger for the insufficiently cultivated.

Buddhist monastics have not been immune from the passions of taste. There are many humorous stories and stereotypes of Buddhist monks as greedy gluttons who relished good-tasting food. Buddhists were criticized and mocked, especially by Jains, for being overly interested in delicious foods.[22] Some, such as the paradigmatic figure Upananda, indulged in quantities of rich foods, like ghee, to the point of death.[23] The Buddha, however, is described as having special powers of taste and digestion that allow him to partake of rich foods, such as brown sugar, that if consumed to excess could be fatal to others.[24] Interestingly, one of the thirty-two marks of the Buddha is a perfect sense of taste, and he evidently also has saliva that improves the taste of bad food.[25]

Buddhist clerics were supposed to eat whatever was put into their begging bowls, but they seemed to have also sought out finer tastes. In South Asia, monastics were not allowed to request specific foods when venturing out for alms (unless they were sick), but they were allowed to partake of delicacies without incurring an offense if they were offered some by their family or an acquaintance.[26] Taste mattered to East Asian monastics as well. Although begging for food was not adopted by Chinese Buddhists, the laity made offerings to monastics by sponsoring maigre feasts (*zhai* 齋). First-person accounts of the pursuit of gustatory pleasures and the avoidance of bad-tasting food in Buddhist literature are hard to come by, but we are provided with a valuable glimpse in the layman Shen Yue's 沈約 (441–513) critique of Chinese monastics who no longer adhere to the single midday meal and "indulge themselves with sweet and rich delicacies and whose larders are full to overflowing." He continues his critique by noting how monastics who are invited to a maigre feast rarely accept the invitation unless there is "absolutely no way out of it. And then with well-oiled mouths they only nibble at the simple vegetable fare. Stretching their necks and furrowing their brows, they are definitely unable to enjoy their food."[27]

Evidence from later sources, like the twelfth-century "Pure Rules for Chan Monasteries" (*Chanyuan qinggui* 禪苑清規), further supports the view that monastics were attentive to the quality of the food they consumed. This set of rules indicates that monastic cooks (*dianzuo* 典座) were charged with preparing tasty foods. "During food preparation the cook must personally make sure the food is natural, carefully prepared, and clean. In buying the ingredients for a meal or choosing the menu, he must consult the prior in advance. Sauces, vinegar, and pickled vegetables are the responsibility of the cook, who must be careful not to miss the appropriate seasons for making them."[28] The section on feasts further states that food should be prepared with three "virtues" (it should be soft, clean, and correctly prepared) and six "tastes" (bitter, sour, sweet, spicy, salty, and mild) (*sande liuwei* 三德六味).[29]

Bad-tasting food, on the other hand, is not only to be avoided but is also depicted as evidence that the period of the decline of the Dharma (*mofa* 末法) has arrived. During that time, when the world deteriorates, people will be "forced to live on bland, tasteless food; for they will be deprived of ghee, honey, oil, salt, and sugarcane."[30] Sweetness is often used as a mellifluous metaphor for the Buddha's teaching, as in the term "sweet dew" (*ganlu* 甘露) referring to the Dharma in the *Lotus Sūtra*.[31] The good taste of sweetness indicates the flourishing of the Dharma, while bad-tasting foods indicate the decline of the Dharma.

It is little surprise, therefore, to find disgusting and abject foods incorporated into Buddhist accounts that describe the worst forms of suffering and punishment. A well-known example includes the types of food that the *preta* (hungry ghosts) are forced to eat. In the *Petavatthu*, when food (rice balls or cakes) is offered to a *preta* it is transformed into disagreeable substances such as blood, pus, worms, and excrement when they attempt to consume it.[32] The *Avadānaśataka* also includes a chapter entitled *Varcaghaṭaḥ* ("A Pot of Shit") that describes a foul preta who eats shit as her punishment after having served excrement to a pratyekabuddha who came begging for alms.[33]

Buddhaghosa's *Visuddhimagga* is filled with graphic sections on the loathsomeness of food that reinforces the negative view of eating as a corporeal practice. In those accounts it is less about food tasting bad or a sense of disgust associated with the food itself and more about the disgust surrounding the processes of gathering food and the ensuing bodily functions of consumption, digestion, and defecation.[34] Buddhaghosa, however, also comments on the disgust that arises upon finding a hair (or anything in the shape of a hair) in one's rice gruel—what disgust theorists refer to as "contamination sensitivity."[35] The contamination of food by a foreign object, especially that of bodily effluvia, seems to be a near-universal cause for disgust, since the consumption of food is a deeply affective act that involves intimate contact with the external environment and that transgresses the boundaries between the outside and inside of our bodies.[36] Taste requires the object of perception to be fully internalized, presenting the ever-present danger of contamination.

• • •

Taste figured importantly within the Buddhist discourse on food, but the tradition also developed intricate regulations about what types of food should not be consumed, which leads the discussion into complex doctrinal and social concerns that shifted over time and across cultures. Vegetarianism, abstaining from meat and fish, has been a topic of perennial interest in discussions of Buddhist food avoidance. This is understandable, since ethical issues related to not killing come into play in deciding what is good and bad food—what is allowed and what is prohibited. The act of eating by its very nature destroys its object (unlike the relationship between the other senses and their objects). The appeasement of appetite entails the destruction of something that is consumed, raising concerns about killing animals.

Considerations of Buddhist vegetarianism are complicated by the fact that early Buddhist monastic regulations did not categorically reject meat eating, but rather countenanced it (with qualifications) and even at times rejected vegetarianism (most notably in Devadatta's failed attempt to institute a stringent vegetarian diet). The key issues that guided what was considered good meat, and therefore acceptable, and what was considered bad meat, and therefore rejected, were ethics and compassion.[37] Indian Vinayas, which elucidate what food and drink are to be avoided and how to comport oneself while eating, say that a Buddhist monastic may consume meat without committing an infraction if it has what is known as the "threefold purity": that the recipient has not seen or suspected that the animal was slaughtered specifically for their benefit.[38] If otherwise, the meat is said to be impure and must not be consumed. Certain animal meats were also prohibited because they were used in sacrificial rituals or because they were eaten either by high-class (those in the king's army) or low-class people. Raw meat was wisely prohibited because of the hazards involved, as was the flesh of animals such as dogs, snakes, lions, tigers, leopards, bears, and hyenas—that is, carnivores who eat flesh and are therefore unclean—as well as humans. In any case, the flexible attitude toward meat eating in the early Indian monastic codes presented interpretive problems for the development of vegetarianism among Buddhists in East Asia.

In East Asia, vegetarianism—which forbids the consumption of meat, fish, and eggs—came to be a widely accepted, and expected, part of the monastic vocation. Even if the avoidance of meat was not mandated in the early Vinayas or was not a normal part of South Asian monastic practice, in East Asia the critiques of meat eating expressed in later Mahāyāna texts, coupled with lay pressures on monastics and legal proscriptions enforced by the state, led to the articulation of a stricter form of vegetarian diet among Buddhists.[39]

Much scholarly attention has already been directed to the shift in attitude toward meat, but East Asian Buddhist texts, in addition to prohibiting meat and alcohol, also prohibit the consumption of a category of plants known as the five pungent (bitter) [vegetables] (*wuxin* 五辛 or *wuhun*

五葷). These are sometimes referred to as the "small meats" (*xiaohun* 小葷), suggesting that the dietary choices were not only related to ethical issues. The *wuxin* include plants in the allium family, like garlic (*dasuan* 大蒜), three kinds of onion (*gecong* 革葱, *cicong* 慈葱, *lancong* 蘭葱), and asafetida (*xingqu* 興蕖 [*hiṅgu*]). Alternative lists include onions (*cong* 葱), leeks (*jiu* 韭), garlic (*suan* 蒜), and scallions (*xie* 薤).[40] All are considered impure foods within Chinese Buddhism, but were, and still are, used extensively in Chinese cooking generally.

The avoidance of the *wuxin* did not develop in China with the arrival of Buddhism. Even pre-Buddhist texts show an avoidance of *wuxin*—for example, Ge Hong's 葛洪 (283–343) *Baopuzi* 抱朴子 (*The Master Who Embraces Simplicity*) stipulates that "those who enter into mountains should fast for one hundred days and not eat the five pungent vegetables (*wuxin*) or live fish."[41] That said, the avoidance of the five pungent vegetables was not entirely an East Asian addition to Buddhist dietary regulations, since prohibitions related to some of the alliums on the *wuxin* lists are found in Indic materials. The Ayurvedic tradition, for example, traces the origin of garlic (*laśuna)* to the drops that fell to the earth when Viṣṇu cut off the head of the king of demons, such that "Brahmins will not eat it, because it is something which flowed from contact with a body."[42] Ayurvedic sources describe garlic as smelly, pungent, hard to digest, and a well-known aphrodisiac, even if it was also used in some medicinal recipes.[43] Additionally, Jains avoided all bulbous roots, including garlic, as they were considered animate living things.[44]

Buddhist monastic regulations, which came to guide East Asian Buddhist conceptions of the proper diet, also contain proscriptions about plants in the allium family. The Mūlasarvāstivāda Vinaya stands out for being the most expansive in prohibiting the consumption of garlic, onions, and leeks due to their strong smell. Other Vinayas focus their attention solely on prohibitions against consuming garlic. The *Cullavagga*, for instance, explicitly states that "garlic should not be eaten" except in the case of illness, such as when Śāriputra had excessive gas.[45] The proscription of garlic is most explicit in discussions of nuns, who are depicted as having a particular fondness for garlic.[46] The offenses for consuming garlic are rather minor, but it is not entirely clear why the punishment for nuns who eat garlic is more severe than that for monks. In either case, the primary reason for avoiding garlic is due to its strong smell, since the scent of garlic on one's breath was socially in bad taste and problematic for other monastics and when encountering lay donors. Some texts describe how those who consumed garlic were required to undergo a seven-day period of isolation and a purificatory bath.

The foundation for East Asian dietary regulations were the Indian Vinayas that were translated into Chinese, but Chinese Buddhists were deeply influenced by the rejection of meat eating in Mahāyāna texts that overturned the earlier flexibility and included explicit proscriptions against eating the *wuxin*.[47] Those rules became canonized in Chinese translations of Mahāyāna texts—most dating to the fifth century—such as the Mahāyāna *Mahāparinirvāṇasūtra* (*Daban niepan jing* 大般涅槃經; T. 376 and T. 374), the *Laṅkāvatārasūtra* (*Lengjia abaduoluobao jing* 楞伽阿跋多羅寶經; T. 670), and apocryphal texts, like the *Scripture of Brahmā's Net* (*Fanwang jing* 梵網經; T. 1484). In general, these Mahāyāna sources developed a new vegetarian framework that excluded meat and the *wuxin* due to their smell and the sense that they were impure.

Regulations concerning the *wuxin* were not just found in canonical texts but were also spread and supported through texts written by Chinese monastics. For example, Zhiyi's 智顗 *Establishing Regulations* ("Lizhifa" 立制法, sixth century CE) says: "Item Seven: Any full monk who has received the Hīnayāna precepts is expressly forbidden to take fish, flesh, leeks and pungent herbs, and liquor on the sly, regardless of whether he is travelling nearby, far away, in residence within the monastery, or outside the monastery. Persons who [violate this prohibition] or who eat at the unappointed times [i.e., after noon], will not be permitted to remain in the community if they are discovered. The only exception to the rule shall be persons who are acutely ill who have been prescribed [forbidden substances] by a physician, or persons who have left the temple to seek cure elsewhere. They are not to be punished."[48]

The eighth-century Chinese translation of the *Śūraṃgamasūtra* (*Shou lengyan jing* 首楞嚴經) contains one of the most explicit statements about the deleterious effects of the *wuxin*.

> Ānanda, these twelve species in the world owe their existence to four ways of feeding: by eating, touching, thinking about, and being conscious of food. Therefore, the Buddha says that all living beings depend on feeding for their stay (in saṃsāra). Ānanda, all beings live if they eat wholesome food and die if they take poison. In their search for samādhi, they should abstain from eating five kinds of pungent roots (i.e., garlic, the three kinds of onions, and leeks)—if eaten cooked, they are an aphrodisiac, and if raw, they cause irritability. Although those who eat them may read the twelve divisions of the Mahāyāna canon, they drive away seers in the ten directions who abhor the bad odor, and they attract hungry ghosts who lick their lips. They are always surrounded by ghosts, and their good fortune will fade away day by day to their own detriment. When these eaters of pungent roots practice samādhi, none of the bodhisattvas, seers, and good spirits come to protect them, while the mighty king of demons takes advantage of the occasion to appear as a buddha as if to teach them the Dharma, defaming and breaking the precepts and praising carnality, anger, and stupidity; at their death, they will join his retinue, and at the end of their time in his realm, they will fall into the unintermittent hell. Ānanda, practitioners of samādhi should never eat these five pungent roots.[49]

This passage clearly connects the five pungent vegetables to claims that they were aphrodisiacs, that their smell would drive away good spirits and impel evil spirits, and that their consumption disturbs meditation practice, which are all claims that have persisted to the present day.

Daoshi 道世 (?–683), in his *Fayuan zhulin* 法苑珠林 (T. 2122), comments extensively on the ban against the consumption of the *wuxin*—along with meat and alcohol—due to its bad smell. In addition to citing other sources, he quotes from the *Wuxin baoying jing* 五辛報應經 (*Sūtra on the Retribution [from Eating] the Five Pungent Vegetables*), which discusses the offense one commits for reciting a sūtra after eating any of the *wuxin*, but that text is no longer extant and is not listed by that title in any Buddhist catalogues. As others have noted, however, there is a similarly titled text, namely the *Wuxin jing* 五辛經 (*Sūtra on the Five Pungent Vegetables*), that is listed as "spurious" (*wei* 僞) in catalogues dating back to Fajing's 法經 (d.u) *Zhongjing mulu* 衆經目錄 (T. 2148), completed in 594.[50] That text has been considered lost, but Fang Guangchang 方廣錩 has identified a fragment from it among the Dunhuang manuscripts in the National Library of China collection (identified as manuscript BD 06951), and there is also a text in the Pelliot collection (P.3777) titled *Wuxin wenshu* 五辛文書 (*Documents on the Five Pungent Vegetables*), which is a Tang Chan interpretation of the five pungent vegetables.[51] These texts, with *wuxin* in their titles, suggest that these pungent vegetables were a topic of more than passing interest.

The Beijing fragment, which is untitled, includes a lengthy story about a practitioner who eats some smelly (*chou* 臭) food and is castigated by spirits who take their leave from him. The god Viśvakarman (Pishou tianshen 毗首天神), speaking to him from the sky, admonishes him: "You fool! You should not have eaten the food given by the lay donor. Why is that? You ate impure smelly food, which forces us spirits to depart and flee to a different location." When he finishes speaking, he vanishes. The practitioner goes to rinse his mouth in a river and thinks to himself: "The five pungent vegetables are scourges that can't be gotten rid of." Later, after returning to his forest retreat, he suffers, dies, is reborn for a thousand *kalpas* in the hell of excrement and urine, is reborn as a dog for another thousand *kalpas*, is reborn as a destitute human who is impure and riven with sores, and finally returns as a human who meets a *kalyānamitra* who helps him attain the aspiration for perfect awakening. The Buddha then says that he has experienced such immeasurable suffering in his own body and tells Śāriputra that he should know that "the *wuxin* are scourges that harm one's good roots, you should definitely not eat them." The Buddha closes by warning that if any of those in his assembly eat the smelly and polluted *wuxin*, they will not obtain . . ."[52] Here the fragmentary text cuts off, but presumably it would have listed all the good things that come from holding firmly to the precepts against eating the *wuxin*.

There is an account of the efficacious powers that the avoidance of those bad foods can have in the *Fayuan zhulin* about a certain Linghu Yuangui 令狐元軌 (fl. seventh century). Linghu copied a set of sūtras after maintaining purity by not consuming bad foods like meat, the pungent vegetables, or alcohol. When a fire broke out where a collection of sūtras were stored, the sūtras Linghu copied miraculously survived, while those copied by another monk, who did not keep pure and ate prohibited foods, were incinerated.[53]

The rejection of meat, alcohol, and the five pungent vegetables as a Buddhist practice spread throughout East Asia. For example, in Japan, the "Regulations for Monks and Nuns" (*Sōniryō* 僧尼令) in the *Yōrō Era Law Codes* (*Yōrō ritsuryō* 養老律令) of 757 includes an article banning the consumption of meat, alcohol, and the *wuxin* (which were considered aphrodisiacs and banned in an effort to curb the illicit sexual activities of the clergy).[54] All of that would later change, and most Japanese clerics no longer refrain from eating meat or fish or drinking liquor.[55] In the seventeenth century, the cleric Chikū 智空 (1634–1718), for instance, protested that "when one visits temples one sees that a small amount of seaweed (*wakame*) is put into a bowl. Saying that they will 'season it with liquor (*sake*),' they pour in liquor and drink heavily from their soup bowls. At first it was done in the above fashion, but then clerics said, 'The seaweed is no good, it is stale' and drank just the liquor. They thus violate the prohibition against entering the temple with liquor, meat, or the five pungent foods."[56]

Some Buddhists may have been unable to resist the seductions of meat, but others were able to satisfy their taste for meat by eating "fake meats" (*fanghun* 仿葷), a product that may go back to at least the tenth century and is still served in monasteries and vegetarian restaurants today.[57] What is particularly noteworthy is that despite East Asian Buddhist prohibitions against meat eating, this type of food, made primarily from wheat gluten (*mianjin* 麵筋, an interesting term meaning something like "wheat tendon") or tofu (*doufu* 豆腐, also an interesting term that during the Song dynasty was sometimes referred to as "small mutton" *xiao zaiyang* 小宰羊), imitates meat and complicates the issue of taste. The consumption of fake meat, about which more research is necessary, suggests that there was an enduring desire for the taste of meat. The place of fake meats in the Buddhist diet seems to be at odds with other statements in Buddhist texts that emphasize that one should not even desire the taste of meat, even if the consumed food was not a product of actual killing. A passage in the *Fo kaijie fanzhi aba jing* 佛開解梵志阿颰經, for example, says: "A monk must not drink alcohol, eat meat, or desire to taste their flavors."[58]

I may be guilty of not having kept to my charge of focusing on "bad taste," since I have occasionally encroached on the topic of "good taste." But taste is relative, subjective, and subject to change. Even more significantly, a later Japanese Zen Buddhist monk questioned the division of taste into that which is good and that which is bad. Dōgen 道元 (1200–1253), in his *Tenzo kyōkun* 典座教訓 (*Instructions for the Cook*), for example, remarks that good and bad taste are a result of dualistic thinking: "What is regarded as the preparation of superb delicacies is not necessarily superior, nor is the preparation of a soup of the crudest greens necessarily inferior. When you select and serve up crude greens, if you do so with a true mind, a sincere mind, and a pure mind, then they will be comparable to superb delicacies. Why is that so? Because when one enters into the pure and vast oceanic assembly of the Buddhadharma, superb delicacies are never seen and the flavor of crude greens does not exist: there is only the one taste of the great sea, and that is all. Moreover, when it comes to the matters of nurturing the sprouts of the way and nourishing the sacred embryo, superb delicacies and crude greens are as one; there is no duality." Thus, "There is an old saying that a monk's mouth is like a stove."[59] A stove consumes all kinds of wood equally, regardless of its quality. A monk, similarly, should eat whatever is served without discriminating taste as good or bad.

• • •

Buddhists developed a monastic cuisine that accepted some foods and rejected others. Yet in some Buddhist sources, normal human food disappears entirely, suggesting its inferiority to miraculous sacred food. In texts that describe sacred food, it is depicted as being ingested by smell rather than through the mouth. Vasubandhu's *Abhidharmakośa*, for example, describes *gandharvas* eating only smells, not solid food. Low-ranking *gandharvas* eat unpleasant odors and higher-ranking ones eat pleasant odors.[60] The *Abhidharmakośa* also draws a distinction between "food by the mouthful" that is "subtle" and "coarse."[61] Subtle food is that which does not result in the production of waste products. Miraculous sacred food is also the topic of the famous chapter of the *Vimalakīrti Sūtra* titled "Fragrance Accumulated" (*Xiangji* 香積),[62] which discusses a special ambrosia-like food that naturally multiplies, never to be exhausted. In the universe Sarvagandhasugandhā (literally "All Smells Are Good Smells"), the *Vimalakīrti Sūtra* says, the "belvederes (*kūṭāgāra*), avenues (*caṅkrama*), parks (*upavana*), palaces (*prāsāda*) and the clothes (*vastra*) are all made of various perfumes (*nānāvidhagandhamaya*), and the perfume of the food eaten by this blessed Lord Buddha and these Bodhisattvas fills (*prasarati*) innumerable universes."[63] It is from that universe, where the Buddha teaches with fragrances rather than words, that an imaginary bodhisattva brings a bowl full of fragrant rice to Vimalakīrti's house in this mundane world (sahā). It can only be digested by those of elevated spiritual attainment lacking "ignoble sentiments," who then give off a perfumed smell through their pores.[64] Therefore, the special food is good for the accomplished but bad for deluded people, who are unable to digest it. The denigration of material food in favor of sacred nourishment—what might be called an anti-cuisine—is a theme that resonates with later Chinese Buddhist and Daoist stories of, for example, abstaining from normal foods (the rejection of sacrificial foods and not consuming grains in particular) and subsisting on *qi* 氣 or "pneuma." Proper self-cultivation and the recitation of texts can result in the provisioning of nourishment by miraculous non-material foodstuffs from celestial realms, the so-called heavenly kitchens (*tianchu* 天廚), resulting in detachment from hunger and the attainment of longevity.[65]

Food is essential to the nutritional sustenance of life, but within the Buddhist tradition there are regulations about what and how much is to be ingested. There is a continuum that runs from base material food to food that transcends material form. One of the most exquisite forms of dining in Japan is known as *kaiseki* 懐石, which originated as a meal served during a tea ceremony (*chanoyu* 茶の湯). The term *kaiseki* (懐石) literally means "breast stone," and one explanation of the origin for this term, popularized by the legendary tea master Sen no Rikyū 千利休 (1522–91), is directly related to Buddhism.[66] Zen monks would ward off hunger by putting a warm stone into the front fold of their robe. Thus, the term that came to refer to the highest form of cuisine began as a warm stone put against the stomach to assuage hunger in the absence of food.

Reflection on the sense of taste in Buddhism also invites us to appreciate how difficult it can be to tease apart the senses, since taste is closely related to smell, vision, and touch. Some have suggested that the senses should not be treated in isolation and that it is better to think of associations between the senses.[67] Food operates in multiple modalities. It can be a feast for the eyes, and smell is crucial to taste. The Buddhist tradition has a rich and complicated discourse on taste and food that is larded with symbolic and social values, but what foods were accepted or rejected changed over time, based on reasons far beyond what the tongue registers through its sense of taste. As is clear from all the sources we have considered, the rejection of meat and the five pungent vegetables was primarily due to distinctions between purity and impurity, social class, smell, the laity's perception of the saṅgha, ethics, and the effect that meat and the five pungent vegetables have on the practitioner. If we are to trust the voluminous body of stories about Buddhist monastics, they seemed to have thought a lot about food—the pure and delicious, and the impure and disgusting—and they also thought a lot about not thinking about food.

Notes

1. Durkheim 1995, 311.
2. Jay 2011, 307.
3. The philosophical implications of the gustatory sense of taste have been redressed in Korsmeyer 1999.
4. Bourdieu 1984. See also Ferry 1993.
5. Douglas 1966; and Fabre-Vassas 1997.
6. Miller 1997, 1; and Darwin 1965.
7. Kolnai 2004.
8. Angyal 1941, 395–97.
9. Rozin and Fallon 1987. See also Korsmeyer 2011; Menninghaus 2003; and Kelly 2011.
10. See, among others, Bynum 1987; Fulton 2006; Olivelle 2011; Khare 1992; Tambiah 1969; Leach 1989; and Smith 1990.
11. Bynum 1985, 245.
12. On Buddhist vegetarianism, see, among others, Ruegg 1980; Schmithausen 2005; Mather 1981; Kieschnick 2005; Heirman and De Rauw 2006; Greene 2016; and Barstow 2019.
13. Jayawickrama 1990, 88.

14. *Lalitavistara*, as translated in Mitra 1881, 285.
15. *Mahāvastu*, as translated in Jones 1952, 112.
16. One might recall here a similar pattern in the life story of Jesus, who fasted for forty days in the desert and resisted the devil's urging him to turn a stone into bread (Luke 4:1–4). On the role of abstinence in Christianity, see Camporesi 1994, 64–91.
17. *Mahāparinibbāna Sutta*, as translated in Walshe 1987, 257.
18. *Mahāparinibbāna Sutta*, as translated in Walshe 1987, 256–57.
19. For a discussion of the order of the senses in South Asian religions, with a focus on smell, see McHugh 2007.
20. Cited in Van Daele 2016, 215.
21. *Milindapañha*, as translated in Warren 1900, 421.
22. Granoff 1998; and Schopen 2007.
23. Schopen 2007, 210.
24. Granoff 1998, 70–71.
25. *Lakkhaṇa Sutta*, as translated in Walshe 1987, 442.
26. Clarke 2014, 58–62.
27. Mather 1981, 19.
28. *Chanyuan qinggui*, as translated in Yifa 2002, 154.
29. Yifa 2002, 261n168.
30. See, for example, *Zhong ahan jing* 中阿含經 *Madhyamāgama*) Taishō 26.15.523a; and *Yujia shidi lun* 瑜伽師地論 (*Yogacārabhūmiśāstra*) Taishō 1579.30.286a. Cited in Kieschnick 2003, 250. On the appeal of sweetness, see Mintz 1985.
31. On the term "sweet dew" in the *Lotus Sūtra*, see Hurvitz 1976, 106.
32. *Paramatthadīpanī nāma Petavatthu-aṭṭhakathā*, as translated in U Ba Kyaw 1980, 46–48.
33. Rotman 2021, 89–92.
34. *Visuddhimagga*, translated in Bikkhu Ñāṇamoli 1975, 396.
35. Kelly 2011, 19.
36. See Angyal 1941, 2.
37. Schmithausen 2005, 183–201.
38. Ruegg 1980, 234–35.
39. Kieschnick 2005; and Heirman and De Rauw 2006.
40. The best overview of the prohibition of the *wuxin* is found in Suwa Gijun 1988.
41. Cited in Suwa Gijun 1988, 195.
42. Wujastyk 1998, 155.
43. Wujastyk 1998, 156 and 229.
44. Schmithausen 2005, 44.
45. Horner 1952, 196.
46. Horner 1942, 243–46.
47. For a convenient summary, see Suwa Gijun 1988, 45–57.
48. Stevenson 2004, 282. For further references see Heirman and De Rauw 2006.
49. Taishō 945.19.120b and Taishō 945.19.141c. Translated in Lu K'uan Yu 1966, 230, with some minor changes for clarity.
50. See the discussion in Heirman and De Rauw 2006.

51. Fang Guangchang 2010, 219–221.
52. Fang Guangchang 2010, 219–221.
53. Taishō 2122.53.421a–b. This story is discussed in Lowe 2017, 38–39.
54. Jaffe 2005, 256.
55. See Jaffe 2011, 1–8.
56. Jaffe 2005, 261.
57. Kieschnick 2005, 205.
58. Taishō 20.1.261b. Translated in Greene 2016, 11.
59. Translated in Foulk 2001.
60. *Abhidharmakośabhāṣyam*, translated in Pruden 1988, 393
61. *Abhidharmakośabhāṣyam*, translated in Pruden 1988, 440ff.
62. *Vimalakirtisūtra*, translated in Watson 1997, 112–20. See also Lamotte 1976.
63. Lamotte 1976, 205.
64. Compare Corbin 1996, 39–40; Harvey 2006; and Albert 1996.
65. See Mollier 2008, 23–54; and Kleeman 2005.
66. If *kaiseki* is written as 会席, the term refers to a "formal occasion" or "get together" and a more lavish-style and aesthetically appealing meal that gained popularity during the Heian period (794–1185).
67. Juravsky 2014, 168–69.

Bibliography

Albert, Jean-Pierre. 1996. *Odeurs de sainteté: La mythologie chrétienne des aromates*. Paris: École des Hautes Études en Sciences Sociales.

Angyal, Andras. 1941. "Disgust and Related Aversions." *Journal of Abnormal and Social Psychology* 36: 393–412.

Barstow, Geoffrey, ed. 2019. *The Faults of Meat: Tibetan Buddhist Writing on Vegetarianism*. Somerville, MA: Wisdom Publications.

Bhikkhu Ñāṇamoli, trans. 1975. *The Path of Purification: Visuddhimagga by Bhadantācariya Buddhaghosa*. Kandy: Buddhist Publication Society.

Bourdieu, Pierre. 1984. *Distinction: A Social Critique of the Judgement of Taste*. Cambridge, MA: Harvard University Press.

Bynum, Caroline Walker. 1985. "Fast, Feast, and Flesh: The Religious Significance of Food to Medieval Women." *Representations* 11: 1–25.

———. 1987. *Holy Feast and Holy Fast: The Religious Significance of Food to Medieval Women*. Berkeley: University of California Press.

Campany, Robert Ford. 2005. "The Meanings of Cuisines of Transcendence in Late Classical and Early Medieval China." *T'oung Pao* 91: 1–57.

Camporesi, Piero. 1994. *The Anatomy of the Senses: Natural Symbols in Medieval and Early Modern Italy*. Cambridge: Polity Press.

Clarke, Shayne. 2014. *Family Matters in Indian Buddhist Monasticisms*. Honolulu: University of Hawai'i Press.

Corbin, Alain. 1996. *The Foul and the Fragrant: Odour and the Social Imagination*. London: Macmillan.

Darwin, Charles R. 1965 [1872]. *The Expression of the Emotions in Man and Animals*. Chicago: University of Chicago Press.

Douglas, Mary. 1966. *Purity and Danger*. London: Routledge & Kegan Paul.

Durkheim, Émile. 1995 [1912]. *The Elementary Forms of Religious Life*. Translated by Karen Flood. New York: The Free Press.

Fabre-Vassas, Claudine. 1997. *The Singular Beast: Jews, Christians, and the Pig*. Translated by Karen Volk. New York: Columbia University Press.

Fang Guangchang, 方廣錩, ed. 2010. *Zangwai fojia wenxian* 藏外佛教文獻 [Extracanonical Buddhist Texts]. vol. 2. Beijing: Renmin daxue chubanshe.

Ferry, Luc. 1993. *Homo Aestheticus: The Invention of Taste in the Democratic Age*. Chicago: University of Chicago Press.

Foulk, T. Griffith. 2001. "Instructions for the Cook (*Tenzo kyōkun*)." In *Nothing Is Hidden: Essays on Zen Master Dōgen's Instructions for the Cook*, edited by Jisho Warner et al., 21–40. New York: Weatherhill.

Fulton, Rachel. 2006. "'Taste and See That the Lord Is Sweet' (Ps. 33:9): The Flavor of God in the Monastic West." *The Journal of Religion* 86.2: 169–204.

Granoff, Phyllis. 1998. "Divine Delicacies: Monks, Images, and Miracles in the Contest between Jainism and Buddhism." In *Images, Miracles, and Authority in Asian Religious Traditions*, edited by Richard H. Davis, 55–95. Boulder, CO: Westview Press.

Greene, Eric M. 2016. "A Reassessment of the Early History of Chinese Buddhist Vegetarianism." *Asia Major* 29.1: 1–43.

Harvey, Susan Ashbrook. 2006. *Scenting Salvation: Ancient Christianity and the Olfactory Imagination*. Berkeley: University of California Press.

Heirman, Ann, and Tom De Rauw. 2006. "Offenders, Sinners, and Criminals: The Consumption of Forbidden Food." *Acta Orientalia Academiae Scientiarum Hungaricae* 59.1: 57–83.

Horner, I. B. 1942. *The Book of Discipline (Vinaya-Piṭaka), Volume III (Suttavibhaṅga)*. London: Luzac and Co.

———. 1952. *The Book of Discipline (Vinaya-Piṭaka), Volume V (Cullavagga)*. London: Luzac and Co.

Hurvitz, Leon, trans. 1976. *Scripture of the Lotus Blossom of the Fine Dharma*. New York: Columbia University Press.

Jaffe, Richard M. 2005. "The Debate over Meat Eating in Japanese Buddhism." In *Going Forth: Visions of Buddhist Vinaya, Essays Presented in Honor of Professor Stanley Weinstein*, edited by William M. Bodiford, 255–75. Honolulu: University of Hawai'i Press.

———. 2011. *Neither Monk nor Layman: Clerical Marriage in Modern Japanese Buddhism*. Princeton, NJ: Princeton University Press.

Jay, Martin. 2011. "In the Realm of the Senses: An Introduction." *American Historical Review* 116.2: 307–15.

Jayawickrama, N. A. 1990. *The Story of the Buddha: The Nidāna-kathā of the Jātakaṭṭakathā*. Oxford: Pali Text Society.

Jones, J. J. 1952. *The Mahāvastu*. London: Luzac and Co.

Juravsky, Dan. 2014. *The Language of Food: A Linguist Reads the Menu*. New York: W. W. Norton.

Kelly, Daniel. 2011. *Yuck! The Nature and Moral Significance of Disgust*. Cambridge, MA: MIT Press.

Khare, R. S. 1992. *The Eternal Food: Gastronomic Ideas and Experiences of Hindus and Buddhists*. Albany: State University of New York Press.

Kieschnick, John. 2003. *The Impact of Buddhism on Chinese Material Culture*. Princeton, NJ: Princeton University Press.

———. 2005. "Buddhist Vegetarianism in China." In Sterckx, *Of Tripod and Palate*, 186–212.

Kleeman, Terry F. 2005. "Feasting without Victuals: The Evolution of the Daoist Communal Kitchen." In Sterckx, *Of Tripod and Palate*, 140–62.

Kolnai, Aurel. 2004. *On Disgust*. Chicago: Open Court.

Korsmeyer, Carolyn. 1999. *Making Sense of Taste: Food and Philosophy*. Ithaca, NY: Cornell University Press.

———. 2011. *The Foul and the Fair in Aesthetics*. Oxford: Oxford University Press.

Lamotte, Étienne. 1976. *The Teaching of Vimalakīrti* (*Vimalakīrtinirdeśa*). London: Routledge and Kegan Paul.

Leach, Edmund. 1989. "Anthropological Aspects of Language: Animal Categories and Verbal Abuse." *Anthrozoös* 2.3: 151–65.

Lowe, Bryan D. 2017. *Ritualized Writing: Buddhist Practice and Scriptural Cultures in Ancient Japan*. Honolulu: University of Hawai'i Press.

Lu K'uan Yu (Charles Luk), trans. 1966. *The Śūraṃgama Sūtra*. Sri Lanka: Buddha Dharma Education Association.

Mather, Richard B. 1981. "The Bonze's Begging Bowl: Eating Practices in Buddhist Monasteries of Medieval India and China." *Journal of the American Oriental Society* 101.4: 417–24.

McHugh, James. 2007. "The Classification of Smells and the Order of the Senses in Indian Religious Traditions." *Numen* 54.4: 374–419.

Menninghaus, Winfried. 2003. *Disgust: Theory and History of a Strong Emotion*. Albany: State University of New York Press.

Miller, William Ian. 1997. *The Anatomy of Disgust*. Cambridge, MA: Harvard University Press.

Mintz, Sidney W. 1985. *Sweetness and Power: The Place of Sugar in Modern History*. New York: Penguin Books.

Mitra, Rajendralala. 1881. *The Lalita-Vistara: Memoirs of the Early Life of the Sakya Siñha*. Calcutta: J. W. Thomas, Baptist Mission Press.

Mollier, Christine. 2008. *Buddhism and Daoism Face to Face: Scripture, Ritual, and Iconographic Exchange in Medieval China*. Honolulu: University of Hawai'i Press.

Olivelle, Patrick. 2011. *Language, Texts, and Society: Explorations in Ancient Indian Culture and Religion*. London: Anthem Press.

Pruden, Leo M., trans. 1988. *Abhidharmakośabhāṣyam*. English translation from the French by Louis de La Vallée Poussin. 4 vols. Berkeley, CA: Asian Humanities Press.

Reischauer, Edwin O. 1955. *Ennin's Diary: The Record of a Pilgrimage to China in Search of the Law*. New York: The Ronald Press Company.
Rotman, Andy. 2021. *Hungry Ghosts*. Boston: Wisdom Publications.
Rozin, Paul, and April E. Fallon. 1987. "A Perspective on Disgust." *Psychological Review* 94.1: 23–41.
Ruegg, David Seyfort. 1980. "Ahiṃsā and Vegetarianism in the History of Buddhism." In *Buddhist Studies in Honour of Walpola Rahula*, edited by Somaratna Balasooriya et al., 234–35. London: Gordon Fraser.
Schmithausen, Lambert. 2005. "Meat-Eating and Nature: Buddhist Perspectives." In *Buddhism and Nature (Bukkyō to Shizen)*, 183–201. Supplement to the *Bulletin of the Research Institute of Bukkyo University*. Kyoto: Research Institute of Bukkyō University.
Schopen, Gregory. 2007. "The Learned Monk as a Comic Figure: On Reading a Buddhist Vinaya as Indian Literature." *Journal of Indian Philosophy* 35.3: 201–26.
Smith, Brian K. 1990. "Eaters, Food, and Social Hierarchy in Ancient India: A Dietary Guide to a Revolution of Values." *Journal of the American Academy of Religion* 58.2: 177–205.
Sterckx, Roel, ed. 2005. *Of Tripod and Palate: Food, Politics, and Religion in Traditional China*. New York: Palgrave Macmillan.
Stevenson, Daniel. 2004. "Making New Monastic Rules." In *Buddhist Scriptures*, edited by Donald S. Lopez Jr., 278–84. London: Penguin Books.
Suwa Gijun 諏訪義純. 1988. *Chūgoku chūsei bukkyōshi kenkyū* 中国中世仏教史研究 [Studies in Medieval Chinese Buddhist History]. Tokyo: Daito shuppansha.
T. Taishō shinshu daizōkyō. 大正新脩大藏經 [Taishō Tripiṭaka]. 1924–35. Edited by Takakusu Junjirō 高順次郎 et al. Tokyo: Taishō issaikyō kankōkai.
Tambiah, Stanley J. 1969. "Animals Are Good to Think and Good to Prohibit." *Ethnology* 8.4: 423–59.
U Ba Kyaw, trans. 1980. *Elucidation of the Intrinsic Meaning: So Named the Commentary on the Peta-Stories (Paramatthadīpanī nāma Petavatthu-aṭṭhakathā) by Dhammapala*. Edited and annotated by Peter Masefield. London: Pali Text Society.
Van Daele, Wim. 2016. "Desiring Foods: Cultivating Non-attachment to Nourishment in Buddhist Sri Lanka." *Appetite* 105: 215.
Walshe, Maurice. 1987. *Thus Have I Heard: The Long Discourses of the Buddha*. London: Wisdom Books.
Warren, Henry Clarke. 1900 [1896]. *Buddhism in Translations*. Cambridge, MA: Harvard University Press.
Watson, Burton, trans. 1997. *The Vimalakirti Sutra, Translated from the Chinese Version by Kumarajiva*. New York: Columbia University Press.
Wujastyk, Dominik. 1998. *The Roots of Ayurveda*. New York: Penguin Books.
Yifa, 2002. *The Origins of Buddhist Monastic Codes in China: An Annotated Translation and Study of the Chanyuan Qinggui*. Honolulu: University of Hawai'i Press.
Zürcher, Erik. 1959. *The Buddhist Conquest of China: The Spread and Adaption of Buddhism in Early Medieval China*. Leiden: E. J. Brill.

Sweetness and Power: The Buddhist Transformation of Taste

D. Max Moerman

Taste, in Buddhist traditions, is a sense shot through with ambivalence. The language of taste is used both to unite and divide the teachings. The unconditioned, undifferentiated, and unadulterated "single taste" of the Dharma, which is likened to the single taste of rainwater wherever it may fall, or to the singular salinity of the ocean wherever it may be tasted, is a common phrase used to describe of the unity of the teachings. In the *Nirvāṇa Sūtra*, the Buddha explains: "I refer to liberation as being 'uniform in its flavor,' like the purity of the uniform taste of rain as it falls from the sky. This purity of being uniform in flavor is but a metaphor for true liberation."[1] Conversely, the Chinese Tiantai and Japanese Tendai traditions divide the Dharma into "five tastes" or "five flavors" that are equated with the five progressive stages in the refinement of dairy: milk, cream, buttermilk, butter, and refined butter. These five tastes are used to distinguish five temporal periods of the Buddha's teaching, which correspond to a fivefold division of the sūtras. In this taxonomy, the taste of milk corresponds to the teachings of the *Avataṃsaka Sūtra*; the taste of cream with the Āgamas; the taste of buttermilk with the Vaipulya sūtras; the taste of butter with the Prajñāparāmitā sūtras; and the taste of clarified butter with the *Mahāparinirvāṇa Sūtra* and the *Lotus Sūtra*. The purpose of this lactic analogy is hierarchical and polemical: it identifies the sūtras valued by the Tiantai tradition as those of the highest flavor and the sūtras of other traditions as those of less refined taste.

Anthropologists have similarly turned to the power of taste to unite, divide, and classify. Claude Lévi-Strauss has argued that taste concerns not only what is "good to eat" (*bonnes à manger*) but also what is "good to think" (*bonnes à penser*); Mary Douglas has charted the connections between dietary practices and cultural systems; Pierre Bourdieu and Jack Goody have examined taste as a source and marker of social distinction.[2] The extensive regulation of food and drink in the Vinaya literature seems to bear out such an anthropological attention to cultural categories. According to the tradition, a great many rules in the Buddhist monastic code were formulated by the Buddha in order to appeal to the sensibilities of the laity. This is clearly the case with taste, where the alimentary prohibitions have far more to do with social expectations and sectarian divisions than with matters of flavor. Even the accusation of gustatory indulgence served polemical purposes and was a common trope within the intrareligious rivalries of renunciant communities in South Asia. The Jains were the famed ascetics of ancient India and were opponents of the Buddhists, often criticizing the Buddha and his followers for what and how much they ate. One Jain critique of a Buddhist monastic, expressed in verse, says: "rice porridge after rising / food at noon and drink in the afternoon / grapes and sugar candy at night / and in the end a Buddhist monk experiences liberation!"[3]

The Taste of Suffering and the Taste of Liberation

As noted throughout this volume, the philosophical and moral hierarchy of the senses within Buddhist traditions prioritizes the "higher senses" of seeing and hearing above the "lower senses" of tasting, smelling, and touching.[4] Such an order of the senses is appropriate for a tradition that extols insight (*vipassanā*) and hearing the voice (*vacana*) of the Buddha, and that identifies craving as the source of suffering, and the senses, especially taste and touch, as the source of craving. Taste, like other sensory pleasures, therefore presents obvious problems for a tradition in which seeking pleasure is the cause of pain. Within the Buddhist "realm of the senses," taste—the sense most closely identified with craving, the sense most commonly associated with sensory indulgence—would naturally tend toward the lower end of the sensory spectrum. The craving for food is inherent to the human condition and the regulation of what and when one is allowed to eat is fundamental to all forms of Indian asceticism. In Abhidharma literature, smell and taste are particularly linked to the generation of desire. According to the *Abhidharmanyāyānusāra Śāstra*, "pleasant feeling is generated through food. Cravings can be created through the pleasant feeling. When cravings are generated, people become attached and treat the cravings as a necessity of life."[5] Indeed, in Buddhist cosmogony, the sense of taste appears as the prime mover and the original sin that leads to human craving. In the beginning, according to the *Aggañña Sutta*:

> There was just one mass of water, and all was darkness, blinding darkness. Neither moon nor sun appeared, no constellations or stars appeared, night and day were not distinguished, nor months and fortnights, no years or seasons, and no male and female, beings being reckoned just as beings. And sooner or later, after a very long period of time, savory earth spread itself over the waters where those beings were. It looked just like the skin that forms itself over hot milk as it cools. It was endowed with color, smell, and taste. It was the color of fine ghee or butter, and it was very sweet, like pure wild honey. And then some being of a greedy nature said: "what can this be?" and tasted the savory earth on its finger. In so doing, it became taken with the flavor, and craving arose in it. Then other beings, taking their cue from that one, also tasted the stuff with their fingers. They too were taken with the flavor, and craving arose in them.[6]

As discussed in the introduction to this volume, in this Buddhist tale of genesis, the taste of something "very sweet, like pure wild honey" is the origin of human craving, and hence the origin of human suffering. And yet, the very same sweet flavor is used to describe the supreme quality of the Buddhist teachings and the goal of Buddhist liberation, which are equated with the sweetness of ambrosia (*amṛta*), the nectar of deathlessness consumed by divinities in the Heaven of the Thirty-Three (*trāyastriṃśa*) on the summit of Mount Meru.

The Sanskrit term *amṛta* is semantically and etymologically related to the Greek term *ambrosia* and in East Asia is rendered with the characters for "sweet dew" (甘露). The *Milindapañha* describes the nirvāṇa state as ambrosia itself and the Buddha as the keeper of an "ambrosia shop" where one is invited to "buy, and feed on, that ambrosial food."[7] In the Mahāyāna *Mahāparinirvāṇa Sūtra*, the Buddha teaches: "The taste of sweet *amṛta* is a metaphor for true liberation."[8] And the *Scripture in Forty-Two Sections*, said to be the first Buddhist sūtra to reach China, states that the Buddha said: "Practicing the Way is like eating honey, which is sweet all the way through."[9] The same honey-like sweetness thus characterizes both the origin and the end of craving; it is the taste of both suffering and liberation. The ability to convert the taste of suffering into the taste of liberation lies, as we shall see, with the power of the Buddha and the saṅgha, and is accomplished through the central act of the lay-monastic relationship: the ritual mechanism of food offering.

Within the pre-Buddhist tradition of the Vedas, the ambrosia of the gods is what remains from sacrifices, which priests are enjoined to consume. According to the *Laws of Manu*, Vedic priests "should regularly eat the leftover offerings and the ambrosia: leftover offerings come from what remains from feasts, but ambrosia comes from what remains from sacrifices."[10] In the *Vimalakīrti Sūtra*, the "sweet dew" of ambrosia is contained in the leftovers of the Buddha's meal. The sūtra's protagonist, the layman-bodhisattva Vimalakīrti, is described as one whose "food is the sweet dew of the dharma and his drink the flavor of emancipation."[11] In one of the sūtra's more extrasensory episodes, he shares this "flavor of emancipation" with the great disciples of the Buddha who have assembled at his home. Vimalakīrti requests "the leftovers from the World-Honored One's meal, which would be given to accomplish the Buddha's work in the *sahā* world," from a buddha named Accumulated Fragrances, who resides in a realm named Host of Fragrances.[12] He then offers this "bowl full of fragrant food" to his assembled guests, saying, "You may eat the Tathāgata's food of the flavor of sweet dew, which is perfumed with the intention of great compassion, and which will not be diminished by its consumption."[13] The remains of the Buddha's meal is both food and remedy. It is said to sustain the body for seven days before it is digested. It is likened to "a medicine called 'superior flavor'" that "eliminates all the poisons of the afflictions."[14] Such leftovers become an inexhaustible source of physical and spiritual strength: an elixir of life, an antidote to afflictions of the mind and body, and a panacea to end all suffering.

How the Buddha Tastes

The Buddha is renowned for having the thirty-two physical characteristics of a great man (*mahāpuruṣa*), the set of corporal qualities shared only by buddhas and universal kings (*cakravartin*). These are sometimes listed from the ground up, beginning with his feet, firmly planted on the ground, and ending with the wondrous crown protrusion (*uṣṇīṣa*) atop his head. Between his full, round shoulders and his jaw like a lion, we find the only instance of a sense organ in the long list: he has a perfect sense of taste. "Whatever he touches with the tip of his tongue," explains the *Lakkhaṇa Sutta*, "he tastes in his throat, and the taste is dispersed everywhere.[15] Among the thirty-two marks, nothing is said about sight, sound, smell, or touch. The list of physical characteristics, as is well known, is otherwise concerned exclusively with the physical attributes of the Buddha's body: his feet, toes, hands, fingers, arms, thighs, penis, shoulders, head, teeth, jaw, eyes, eyelashes, hair, and tongue. The iconographic, even iconometric, qualities of the thirty-two physical characteristics have led some scholars to suggest that they may be related to the early production of Buddhist images. Yet there is nothing visible about the Buddha's superior sense of taste. It is a sense that cannot be seen and must therefore be described in the sensory language of Buddhist literature.

The *Mahāratnakūṭa Sūtra* explains the transformative power of the Buddha's sense of taste as follows: "There is no delicacy in the world which the Tathāgata does not enjoy. Even if the Tathāgata ate grass, a piece of wood, a clod of earth, or a broken tile, no dish in the billion-world universe would be as delicious as the grass, the piece of wood, the clod of earth, or the broken tile eaten by the Tathāgata. Why? Because the Tathāgata, the Great Man, has attained supreme taste among all tastes. Even when the Tathāgata eats the coarsest food, it tastes better than any celestial ambrosia."[16]

The narrative context for this discourse on the Buddha's supreme sense of taste, a sense of taste that transforms the coarsest food into celestial ambrosia, is a tale of food offered to the Buddha and his community of monks. Or rather a tale of a failed food offering. According to the story, a certain horse trader had promised to provide the Buddha and his community with food during the rainy season retreat but failed to do so, and thus the Buddha and his community were forced to subsist on horse feed. "At that time Ānanda felt grief-stricken because the Tathāgata, who belonged to the royal caste and had left the household life to follow the path, ate horses' wheat just like lowly people." The Buddha then gave Ānanda a grain of wheat that was stuck between his teeth and said, "Try this grain of wheat and see how it tastes." When Ānanda tried it, he found it marvelous and said to the Buddha, 'World-Honored One, I was born and brought up in a royal family, but I have never before experienced such a good taste.' For seven days and nights after he ate that grain of wheat, Ānanda did not eat or drink anything and was free of hunger and thirst."[17] The Buddha's supreme sense of taste has a transformative effect on anything touched by his tongue. Even the most abject of foodstuffs—the interdental debris of animal feed—assumes a marvelous taste and a miraculous sustenance.

This account of the Buddha's supreme sense of taste not only addresses what anthropologists of food would identify as the social and dietary distinctions of caste, class, and status. It also underscores the central relationship between laity and monastics in Buddhist cultures: the link between food offering and religious attainment. At the center of this tale is the gift of food, which is perhaps the most fundamental ritual act binding Buddhist renunciants and their lay supporters. This moral economy of exchange—the transformation of food into religious merit—represents the formative act of Buddhist devotion, the social and symbolic interdependence of lay and monastic communities, and the material sustenance and ceremonial function of Buddhist institutions.

Whether in the Therāvada traditions of South and Southeast Asia, where monks beg for their daily food from lay devotees, or in the Mahāyāna traditions of East Asia, where begging was considered degrading and was replaced by communal monastic feasts, food transactions define the relationship between the saṅgha and the lay community. In this transactional economy, the currency of food is converted into the currency of merit whereby the laity provide monastics with flavorful food to feed their spiritual development, and the monastics, in turn, provide the laity with religious merit to feed their moral progress.

What the Buddha Tastes

The gift of food and its spiritual effects is foundational to the Buddhist tradition. It is what allowed Śākyamuni to attain liberation and to formulate the middle way as a religious path between the renunciation and indulgence of the senses. When Śākyamuni, following the strict ascetic regime of traditional Indian renunciants, was emaciated and near death, his acceptance of a bowl of rice cooked in milk marked his departure from the mortification of the senses and initiated the bodhisattva's process of enlightenment.[18] Provided by local lay women—in some accounts by Sujātā, in others by the sisters Nandā and Nandabalā—the sweet milk-rice revived and sustained the starving Śākyamuni, allowing him to achieve enlightenment under the bodhi tree the next day and not to require any food for the next forty-nine days. The gift of "sweetened milk-rice condensed sixteen times," enabled the Buddha's religious realization and realized the intent of the donors, who vowed, according to the Mūlasarvāstivāda Vinaya, "Let the meritorious fruit of this act of giving be your highest enlightenment."[19] In some accounts, during the forty-nine days, a monkey offers him honey to sustain him. In others, it is at the end of the forty-nine days that he accepts his first meal after his enlightenment, in a bowl provided by the gods. Two merchants, Bhallika and Trapuṣa, who are passing by offer him sweet cakes of rice and honey. In return, the Buddha has them take refuge in the Buddha and the Dharma (there was no saṅgha). He does not teach them but gives them some of his hair, which, according to Burmese Buddhism, they take back to their native land, where it is enshrined in the Shwedagon Pagoda, the most sacred stūpa in Myanmar.[20] In all cases it is the sweetness of its taste that distinguishes the flavor of Buddhist liberation.

Buddhist cultures across Asia have celebrated the sweet taste of enlightenment in many ways. In contemporary Northern Thailand, for example, forty-nine small bowls of rice cooked in milk and sweetened with honey are presented to buddha images during the rites of consecration that transform inert matter into living buddhas. Bowls of sweet milk-rice, one for each of the forty-nine days, are ritually "fed" to the buddha image by lay and monastic participants and then later fed to the participants so that they too might taste the Buddha's enlightenment.[21] Buddhists in China and Japan also commemorate the Buddha's enlightenment with the taste of his pre-enlightenment meal of sweet rice porridge. On the eighth day of the twelfth lunar month East Asian monastics prepare and consume a version of Sujātā's milk-rice, but one that is usually made without milk. As the consumption of dairy was far less common in East Asia than in India, and the availability of fresh cow's milk more limited, Chinese and Japanese Buddhists, from at least the fourteenth century, enriched their commemorative rice porridge with fermented rice, nuts, sesame, fruits, and beans.[22]

The taste of rice porridge is seen to have physical and spiritual benefits across Buddhist Asia. In the *Yūga Sutta* (*Porridge Sūtra*) preserved in the Pāli canon, the Buddha teaches: "There are five advantages from rice porridge. What five? It checks hunger, keeps off thirst, regulates wind, cleanses the bladder, and digests raw remnants of food."[23] The *Sūtra Spoken by the Buddha on the Five Blessings Reaped from the Bestowal of Food* (佛說食施獲五福報經) extends the benefits beyond the physiological: "When people take rice food and offer it to people, there are five advantageous virtues that make people attain the Way. If the wise settle into a broadminded view, then they will reap the five blessings. What are the five? The first is the bestowal of life, the second is the bestowal of appearance, the third is the bestowal of strength, the fourth is the bestowal of ease, and the fifth is the bestowal of wit."[24]

In the *Porridge Sūtra*, the five advantages benefit the monks who consume the porridge; in the *Sūtra on the Bestowal of Food*, the five advantageous virtues that make people attain the Way accrue to those who offer it. In the Mahāsāṅghika Vinaya, the number of benefits is doubled, as are classes of beneficiaries. When the laity offer rice porridge to monastics: "Ten benefits profit those on the path: appearance, strength, longevity, joy, eloquence, removal of undigested foods and of wind [pathologies], [elimination of] hunger and of thirst, and [benefits to] digestion. These names are what was spoken by the Medicine Buddha. Those wanting to be born in the human and heavenly realms and obtain everlasting joy should give rice porridge to the saṅgha."[25] The giving and receiving of food, in particular that which carries the sweet taste of the Buddha's enlightenment, brings physical and spiritual blessings to monastics and laity alike. The ritual exchange is mutually beneficial and productive as well. Rice offered to the Buddha and the monks is transformed into something more. It generates physical, emotional, and medical benefits in the present life and an auspicious rebirth in the human and heavenly realm in the next.

More famous than the meal of horse feed, more famous than the gift of Sujātā, is the Buddha's final meal. Indeed, it is the most famous meal in the history of Buddhism. As recounted in the *Mahāparinibbāṇa Sutta*, in the Buddha's final days, and after he had intentionally renounced his life force, he and his monks accepted a meal from a blacksmith named Cunda. The Buddha instructed Cunda to offer the food only to him and not to his monks, telling him to bury the remainder of the dish. The dish is described as *sūkaramaddava*, a term that has been the subject of much scholarly debate. Literally meaning "soft pig" in Pāli (and translated in some sources as "pig's delight"), the central question is whether the pig in question is the eater or the eaten. That is, is it some kind of truffle eaten by pigs (the Chinese rendering of the term means "sandalwood tree fungus") or is it pork? Perhaps not surprisingly, those Buddhist traditions that promote a vegetarian diet prefer the former interpretation; those that allow monks to eat meat (as the Buddha did on other occasions) prefer the latter. Nothing is said in the Pāli account about how it tasted but much is said about its effect. After eating the dish, the Buddha suffered a severe attack of dysentery, so severe that it appeared to be the cause of his death, confirmed by the fact that the Buddha made a point of having Ānanda send word to Cunda that he should not feel responsible for the Buddha's demise, that there is in fact great merit in having served the Buddha his final meal.[26]

Feeding the Saṅgha, Feeding the Dead

The reciprocal benefits of Sujātā's gift, redounding to those on both sides of the transactional exchange, is found not only in the food offering commemorating the Buddha's enlightenment but also in food offerings memorializing the Buddhist dead. As John Strong has observed, the food offered to the Buddha and the food offered to the dead share common patterns of practice. Strong notes that in the Pāli tradition, Śākyamuni divides the milk-rice he receives into forty-nine rice balls, one for each of the forty-nine days after his enlightenment.[27] The term for these rice balls is the same as for the offerings given to monks and for the offerings given to the spirits of the dead, for whom forty-nine days marks the period between death and rebirth and the period of mourning observed in Buddhist mortuary rites.

The East Asian midsummer ceremony known as the Ghost Festival (Ch. *yulan pen*; J. *urabon*) ritualizes the exchange of food between laity and monastics in order to satisfy the alimentary and soteriological needs of the unattended dead.[28] The legendary origin of the festival finds the Buddha's great disciple Maudgalyāyana seeking to aid his deceased mother who has been reborn in the underworld as a hungry ghost, forever craving and forever deprived of food and drink. The *Transformation Text on Mahāmaudgalyāyana Rescuing His Mother from the Underworld* (大目乾連冥間救母變文) describes her plight as follows: "She might see in the distance some clear, cool water but, when she came near it, it would turn into a river of pus. Even though she obtained delicious food and tasty meals, they would immediately be transformed into fierce flames."[29] Maudgalyāyana returns to the human world to beg for rice to feed his mother, "but, before it entered her mouth, the food was transformed into a fierce fire."[30] The Buddha then teaches his disciple that only by providing a feast for monastics can his food offerings be transubstantiated into fare fit for the dead. In the Ghost Festival, as in its origin narrative, the saṅgha is inserted as a requisite mediator in the circuit of exchange necessary for the care and feeding of the ancestral dead.[31]

The hungry ghost, before whom food and drink burst into flames just before they can satisfy their most basic cravings, is one of the more haunting Buddhist images of insatiable desire. With needle-thin throats and enormous stomachs, alimentary satisfaction is a physiological impossibility. Like the denizens of Buddhist hells who are forced to swallow flaming iron balls, molten copper, and drink from a sea of burning excrement, they are condemned to a somatic fate of embodied imprisonment and sensory suffering. Japanese illustrated scrolls from the twelfth century vividly depict hungry ghosts consuming the most abject of fare: excrement, urine, and

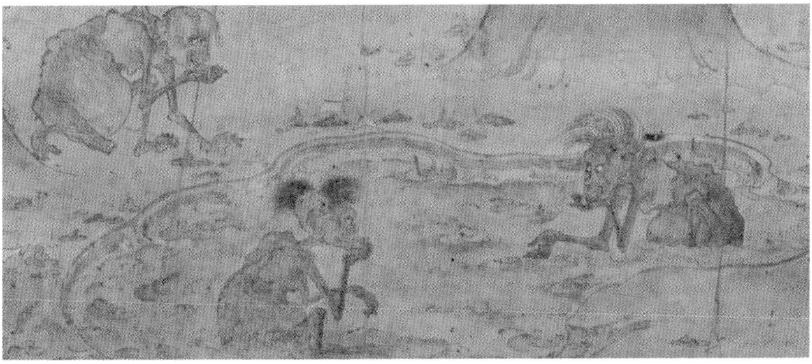

FIGS. 1 AND 2. Sections from *Hungry Ghost Scroll*, twelfth century, ink and color on paper, H. 27 cm., Tokyo National Museum.

all forms of human discharge and decay. They are shown eating and drinking out of cesspools with smiling faces and cupped hands, clustered beside squatting townspeople engaged in acts of public urination and defecation, eagerly following men performing ambulatory masturbation, salivating over the placenta at scenes of childbirth, devouring mortuary offerings, and gnawing on human bones in charnel grounds (figs. 1 and 2).

Only at the end of these scroll of the gustatory grotesque are there scenes in which the cravings of hungry ghosts are sated. In the final segment of one such scroll, bowls filled with cooked rice and glutinous rice cakes are laid out on a table, behind which monastics are seated in prayer, as other monks and attendants distribute their contents to an eager gathering of hungry ghosts. When prepared by the saṅgha and ritually distributed by buddhas and monastics, the food that had previously been consumed in flames can now satisfy their otherwise insatiable hunger (fig. 3).

FIG. 3. Section from *Hungry Ghost Scroll*, twelfth century, ink and color on paper, H. 27 cm., Kyoto National Museum.

Such a conversion of comestibles and their taste is invoked daily in monastic refectories. When washing out their bowl after a meal, the *Baizhang Chan Monastic Regulations* instruct monks to "intone the following verse from memory: This water with which I have cleansed the bowl tastes like ambrosia. I offer it to the hungry ghosts, wishing that they all be gratified by it."[32] As with the conversion of food offerings enacted in the Ghost Festival, in which the feeding of the saṅgha enables the feeding of the dead, the dirty dishwater of the refectory meal takes on, through the mechanism of monastic mediation, the sweet taste of ambrosia that quenches the ravenous cravings of hungry ghosts.

Similar scenes of food offering, hungry ghosts, and celebrating monks are to be found in a type of Korean Buddhist painting known as Sweet Dew paintings (*Kamnodo* 甘露圖), which are displayed in temples during rituals to assuage the suffering of hungry ghosts and deceased family members. As the name suggests ("sweet dew" is the East Asian translation of the Sanskrit *amṛta*), these paintings, and the rituals they attend, emphasize the ambrosial taste of the food bestowed by monks on hungry ghosts. In Sweet Dew paintings, a low altar-like table is covered with numerous bowls of rice and other offerings and an enormous hungry ghost with flaming red hair is seated before it. In scale, the hungry ghost dwarfs the other figures in the scene. He faces a group of monks performing ceremonial music and armed with the ritual implements of vajra and prayer beads. Behind the group of monks are smaller hungry ghosts eating and holding up bowls of rice. Surrounding the altar of food offerings are scenes of unfortunate deaths—by drowning, fire, falling rocks, falling buildings, or the hooves of horses—while descendants of the dead kneel in prayer before the altar. In the clouds above, flanked by the buddha Amitābha and the bodhisattvas Avalokiteśvara and Kṣitigarbha, stand the seven buddhas of the Korean tantric tradition with the buddha named Sweet Dew King (K. Kamnowang yorae 甘露王如來; Skt. Amṛta Rājāya Tathāgata) at the very center holding in his hands a medicinal flask of ambrosia. The liturgical task of this King of Ambrosia, according to contemporaneous ritual manuals, is to "open the needle-like throats of the hungry ghosts so that they can receive the wonderful taste of the sweet dew."[33] This "wonderful taste of the sweet dew" brings an end to the suffering of hungry ghosts, the very embodiment of human craving. In the words of the *Nirvāṇa Sūtra*, "the taste of sweet *amṛta* is a metaphor for true liberation." The painting, the liturgy, and the Buddha Sweet Dew King at its center are thus emblematic of the Buddhist transformation of taste: a ritual alchemy that can change the humble offerings of the laity into the sweet taste of true liberation (fig. 4).

In Buddhist literature and ritual across Asia, the sweet flavor of ambrosia is celebrated as the taste of enlightenment and characterizes the highest qualities of the Buddha, the Dharma, and the Saṅgha. With his perfect sense of taste, the coarsest food is transformed in the Buddha's mouth into celestial ambrosia and the leftovers of his meal impart the flavor of sweet dew. His teachings are similarly described as the sweet dew of the Dharma, and even the dishwater of the saṅgha, like the leftovers of the Buddha, tastes like ambrosia. Sweetness is the flavor of the food that is offered to him before and after his awakening, which sustains and transforms him throughout the process of his enlightenment. Such ambrosia is produced from the food offered to the saṅgha as well, which in turn sustains and transforms hungry ghosts and ancestral spirits. Sweetness is the taste that produces buddhas: in the hagiography of Śākyamuni, in the consecration of buddha images, in the rituals of the monastic refectory, and in the salvation of the dead. Yet in all of these cases such heavenly taste is produced through human effort. The food of the gods is the result of the interaction between lay and monastic communities. In the essential collaborative act of Buddhist communities, the exchange of food for the promise of liberation, celestial ambrosia is a

Fig 4. Sweet Dew Painting, 1744, ink and color on silk, 290 × 270 cm., Peabody Essex Museum.

necessarily social construction. As depicted in the Sweet Dew Painting, lay donors and monastic officiants, buddhas, bodhisattvas, and hungry ghosts, the bodies of the living and the spirits of the dead must all work collectively to generate the taste that brings an end to craving.

Notes

1. Blum 2013, 153.
2. Lévi-Strauss 1963, 89; Douglas 1972; Bourdieu 1984; Goody 1982.
3. Lang 2015, 187.
4. James McHugh speculates that the Buddhist order of the senses—sight, hearing, smell, taste, touch—"may well be based on the spatio-temporal relationship between the perceiver and the perceived," and as such suggests a theoretical concern with "the phenomenological explanation of the world" (McHugh 2007, 403).
5. Saṃghabhadra, *Abhidharmanyāyānusāra Śāstra,* Taishō 1562, 29: 513a.
6. Walshe 1995, 410.
7. Rhys Davids 1890, 220.

8. Blum 2013, 155.
9. Sharf 1996, 371.
10. Doniger and Smith 1991, 89.
11. McRae 2004, 136.
12. McRae 2004, 150.
13. McRae 2004, 152.
14. McRae 2004, 159.
15. Walshe 1995, 453.
16. Chang 1983, 461–62.
17. Chang 1983, 462.
18. Strong 2001, 69.
19. Strong 1995, 17.
20. Mastrocinque 2021, 6–10.
21. Swearer 1995, 275–76.
22. Toleno 2017, 142.
23. Toleno 2017, 145.
24. Toleno 2017, 166; *Sūtra on the Bestowal of Food*, Taishō 132, 2: 854c8–11.
25. Toleno 2017, 146–47; Yifa 2002, 59; *Mahāsāṃghika Vinaya*, Taishō 1425, 22: 462c19–24.
26. For a discussion of the Buddha's last meal, see Strong 2001, 134–37.
27. Strong 2001, 69.
28. On the historical, textual, and cultural history of the festival, see Teiser 1988.
29. Mair 1983, 114.
30. Mair 1983, 117.
31. Teiser 1988.
32. Ichimura 2007, 274.
33. Pak 2020, 20.

Bibliography

Blum, Mark L. 2013. *The Nirvana Sūtra (Mahāparinirvāna-Sūtra)*, vol. 1. Moroga, CA: BDK America.

Bourdieu, Pierre. 1984. *Distinction: A Social Critique of the Judgement of Taste*. Translated by Richard Nice. Cambridge, MA: Harvard University Press.

Chang, C. C. 1983. *A Treasury of Mahāyāna Sūtras: Selections from the Mahāratnakūṭa Sūtra*. University Park: Pennsylvania State University Press.

Doniger, Wendy, and Brian K. Smith 1991. *The Laws of Manu*. London: Penguin Books.

Douglas, Mary. 1972. "Deciphering a Meal." *Daedelus* 101.1: 61–81.

Goody, Jack. 1982. *Cooking, Cuisine, and Class: A Study in Comparative Sociology*. Cambridge: Cambridge University Press.

Ichimura Shohei. 2007. *The Baizang Zen Monastic Regulations*. Moraga, CA: BDK America.

Lang, Karen C. 2015. "When the Vindhya Mountains Float in the Ocean: Some Remarks on the Lust and Gluttony of Ascetics and Buddhist Monks." *International Journal of Hindu Studies* 19.1/2: 171–92.

Lévi-Strauss, Claude. 1963. *Totemism*. Translated by Rodney Needham. Boston: Beacon Press.

Mair, Victor H. 1983. *Tun-huang Popular Narratives*. London: Cambridge University Press.

Mastrocinque, Attilio 2021. "Philostratus, the Cup of Tantalus and the Bowl of Buddha." *Ancient Narrative* 18: 1–38.

McHugh, James 2007. "The Classification of Smells and the Order of the Senses in Indian Religious Tradition." *Numen* 54.4: 374–419.

McRae, John R. 2004. *The Vimalakīrti Sūtra*. Moraga, CA: BDK America.

Pak, Taylor 2020. "Picturing the Divine Agents of Food Bestowal: The Seven Buddhas in the Sweet-Dew Painting of the Chosŏn Period." *Korean Journal of Art History* 307: 5–33.

Rhys Davids. T. W. 1890. *The Questions of King Milinda*. Sacred Books of the East 35. Oxford: Oxford University Press.

Sharf, Robert 1996. "Scripture in Forty-Two Sections." In *Religions of China in Practice*, edited by Donald S. Lopez Jr., 360–71. Princeton, NJ: Princeton University Press.

Strong, John H. 1995. *The Experience of Buddhism: Sources and Interpretations*. Belmont, CA: Thomson/Wadsworth.

———. 2001. *The Buddha: A Short Biography*. Oxford: Oneworld.

Swearer, Donald K. 1995. "Hypostasizing the Buddha: Buddha Image Consecration in Northern Thailand." *History of Religions* 34.3: 263–80.

Teiser, Stephan F. 1988. *The Ghost Festival in Medieval China*. Princeton, NJ: Princeton University Press.

Toleno, Robban A. J. 2017. "The Celebration of Congee in East Asia Buddhism. *Journal of Chinese Buddhist Studies* 30: 125–68.

Walshe, Maurice. 1995. *The Long Discourses of the Buddha: A Translation of the Dīgha Nikāya*. Boston: Wisdom Publications.

Yifa. 2002. *The Origins of Buddhist Monastic Codes in China: An Annotated Translation and Study of the Chanyuan qinggui*. Honolulu: University of Hawai'i Press.

Infectious Touch and the Buddha's *Seven Zombies Spell* (*Saptavetāḍaka-dhāraṇī*)

Bryan J. Cuevas

Touch is our most fundamental sense. In Buddhism, touch (Skt. *sparśa*; Tib. *reg pa*) is said to be the very first sense that we acquire at birth and the very last sense that we lose at death.[1] But unlike our other senses (seeing with our eyes, hearing with our ears, smelling with our nose, tasting with our tongue), there is no single localized organ in the body that touches. The body (*kāya*; *lus*) as a whole is our organ of touch, and more specifically, our skin, covering the entire body. Would it be possible to live without a body, without skin, without the sensation of touch, as we most certainly can without the other senses? The body is the basis of all those other senses, in addition to being the singular sense faculty or "controlling power" (*indriya*; *dbang po*) of touch. Touch (body), like the faculty of taste (tongue), apprehends its sensory object only after making direct contact with it. Indeed, contact is synonymous with touch, both identified by the same word in Buddhism. The sense faculties of sight (eye), hearing (ear), and smell (nose) apprehend their sensory objects indirectly from a distance.

The need for a body to touch its object in order to sense it, to feel it, makes the sensing subject, whether touching or being touched, vulnerable, and even more so if the object is noxious, or worse, malicious. We might qualify the latter as an instance of "bad touch." But what exactly would that mean in Buddhist terms? My task in this brief chapter is to introduce one peculiar case of bad touch from Buddhist canonical sources in an effort to isolate and clarify such a sensate category. To do so, I will highlight what this one case might tell us about certain Buddhist notions pertaining to infection or contagion and the transmission of disease through physical contact—a touch that is quite obviously bad.

The case under consideration is an odd little tale about the Buddha's favored disciple Ānanda, who one day is assaulted by a horde of seven zombies (*vetāla*; *ro langs*) dispatched by a gang of anti-Buddhist villains intent on harming the Buddha. Ānanda is afflicted instead and experiences an unbearable feverish pain resulting directly from the zombies' touch. The agonized monk is quickly rushed to see the Buddha, who offers him a series of spells (*dhāraṇī*; *gzungs*) guaranteed to relieve him (and every other person afflicted thereafter) of such a terrible malady. This is the *Noble "Seven Zombies" Spell* (*Saptavetāḍakadhāraṇī*; *'Phags pa ro langs bdun pa zhes bya ba'i gzungs*), and it is preserved twice in the Tibetan Kangyur: once in the *kriyā-tantra* division and repeated in the *dhāraṇī* section.[2] I include a full translation of this work from the Tibetan at the end of the chapter. First, it will be important to define our terms.

As one scrolls through the many definitions of "bad" in the *Oxford English Dictionary*, one eventually comes to the definition most germane to our interests: "tending to have a deleterious or damaging effect, esp. on health; injurious, hurtful, noxious, hazardous." The relevant Sanskrit terms (with their Tibetan equivalents) might begin with *pāpa* (*sdig pa*), whose basic meaning is simply "bad, unfortunate, unfavorable." It is used typically in reference to the ordinary afflictions and misfortunes of saṃsāra. There are contexts in which it connotes a moral wrong, bearing the weightier meaning of "evil" as is conventionally understood in English.[3] It is mostly in this sense, for example, that the term is used to describe Māra, the arch-antagonist of the Buddha and his followers.[4] The Sanskrit term *duṣṭa* (*ngan pa*) is another word for "bad" that refers more precisely to "evil" in this stronger sense, to something "wicked, malignant." Other significant Buddhist terms include *doṣa* (*nyes pa*), "faulty, deficient, criminal"; *mithyā* (*log pa*), "wrong, perverse"; *akuśala* (*mi dge ba*), "non-virtuous, unwholesome"; *aśubha* (*mi sdug pa*), "unpleasant, repulsive"; and *apakāra* (*gnod pa*), "harmful, injurious." Any one of these words could be used to describe the sense of touch negatively in Buddhism.

The meaning of "bad touch," however, can be somewhat ambiguous. This may be because "bad touch" can refer in varied contexts to either a quality of *feeling*, a *sensation*, or to a particular type of *action*. In terms of the latter, we have to recognize that there is an important distinction to be made between *active* and *passive* "bad touch"—that is to say, *actively* "touching (something) bad" (e.g., a thorn or hot stove) contrasted with *passively* "being touched (by something) bad" (e.g., bitten by a snake); or alternatively, in reference to persons, *passively* "being touched (by someone) badly," including, more perversely (*'dod log*), being touched inappropriately, molested, or raped (*btsan g.yem*), or other such unspeakably violent, terrorizing contacts. One's own touch could be "bad" to or for others as well, in the same manner as "bad speech," and this would be an instance of *actively* "touching (someone) badly," a type of bad action we would expect to find set apart and proscribed, for example, in the Buddhist monastic code. This sort of inappropriate or prohibited touch is discussed (but read in reverse) in Reiko Ohnuma's chapter in this volume. My focus here, however, is on a particular example in Buddhism of unpleasant or harmful touch that better fits the category of "being touched (by something) bad"—specifically, infectious zombies.

Infectious or Contagious Touch in Buddhist Terms

The *Seven Zombies Spell* has unambiguous medical connotations with its notions of disease and infection or contagion. Ānanda is sickened by the touch of seven zombies. "Touching" is thus recognized as a source of bodily affliction. Ānanda's main symptoms include physical pain, intense burning sensations, and severe headache (*klad gzer*); "fever" (*jvara*; *rims*) is mentioned explicitly. The etiology of these ailments plainly involves ideas connecting touch with transmission, but not necessarily with transference, transitiveness, or communicability. In other words, there is no indication here that Ānanda becomes *contagious* after being afflicted (*gnod bya*), transferring his zombie sickness to others, and there does not appear to be even the threat of that possibility. In this text, therefore, we find no clear conception of "sharing the touch" by those already afflicted, suggesting that *infection* may be distinct from *contagion*.[5] Although disease is understood here to be transmitted by physical contact, which is the standard characterization of infection, no contagion is implied. In fact, as far as I can discern, rarely in traditional Buddhist sources is illness attributed to contamination by contact with a physically diseased person or by being in close proximity to the sick, and certainly never by the transmission of pathogens we now call germs. When we find some notion of contagiousness in Buddhist contexts, if the transference or communicability of an affliction is not instigated by demonic assault or by other polluting agents (*grib/sgrib*), the underlying cause is most often expressed in terms of conventional Buddhist theories of moral or karmic retribution.[6] Here, sickness is almost invariably the result of low merits or unethical conduct, but may also be due to poor diet or imbalances of the three bodily humors (*doṣa*; *nyes pa*—i.e., wind, bile, and phlegm).[7] These humoral elements too can be a contributing cause of one's moral vulnerabilities, beyond just affecting one's overall physical and mental health.

If we consult the foundational text of Tibetan Buddhist medicine, the *Four Treatises* (*Rgyud bzhi*), which draws much from classical Indian Āyurveda, we learn that there are generally two main categories of illness or "fever" that can be caused by demonic touch (*gdon nad/gnod pa*).[8] Sickness of these sorts starts out on the surface of the skin, the site of first contact, and then enters the body gradually by stages through various pathways: first from skin to muscle, then through the channels to the bones, and from there impacting finally the body's most sensitive internal organs. The first type of demonic illness, called "agitated fever" (*'khrugs pa'i tshad rims*), involves disturbance of one or more of the three bodily humors—wind (*rlung*) in the lower body, bile (*mkhris*) in the midsection, and phlegm (*bad kan*) in the upper body—though too much bile is usually diagnosed as the main culprit. This humoral imbalance is said to increase blood and bodily heat and thus leads to pathological inflammation in the body.[9]

The second type of demonic illness, known as "infectious fever" (lit. "tainted sickness," *'go ba'i rims*), is said to be of five types, all predominantly caused by the noxious breath or vapors (as in the Greek *miasma*) of particular classes of (mostly) female spirits.[10] The first of these fevers is the so-called *belné* (*bal nad*) disease, which is distinguished by its symptoms: shivering, insomnia, jaundice, migraine, confusion, and dementia. The other categories of infectious fever are more familiar maladies: smallpox (*'brum bu*); intestinal colic (*rgyu gzer*); angina, muscular spasm, or swelling of the throat (*gag lhog*); and the common cold (*cham pa*).

The symptomologies of affliction by demonic agents are varied throughout Buddhist cultural traditions. One early Tibetan practical source from the fourteenth century describes the sensations of demon-caused illness in vivid detail: "Your body feels various unpleasant sensations such as roughness, cutting, numb flesh, quivering flesh, crawling flesh, boiling, swelling, abscessing, bursting blisters, fire blades, and heat pricks."[11] In the *Seven Zombies Spell*, Ānanda complains of similarly excruciating symptoms, though not as precisely expressed. Could he have been suffering from one of the various types of demonic fever so meticulously delineated in the Buddhist medical literature? What prescriptions in the end are provided for his relief?

Buddhist Spells and Magical Defenses against Demonic Touch

The *Seven Zombies Spell* bears the characteristics of a typical Buddhist *dhāraṇī* scripture.[12] It introduces, within the frame of a short narrative discourse between the Buddha and one of his disciples, a special and potent grouping of Sanskrit words and meaning-free syllables (akin to mantras) that are to be used as incantations, either spoken or copied in writing, to guard against malign spirits, to cure disease, to assure good fortune, and to promote other similarly beneficial, preventative, and therapeutic aims. In other related Buddhist works, *dhāraṇī* may also serve as mnemonic devices encoding in their syllables the essential meaning of a larger sūtra (or tantra) and thereby preserving the memory of its teaching. In this regard, it is the teaching's concentrated truth power (*satyavacana*; *bden tshigs*) that provides protection for the one who knows and recites its formula. The use of *dhāraṇī* in South Asian Buddhism is indisputably ancient (the earliest material evidence dating to the first century CE) and the scriptures that contain them were widely copied, recited, and disseminated by followers of the Śrāvakayāna and Mahāyāna (including also later the Mantranaya/Vajrayāna) traditions. Even today, throughout the Buddhist world, recitation of *dhāraṇī* scriptures accompanies all sorts of popular Buddhist ceremonies, from weddings to funerals to house blessings. I have found no historical evidence, however, that the *Seven Zombies Spell* enjoyed the same widespread success. Nevertheless, it remains a significant work that is worthy of our curiosity.

Keeping its incantatory and apotropaic features in mind, I would like also to suggest that we approach the *Seven Zombies Spell* as a work of Buddhist *demonology*, appropriate to what is traditionally categorized in South Asia as *bhūtavidyā* or "the science of malign spirits." This is a common body of practice aimed at the pacification of harmful forces and the elimination of various types of human misery and disease.[13] Texts in this category typically include long lists of the names and attributes of malevolent spirits that attack and invade the bodies and minds of human beings. They usually also contain brief ritual instructions. We see all such elements in the text of the *Seven Zombies Spell.*

Buddhist demonology is not a subject that has garnered much popular attention, nor is it one that scholars in Buddhist studies, with few exceptions, tend even to recognize as a valuable interest.[14] This is unfortunate given the remarkable prevalence of demons and demon-like spirit beings in Buddhist discourse, literature, and ritual from its earliest formations in India to everywhere else in the Buddhist world.[15] This lack of regard for the topic seems to derive from an outmoded assumption from earlier times, still stubbornly persistent, that Buddhism in essence is a purely rational, empirical philosophy or a science of the mind. In recent years, in some corners of the academy, this reductive interpretation of Buddhism and the modernist or scientistic presumptions underlying it have begun to be reappraised and remedied. On this matter, I enthusiastically endorse Bruce Lincoln's hypothesis that "the demonological components of any religion are no less intelligent than those of its other constituent parts and (therefore) deserve equally serious study."[16]

As a Buddhist demonological text, the *Seven Zombies Spell* expounds the sets of *dhāraṇī* that provide protection from a variety of demons or malign spirits, but focuses especially on a category of *bhūta* spirit called *vetāla* (alt. *vetāḍa*), translated here in the usual fashion as "zombie."[17] The *vetāla* is a kind of vile spirit-deity that inhabits and animates dead bodies; in Tibetan it is thus referred to literally as a "standing corpse" (*ro langs*). Although quite formidable, this breed of spirit can be easily manipulated by more powerful beings, including both non-Buddhist conjurers (identified in our text as *tīrthika*; *mu stegs pa*) as well as the Buddha himself and those among his followers who have been properly equipped. There are many popular stories about *vetāla* in Indian, Tibetan, and Central Asian literature, the *Vetālapañcaviṃśati* ("Twenty-Five Vetāla Tales") and its multiple variations being perhaps the most familiar and widely circulated collection.[18]

The *vetāla* are also the focus of a specialized class of tantric cremation-ground rituals in which these spirit-animated corpses are employed as servants and/or used to obtain supernormal powers (*siddhi*; *dngos grub*).[19] Tantric manuals dealing with such practices describe an assortment of methods for reviving corpses. One type in particular requires what we might call a "tantric touch." The practitioner is first instructed to procure a fresh, unmutilated corpse from the cremation ground, consecrate it with various perfumes and flowers, and position it with its head pointed south. Next, the tantric practitioner, with his hand smeared with red sandal or mustard paste, touches the head or chest of the corpse while reciting the specified mantra. This is said to cause the corpse to stand up and speak: "What shall I do?" The practitioner can then exploit the enlivened corpse to his benefit as either a servant or assassin.[20] A magical ritual of this sort seems to be implied in the opening episode of the *Seven Zombies Spell*, which recounts that the seven *vetāla* who initially attacked Ānanda (each of them are named in the text) were (magically?) dispatched by a group of non-Buddhist conjurers. This clearly draws on popular South Asian notions of the *vetāla* as a harmful creature who carries out the commands of its master. But unusually, we should note, there is no explicit evidence in our text indicating that these seven *vetāla* were in fact reanimated corpses. Other malign spirits identified in the scripture by name include mainly an assortment of *graha* demons (lit. "seizers"; *gdon* in Tibetan, but also *gza'* and *'dzin*). This class of spirit has long been associated in South Asian traditions with certain neurological disorders and physical ailments, especially those that afflict children.[21]

The Buddha's curative and protective measures offered in defense against these various demons and their infectious assaults include not only the specific *dhāraṇī* to be recited but also ritual instructions for the magical use of different hand signs (*mudrā*; *phyag rgya*), knots (*granthi*; *mdud*), and threads (*sūtra*; *skud pa*). When recited in conjunction with these manual binding devices, the series of *dhāraṇī* provided in the *Seven Zombies Spell* is guaranteed ultimately to effect the paralysis (*stambhana*; *rengs pa*) of every class of *vetāla*, *bhūta*, *graha*, and any number of other virulent demon. Thus, through this special teaching of the Buddha, "all that threatens, frightens, and harms us" is effectively rendered powerless.[22]

TRANSLATION: *THE NOBLE "SEVEN ZOMBIES" SPELL*

(52b) Homage to all buddhas and bodhisattvas!

This is what I have heard. Once the Fortunate One was staying in Rājagṛha on Vulture Peak, together with a large community of some 1,250 monks, and with his attendant the venerable monk Ānanda at his side.

At that time, a group of wandering non-Buddhist rivals[23] (53a) dispatched seven giant zombies to bring harm to the Fortunate One. These zombies approached the Fortunate One but found no opening to get hold of him; they could not perceive the Fortunate One.

Having found no opening, having not perceived him, they left and went to the spot where the venerable Ānanda was resting and touched the body of that venerable monk. The very instant Ānanda was touched by the seven zombies, he experienced intolerable, severe, burning pain that made him feel he was on the verge of dying. The venerable Ānanda then thought, "I am experiencing intolerable, severe, burning pain that makes me feel I am on the verge of dying. The Fortunate One did not intend for this to happen to me! The Tathāgata did not want me to be in such distress!"

At that moment, the venerable Śāriputra and venerable Maudgalyāyana, who were sitting not far from Ānanda, heard the monk's urgent cries. The two went over to him and asked, "Venerable Ānanda, did you say that you were experiencing intolerable, severe, burning pain and that the Tathāgata did not intend for this to happen to you?"

Ānanda responded, "Venerable Ones, my body feels as if my head is being sawed into pieces; just that touch made me feel this way!"

"Ānanda, do not fear! We will place you upon a palanquin and respectfully carry you before the Tathāgata. The Fortunate One will shelter and protect you."

The venerable Śāriputra and venerable Maudgalyāyana then placed Ānanda upon a palanquin (53b) and went to the place where the Tathāgata was staying. There they set him before the Fortunate One.

Then the Fortunate One spoke to Ānanda: "Ānanda, do you have intolerable, severe, burning pain? Is that how you feel?"

"Yes, Fortunate One, that is so," the monk replied.

"Ānanda, that being so, listen very carefully and keep in mind what I am going to tell you. Ānanda, you were touched by seven giant zombies, extremely powerful and difficult to tame. The mere sight of them is deadly. They possess seven afflictions. Who are these seven zombies, you ask? They are called Garland-grabber, Jewel-grabber, Brutal One, Vile One, Peacock Heart, Life-depleter, and Blanketed.[24] These seven giant zombies are extremely powerful, difficult to tame, difficult to approach, and their magical and wonder-working powers are substantial. Ānanda, each one of these zombies, if it wanted to, could with the toe of its left foot cast down even Mount Meru, king of mountains; that mountain would be completely reduced to the size of a mustard seed. Each one of them has only to fix its gaze upward to split it open; if it gazes in the cardinal directions, all who are present will die; if it gazes in the intermediate directions, all who are present will be burned by fire. It is they who have touched you. Nevertheless, that being so, it is by the power of the Tathāgata, by the reverence with which you have heard the Dharma, and by the Tathāgata's blessings that your body is still alive."

Ānanda pleaded, "Fortunate One, I beg you to make me well, clear me of this. Please, I beg you, cast these zombies out, bind them with *mudrā*, bind them with thread!"

The Fortunate One then said to him, "Ānanda, for that purpose, listen very carefully and keep in mind what I am going to teach you, as here follows:

HARA | MAHĀGERE | GHASARAPATI | DHARA DHARI | DHARAṆI | CHORA CHORAṆI | KAROTITI | SATOTA SAMĀDHINI | SAMARA

SARAṆI | SARANA KOTAMATI | SAMABHAVE | BHAVANA | NĀGARE | BHADINA SADHANITI SVĀHĀ |

"Ānanda, if you recite the syllables of this mantra-spell (*gzungs sngags*) fifty-two times (54a), while casting fifty-two knots, it will bring harm to the hearts of all demons who cause forgetfulness[25] and all malignant ghosts;[26] you will be delivered from the attacks of all the seizing spirits."[27]

"Excellent, O Fortunate One! Please make it so! A second request—please don't let these evil spirits draw near."

"Ānanda, for that purpose, listen and again remember well, as follows:

BAD CALE BALE | MAHĀBAD CALE BALE | BHILE BHILE | MAHĀBHIRIṆI | NIMIRINI | HANAHANA HATIRI | MACATHĀ | MAVICARATHĀ | STIRISTHIRAMULE | MATHANIRMATHANI | CALANI | MĀKANĪ | JAṂBHANI | PĪDĀNI | VAYASVASKṚṆĪ | BHAGAVATI | TATHĀGATA | VITATHE | TIVEGHADHARE | PARAPRADE | HARE TIṢṬHI | NĪLĀVASINA SVĀHĀ |

"Ānanda, these zombies are thrashers, malignant; they come full of rage, murderous. To counter them with this knowledge-mantra,[28] repeat it twenty-one times on Kemuruka thread while casting twenty-one knots.[29] Thereafter, the great malignant ghosts will become extremely troubled. By this mantra they will all surrender, they will recoil, and they will be pacified. By this also every malignant ghost will be brought under control, all of them thoroughly pacified.

"Listen, Ānanda, to what I am going to teach you, as follows:

DARA DARA DARA | KARA KARA KARA | MAHĀKAKKARA | CARA CARA | CADA CARA MAHĀCADA CARA | HALA HALA HALA | HILI HILI | HULU HULU | HIRE VIRE | HIRI KIRI | VAIRAIVICINI KARA NAKARI | SARVABHŪTĀNĀNA | PRAJAṂ BHANI | NĪLA BARASANI | CACCHU | CAKRA CAKRA | ĀYUDHE SVĀHĀ |

"Ānanda, these syllables thoroughly pacify all harming spirits[30] and cannibal demons,[31] all secret mantras, ghosts,[32] curses and evil doers; they repel those selected by the king and toll collectors.[33] To counter them with this knowledge-mantra, if you repeat it thirty-seven times on red thread while casting thirty-seven knots, every one of them will be debilitated. Ānanda, take these secret mantra syllables. (54b) Hold onto them. Remember them well and completely. Apply them!

"And so, Ānanda, you should take hold of these mindfully, as follows:

DHARADHA | DHADHARA | KHARA KHARA | MAHĀKĀRA | MAHĀVALE | VAVANAŚANI | GODAṬA | KUṬṬANI | KUṬṬANĪ | SAMAHĀRE | KŪṬADAṂṢṬE | KAKHAKHARE | MUKUṬA | DHAREṆI | MULUKAKA | KṢAṆE KANĪKE | SAMESMRAŚĪNI | KINI | GIRIṆI | BHOGISARE | SĀSĀBETAḌA | KUMĀRAKA | KRITISVĀSI | KINANIVA BUDDHASI | VIBUDHYA | VIBUDHYA GRIHANABHYE | KṚTAB[H]AIRAVA | VIKRITEBHAIRAVA | MAHĀVAYE | KṚTONA | HARASI | KINANA MĀRAYASI KINANI SARVADEVA | NĀGA | YAKṢA | GANDHARVA | ASURA | SARVA ASURA | SARVA BHAYAŚAMANA | MATASARA SVĀHĀ |

"Ānanda, if you bind this knowledge-mantra with a fire offering or with a thread, every one of those you wish to target is struck with fear, collapses, and is consumed. Ānanda, remember the knowledge-mantra that paralyzes all zombies, as follows:

SEMELE | MAHĀHAHALE | HARADHARE | GHORADHARE | DHARITTI | RITTI | VIROTTI | KUṆATTI | KUTANI | SAṂGOCANI | KACARI | KHACARA | KHACARI | MAHAṆE | HUHU | MAREṆA | MAHĀMĀLADHARE | NAYONAMATI SVĀHĀ |

"Ānanda, these secret mantra syllables are similar and identical to a terrible curse. To thoroughly destroy all malignant ghosts, repeat these syllables twenty-four times on pure woolen thread while casting twenty-four knots. Should you do so, no harm will come from any negative forces.

Ānanda, take hold of these secret mantra syllables. Remember them well and completely.

"Ānanda, this secret mantra cannot be grasped by just anyone. Therefore, Ānanda, remember it well, as follows:

> CATA CARA | MAHĀCATA CARA | CIRI CIRI | BURU BURU | MAHĀBURU | SAṂBHALE | MAHĀSAṂBHALE | MAHĀVELE SVĀHĀ |

"Ānanda, whoever in this world—with all its gods, demigods, Brahmā, ascetics, brahmins, (55a) and all living beings—does not rejoice in this secret mantra, I do not look at them, protect them, or follow after them. This secret mantra is inexhaustible, whether it be burned, whether it be boiled, whether it be ensnared, whether it be crushed, whether it be set ablaze. Repeating the knowledge-mantra sixty-one times while casting sixty-one knots thoroughly pacifies all evil doers and nullifies their own knowledge-mantras."

Then Ānanda spoke these words to the Fortunate One: "That is good, O Fortunate One! I understand it well. Please cast the knot. I beg you to perform the *mudrā*."

"Ānanda, for that purpose, as follows:

> BHABHARE | BHARE | BHARAṆI HARE | PRAHARE | HARAṆI | KUTHANI TAḌI | LED CHADDATI |

"The knowledge-mantra produced by Brahmā is nullifed; the knowledge-mantra produced by Maheśvara is nullifed; the knowledge-mantra produced by Viṣṇu is nullifed; the knowledge-mantra produced by Indra is nullifed; the knowledge-mantra produced by the four great kings is nullifed; the knowledge-mantra produced by the commander-in-chief of the haunting spirits is nullifed; the knowledge-mantra produced by Sūrya (Sun) and Candra (Moon) is nullifed; the knowledge-mantra produced by Rāhu and Sūrya is nullifed; the knowledge-mantra produced by Rāhu and Nakṣatra is nullifed; the knowledge-mantra produced from the cardinal directions is nullifed; the knowledge-mantra produced from the intermediate directions is nullifed; the knowledge-mantra produced from above and from below is nullifed; the knowledge-mantra produced by the gods is nullifed; the knowledge-mantra produced by the serpent spirits[34] is nullifed; the knowledge-mantra produced by the harming spirits is nullifed; the knowledge-mantra produced by the *garuḍas* is nullifed; the knowledge-mantras produced by the ghouls,[35] by the feelers,[36] the ascetics, the brahmins, the warriors, the merchants, the commoners, the men, the women; and those knowledge-mantras produced by the outcasts and the barbarians; those produced by the hermits, the lions, and (55b) those produced by phantoms and by the minds of *drāmiḍas* (?); those produced by the servants, by the *tongsalapa* (?) and by the *mudaga* (?) hermits; the knowledge-mantras produced by all sentient beings who hold the knowledge-mantras, all of them are nullifed, as follows:

> GAGAGĀRALIPHU | MAHĀGAGAGĀRILAPHU | VIŚEPHU | ŚAPARASIDDHEPHU | CAṆḌALIPHU | MAHĀCAṆḌALIPHU | COGIPHU | CIMIREPHU | CICIMIREPHU | CAKREPHU | CAKRADHAREPHU | KṚṢṆAPHU | KṚṢṆAPHU | KṚṢṆARUPEPHU | CAṆḌEPHU | SOGEPHU | PAÑCAPRALIPHU | PAÑCALEPHU | BHIMIPHU | BHIPĀPALEPHU | VIṂGALEPHU | VIṂGALA AKṢEPHU | ĀNANDEPHU | SAMANTEPHU | NĀŚANIPHU | CCHEDANIPHU | VICCHEDANIPHU SVĀHĀ | KRISANI | VAKṢANI | MĀRANI | PANDANI | VINDYANAN | VAKṢAṆI | NĀŚANI | KHĀDADYAKANAN | GĀLABHINAŚANI | DĀHĀMASI | BHASMA | BHASMANI | MASANI | BANDHANI SVĀHĀ |

"Ānanda, when the sun rises, there is a giant zombie called Harmbringer.[37] During autumn that zombie follows after the rays of the sun; whomever those rays of the sun have touched, wherever the network of rays have touched, will become infected with fever (*rims*). That too is nullifed.

"Ānanda, there is a giant zombie called One Mouth;[38] it too is to be subsumed within this very mantra. The king of serpent spirits called Earthgrabber[39] is also to be subsumed within this very mantra. Every serpent spirit, every ghoul, every harming spirit, and every flesh-eating demon[40] is to be subsumed within this very mantra; the *garuḍas* as well, also the

Jewel-grabber, Vāyudeva too. The son of Illusion-clinger,[41] fallen Parapaḍiśe,[42] Skandhagraha,[43] and Śaktigraha[44] are likewise subsumed, and similarly their accompanying ministers and retinue, all subsumed within this very mantra.

"From every direction, for a hundred miles,
I (56a) performed the nullifications.
What can the malignant ghosts do to me?
I defeated all the hostile ones,
those to be slayed, the mighty ones.

All the zombies, what can they do?
They too with my noose
are wrapped up from all sides.
With all my nooses, they are also
numbed and stupefied.

Through this I have accomplished everything.
May these secret mantra syllables be successful!

NAMAḤ SIDDHANĀN | SIDDHYANTU MANTRAPĀDĀ
SVASTIR ME SARVASATVANAÑCA SVĀHĀ |

By that power of all the buddhas,
by that power of all the arhats,
by the majesty of the True Dharma,
whoever it is, may they be abundant in peace and happiness!
By the splendor of the noble buddhas,
to all who are forever fearful, *svāhā*! Be blessed!

The ritual:
"Recite this sixty-one times on red Kemeru thread, on pure woolen thread, and the like, while casting knots. Repeat it again in the same way. Those who do this against all the malignant ghosts, against the demons who cause forgetfulness, against the spirits who create mental distractions,[45] and all

the others; against the deliverers of poison[46] and against the producers of poison,[47] against the two-legged and the four-legged ones, they (the performers of this ritual) are supremely successful everywhere they go."

After the Fortunate One delivered these words, the venerable Ānanda, together with the gods, humans, demigods, and *gandharvas*, all those within this world, profusely praised the speech of the Fortunate One.

This concludes the *Noble "Seven Zombies" Spell.*

Notes

1. La Vallée Poussin 1988, vol. 1, 175–76.
2. Toh 616, rgyud *ba*, 52v6–56r7; Toh 1083, gzungs *waṃ*, 247v3–251r6. To date this Buddhist *dhāraṇī* scripture has not received much scholarly attention. A very early French translation of the text can be found in Feer 1883, 453–60, but with minimal commentary. A portion of the Tibetan text's opening section is paraphrased and briefly analyzed in Walter 2004, 14–16 (transcription of the Tibetan passage, 30–31). A short summary of its main plot appears in Cuevas 2008, 96.
3. Southwold 1985.
4. On Māra, see Ling 1997; Boyd 1975; Nichols 2019.
5. See Das 2000 and Zysk 2000 on the boundaries between infection and contagion in classical South Asian medical discourse.
6. Regarding the range of meanings of the Tibetan term *grib/sgrib* and notions of moral pollution, see Epstein 1977, 89–92; Schicklgruber 1992; and Millard 2007, 259–60.
7. Such moral and physical causes of disease are explicated, for example, in the Tibetan Buddhist medical literature, as in *Rgyud bzhi*, 40–42, 49–50, 51, 54–56; translation in Clark 1995, 75–76, 90–92, 94, 99–103; cf. Parfionovitch, Gyurme Dorje, and Meyer 1992, 53–56 (plates 19–20). For general Buddhist conceptions, see Demiéville 1985, 65–76. On the Tibetan humoral system, see Clifford 1984, 90–96.
8. *Rgyud bzhi*, 247–85; see also 420–37 for other varieties of demon-caused illnesses; cf. Parfionovitch, Gyurme Dorje, and Meyer 1992, 99–100 (plate 42), and 107–8 (plate 46). General introductions to the subject of spirit sickness in the Tibetan-speaking world can be found in Clifford 1984, 145–70; Samuel 2007; and Millard 2007. The Āyurvedic sources of the Tibetan medical literature are examined in Emmerick 1977; see also Czaja 2005/2006.
9. *Rgyud bzhi*, 247–54; cf. Parfionovitch, Gyurme Dorje, and Meyer 1992, 99–100 (plate 42).

10. *Rgyud bzhi*, 255–85; cf. Parfionovitch, Gyurme Dorje, and Meyer 1992, 99–100 (plates 42–43).
11. Harding 2003, 248 and 324n40. The Tibetan reads: *lus la reg bya rnams rtsub cing btsad* [=*bcad*] *pa dang / sha ro / sha 'phrig / sha 'gul dang / snyom khol dang / skrang 'bur / glo shu / ba lta / shu 'thor me dbal / tshab tsag rnams kyi lus mi bde bar byed do*. The obscure word *ba lta* is omitted in Harding's translation. See *Phung po gzan skyur gyi rnam bshad gcod kyi don gsal byed* (modern Lhasa edition, 2016; BDRC W1KG24644), 315.
12. The scholarship on *dhāraṇī* in Buddhist literature is now quite vast and appears to be growing exponentially. For a sound introduction to the subject, see Hidas 2015 and references cited therein.
13. Bhattacharyya 2000, 37; Smith 2006, 474–530; and White 2021, 32–33.
14. The few exceptions of note include Kapferer 1991; Sutherland 1991; Strickmann 2002, 62–68; Bhattacharyya 2000, 54–77; Bell 2020; and Faure 2016a, 2016b, and 2021.
15. This fact is established most eloquently in DeCaroli 2004.
16. Lincoln 2012, 31.
17. On *vetāḍa* as an alternate Buddhist Sanskrit spelling of *vetāla*, see Skilling 2007, 315n7. In some studies, this word *vetāla* is frequently but inaptly rendered as "vampire," following perhaps its first translated appearance in English in Burton 1870. However, the South Asian *vetāla* bears little resemblance to those blood-drinking creatures so popular in Eastern European lore and in modern British and American literature and film. On the other hand, the general features commonly associated in popular culture with the French Creole word "zombi/zombie"—that is, a walking corpse reanimated by various means, sometimes willfully controlled for greedy or malevolent purposes, and so on—provide a much more fitting match. In truth, though, the zombie concept is a rather more complex matter, as is made clear by Ackermann and Gauthier 1991.
18. Studies and translations of the *Vetālapañcaviṃśati* and corresponding literature include Emeneau 1936; Macdonald 1967; Lőrincz 1968; Śivadāsa 1995; Riva 1999; Benson 2006; Tenzin Wangmo 2014; and Mikos 2018. For vernacular accounts of Tibetan zombies, see Wylie 1964; Berglie 1982; Cuevas 2008, 93–104; Zivkovic 2013; and Richmond 2016.
19. Walter 2004; Huang 2009; and Dezső 2010. Early references to non-tantric *vetāla* rites in Buddhist literature are discussed in Skilling 2007; and Davidson 2017, 10–13.
20. Dezső 2010, 392–93.
21. Smith 2006, 483–86; and White 2021, 33–36; on the Tibetan *gdon*, see Lin Shen-Yu 2013 and Sárközi 2012.
22. I refer here to Bruce Lincoln's handy definition of demonology as "an unflinching attempt to name, comprehend, and defend against all that threatens, frightens, and harms us." Lincoln 2012, 31.
23. Skt. *tīrthika*; Tib. *mu stegs can*. On translations of this term and its complications, see Jones 2021.

24. The seven *mahāvetāla*: (1) *mālāgraha*; *phreng ba 'dzin*; (2) *maṇigraha*; *nor bu 'dzin*; (3) *caṇḍa*; *gtum po*; (4) *caṇḍāla*; *gtol pa*; (5) *mayūrahṛdaya*; *rma bya'i snying*; (6) *āyuḥkṣaya*; *tshe zad*; (7) *kocavaka*; *la ba can*.
25. *apasmāra*; *brjed byed.*
26. *bhūta*; *'byung po.*
27. *graha*; *gdon.*
28. *vidyāmantra; rig sngags.*
29. This likely involves a procedure similar to the one described in the *Susiddhikāra Sūtra*, according to its Chinese translation (Taishō 893): "Next take some cotton thread and hemp fiber, have a young girl dye them red in color or saffron in color, twist them into a string, knot it, and make a mantra-cord. With each knot recite the [following] mantra seven times, making seven knots." And again: "Have a young girl twist together a cotton string or a cloth string, take it, and make seven knots, reciting the mantra once for each knot; when the seven knots have all be completed, again recite the mantra seven [times]." In Giebel 2001, 152–53 and 225. One could say that this mantra-cord is comparable to what Catholics call a "cord rosary."
30. *yakṣa*; *gnod sbyin.*
31. *rākṣasa; srin po*
32. *preta; yi dwags*
33. Tib. *la gcan pa*
34. *nāga*; *klu.*
35. *kumbhanda*; *grul bum.*
36. Tib. *tshor ba po.*
37. Tib. *gnod byed.*
38. Tib. *kha gcig pa.*
39. Tib. *sa 'dzin.*
40. *piśaca*; *sha za.*
41. Tib. *sgyu ma len gyi bu*; Skt. *māyodgraha* (?).
42. Tib. *pa ra pa ḍi shes rud dro* (?).
43. Tib. *phung po 'dzin.*
44. Tib. *mdung thung 'dzin.*
45. Tib. *sems rnam par g.yeng byed.*
46. Tib. *dug byin pa.*
47. Tib. *dug byas pa.*

Bibliography

Ackermann, Hans-W., and Jeanine Gauthier. 1991. "The Ways and Nature of the Zombi." *The Journal of American Folklore* 104.414: 466–94.

Bell, Christopher. 2020. *Tibetan Demonology*. Cambridge: Cambridge University Press.

Benson, Sandra. 2006. *Tales of the Golden Corpse: Tibetan Folk Tales*. Northampton, MA: Interlink Books.

Berglie, Per-Arne. 1982. "When the Corpses Rise: Some Tibetan Ro langs Stories." *Indological Taurinensia* 10: 37–44.

Bhattacharyya, Narendra Nath. 2000. *Indian Demonology: The Inverted Pantheon*. Delhi: Manohar.

Boyd, James. 1975. *Satan and Māra: Christian and Buddhist Symbols of Evil*. Leiden: Brill.

Burton, Richard F. 1870. *Vikram and the Vampire or Tales of Hindu Devilry*. London: Longmans, Green, and Company.

Clark, Barry. 1995. *The Quintessence Tantras of Tibetan Medicine*. Ithaca, NY: Snow Lion.

Clifford, Terry. 1984. *Tibetan Buddhist Medicine and Psychiatry: The Diamond Healing*. York Beach, ME: Samuel Weiser.

Cuevas, Bryan J. 2008. *Travels in the Netherworld: Buddhist Popular Narratives of Death and the Afterlife in Tibet*. New York: Oxford University Press.

Czaja, Olaf. 2005/2006. "Zurkharwa Lodro Gyalpo (1509–1579) on the Controversy of the Indian Origin of the *Rgyud bzhi*." *The Tibet Journal* 30.4/31.1: 131–52.

Das, Rahul Peter. 2000. "Notions of 'Contagion' in Classical Indian Medical Texts." In *Contagion: Perspectives from Pre-Modern Societies*, edited by Lawrence I. Conrad and Dominik Wujastyk, 55–78. Burlington, VT: Ashgate.

Davidson, Ronald M. 2017. "Magicians, Sorcerers and Witches: Considering Pretantric, Non-sectarian Sources of Tantric Practice." *Religions* 8.188: 1–33.

DeCaroli, Robert. 2004. *Haunting the Buddha: Indian Popular Religion and the Formation of Buddhism*. New York: Oxford University Press.

Demiéville, Paul. 1985. *Buddhism and Healing: Demiéville's Article "Byō" from Hōbōgirin*. Translated by Mark Tatz. Lanham, MD: University Press of America.

Dezső, Csaba. 2010. "Encounters with *Vetālas*: Studies on Fabulous Creatures I." *Acta Orientalia Academiae Scientiarum Hungaricae* 63.4: 391–426.

Emeneau, M. B. 1936. "Central Asiatic Versions of the *Vetālapañcaviṃśati*." *Poona Orientalist* 2.3: 38–41. Reprinted in *Sanskrit Studies of M. B. Emeneau: Selected Papers*, edited by B. A. van Nooten, 98–101. Berkeley, CA: Center for South and Southeast Asia Studies, 1988.

Emmerick, Ronald. E. 1977. "Sources of the *Rgyud-bzhi*." In *Zeitschrift der Deutschen Morgenländischen Gessellschaft*, edited by Wolfgang Voigt, 1135–42. Supplement 3.2. Wiesbaden: Franz Steiner.

Epstein, Lawrence. 1977. "Causation in Tibetan Religion: Duality and Its Transformations." PhD dissertation, University of Washington.

Faure, Bernard. 2016a. *Gods of Medieval Japan*, vol. 1, *The Fluid Pantheon*. Honolulu: University of Hawai'i Press.

———. 2016b. *Gods of Medieval Japan*, vol. 2, *Protectors and Predators*. Honolulu: University of Hawai'i Press.

———. 2021. *Gods of Medieval Japan*, vol. 3, *Rage and Ravage*. Honolulu: University of Hawai'i Press.

Feer, Léon. 1883. *Annales du Musée Guimet*, vol. 5, *Fragments: Extraits du Kandjour: Traduits du Tibétain*. Edited by Ernest Leroux. Paris. https://archive.org/details/fragmentsextraitoofeer/page/n5/mode/2up.

Giebel, Rolf W., trans. 2001. *Two Esoteric Sutras*. [The *Adamantine Pinnacle Sūtra* and the *Susiddhikara Sūtra*.] BDK English Tripiṭaka series 29-II, 30-II. Berkeley, CA: Numata Center for Buddhist Translation and Research.

Harding, Sarah, trans. 2003. *Machik's Complete Explanation: Clarifying the Meaning of Chöd, A Complete Explanation of Casting Out the Body as Food*. Ithaca, NY: Snow Lion.

Hidas, Gergely. 2015. "Dhāraṇī Sūtras." In *Brill's Encyclopedia of Buddhism*, vol. 1, *Literature and Languages*, edited by Jonathan A. Silk, 129–37. Leiden: Brill.

Huang, Po-chi. 2009. "The Cult of Vetāla and Tantric Fantasy." In *Rethinking Ghosts in World Religions*, edited by Mu-chou Poo, 211–35. Leiden: Brill.

Jones, Christopher V. 2021. "Translating the *Tīrthika*: Enduring 'Heresy' in Buddhist Studies." In *Translating Buddhism: Historical and Contextual Perspective*, edited by Alice Collett, 195–225. Albany: State University of New York Press.

Kapferer, Bruce. 1991 [1983]. *A Celebration of Demons: Exorcism and the Aesthetics of Healing in Sri Lanka*. London: Routledge.

La Vallée Poussin, Louis de. 1988. *Abhidharmakośa Bhāśyam*, vols. 1 and 2. Translated by Leo M. Pruden. Berkeley, CA: Asian Humanities Press.

Lincoln, Bruce. 2012. "The Cosmo-logic of Persian Demonology." In *Gods and Demons, Priests and Scholars: Critical Explorations in the History of Religions*, 31–42. Chicago: University of Chicago Press.

Lin Shen-Yu. 2013. "The Fifteen Great Demons of Children." *Revue d'Etudes Tibétaines* 26: 5–33.

Ling, Trevor. 1997 [1962]. *Buddhism and the Mythology of Evil*. Oxford: Oneworld.

Lőrincz, László. 1968. "Les recueils Ro-sgrun tibétains contenant 21 contes." *Acta Orientalia Academiae Scientiarum Hungaricae* 21: 317–37.

Macdonald, Alexander W. 1967. *Matériaux pour l'étude de la littérature populaire tibétaine. Édition et traduction de deux manuscrits tibétaines des "Histories du cadavre."* 2 vols. Annales du Musée Guimet Bibliothéque d'Études 72. Paris: Presses Universitaires de France.

Mikos, Rachel. 2018. "The Tibetan and Mongolian Vetāla Tales as Nomadic Narrative." In *Mongolia and the Mongols: Past and Present*, edited by Agata Bareja-Starzyńska, Magdalena Szpindler, and Jan Rogala, 137–65. Warsaw: Dom Wydawniczy Elipsa.

Millard, Colin. 2007. "Tibetan Medicine and the Classification and Treatment of Mental Illness." In *Soundings in Tibetan Medicine: Anthropological and Historical Perspectives*, edited by Mona Schrempf, 247–83. Leiden: Brill.

Nichols, Michael. 2019. *Malleable Māra: Transformations of a Buddhist Symbol of Evil.* Albany: State University of New York Press.

Parfionovitch, Yuri, Gyurme Dorje, and Fernand Meyer, eds. 1992. *Tibetan Medical Paintings: Illustrations to the Blue Beryl Treatise of Sangye Gyamtso (1653–1705).* vol. 1, *Plates.* vol. 2, *Text.* London: Serindia Publications.

Rgyud bzhi: G.yu thog Yon tan mgon po. 2005. *Grwa thang rgyud bzhi* [=*Bdud rtsi snying po yan lag brgyad pa gsang ba man ngag gi rgyud*]. Arura series 20. Beijing: Mi rigs dpe skrun khang. Partial translation in Clark, *Quintessence Tantras of Tibetan Medicine.*

Richmond, Keith. 2016. "The Reluctantly-Rising Corpses of Dolpo: Ro-Langs and the Oral Tradition of the Tibetan Bon-pos." In *Reminiscences of a "Gonpa Thief" or Wanderings in Lower Dolpo: An Account of a Journey in 1995*, 91–105. York Beach, ME: The Black Jackal Press.

Riva, Raffaella. 1999. "The *Tales of the Bewitched Corpse*: A Literary Journey from India to China." In *India, Tibet, China: Genesis and Aspects of Traditional Narrative*, edited by Alfredo Cadonna, 229–56. Orientalia Venetiana 7. Firenze: Leo S. Olschki Editore.

Samuel, Geoffrey. 2007. "Spirit Causation and Illness in Tibetan Medicine." In *Soundings in Tibetan Medicine: Anthropological and Historical Perspectives*, edited by Mona Schrempf, 213–24. Leiden: Brill.

Sárközi, Alice. 2012. "The Fifteen Demons Causing Child-Disease." *Acta Orientalia Academiae Scientiarum Hungaricae* 65.2: 223–34.

Schicklgruber, Christian. 1992. "Grib: On the Significance of the Term in a Socio-Religious Context." In *Tibetan Studies: Proceedings of the 5th Seminar of the International Association for Tibetan Studies (Narita 1989)*, edited by Ihara Shōren and Yamaguchi Zuihō, vol. 2, 723–34. Tokyo: Naritasan Shinshojji.

Śivadāsa. 1995. *The Five-and-Twenty Tales of the Genie.* Translated by Chandra Rajan. London: Penguin Books.

Skilling, Peter. 2007. "Zombies and Half-Zombies: Mahāsūtras and Other Protective Measures." *The Journal of the Pali Text Society* 29: 313–30.

Smith, Frederick M. 2006. *The Self Possessed: Deity and Spirit Possession in South Asian Literature and Civilization.* New York: Columbia University Press.

Southwold, Martin. 1985. "Buddhism and Evil." In *The Anthropology of Evil*, edited by David Parkin, 128–41. Oxford: Basil Blackwell.

Strickmann, Michel. 2002. *Chinese Magical Medicine.* Edited by Bernard Faure. Stanford, CA: Stanford University Press.

Sutherland, Gail Hinich. 1991. *The Disguises of the Demon: The Development of the Yakṣa in Hinduism and Buddhism*. Albany: State University of New York Press.

Tenzin Wangmo. 2014. *The Prince and the Zombie: Tibetan Tales of Karma*. Boston: Shambhala Publications.

Walter, Michael. 2004. "Of Corpses and Gold: Materials for the Study of the Vetāla and the Ro langs." *Tibet Journal* 29.2: 13–46.

White, David Gordon. 2021. *Dæmons Are Forever: Contacts and Exchanges in the Eurasian Pandemonium*. Chicago: University of Chicago Press.

Wylie, Turrell. 1964. "Ro-langs: The Tibetan Zombie." *History of Religions* 4.1: 69–80.

Zivkovic, Tanya. 2013. "Returning From the Dead: Contested Continuities in Tibetan Buddhism." *Mortality* 18.1: 17–29.

Zysk, Kenneth G. 2000. "Does Ancient Indian Medicine Have a Theory of Contagion?" In *Contagion: Perspectives from Pre-Modern Societies*, edited by Lawrence I. Conrad and Dominik Wujastyk, 79–95. Burlington, VT: Ashgate.

A Science of Pleasurable Touch? Sex Rules in the Vinaya

REIKO OHNUMA

SEEING, HEARING, SMELLING, tasting, and touching: although there is no single hierarchy of the senses that is universally valid across all cultures, in many contexts, *touch* is seen as the earliest, the most primary, the most primitive and uncivilized of the senses. To take just a single example, the early nineteenth-century German naturalist Lorenz Oken (a leading figure of the German *Naturphilosophie* school of thought) classified all animals into five basic types, arranged hierarchically and characterized by the successive addition of each basic sense, from the lowest to the highest—from touch, to taste, to smell, to hearing, to sight. While sight was most characteristic of mammals (including humans), it was invertebrates who were condemned to a blind and stumbling existence largely limited to touch alone.[1] Further extending this paradigm from the realm of nature to that of culture, Oken devised a sensory scale of races in which "the 'civilized' European 'eye-man,' who focused on the visual world, was positioned at the top and the African 'skin-man,' who used touch as his primary sensory modality, at the bottom."[2] Touch, on its own, immediately calls to mind the image of a bumbling and benighted being—blind and deaf, with its limbs helplessly extending outward into the unknown, trying to feel its way around.

The lowly position of touch within the hierarchy of the senses perhaps derives from some of the basic features of touch as a modality of sense perception. One basic feature regards the permissible distance between the stimulus and the sense organ that perceives it: sight and hearing can take place when the stimulus exists at a distance; smell can also take place at a distance yet requires molecules of odor to travel and make contact with sense receptors in the nose; but only taste and touch require direct physical contact between the stimulus and the sense organ. Moreover, the sense organ itself is disturbingly diffuse and non-specific in the case of touch: whereas sight occurs through the eyes, hearing through the ears, smell through the nose, and taste through the mouth—all specific organs located on the head, the highest and most culturally valued part of the human body—touch takes place through the skin, which covers the entire body and constitutes the body's largest organ. With the skin being the largest and most diffuse sense organ, and touch being the sense that requires the most direct contact with its stimulus, perhaps it is no wonder that touch has been seen as the crudest and most primitive mode of sense perception.

These anomalous features of touch as a sense are recognized in the Buddhist Abhidharma understanding of sense perception, although naturally they are expressed in culturally specific ways. Buddhaghosa's fifth-century treatise, the *Path of Purification* (*Visuddhimagga*), for example, in speaking of the distance between the stimulus and its corresponding sense organ, notes that the eye and the ear apprehend "non-contiguous" objects, whereas the nose, tongue, and body apprehend only "contiguous" objects, meaning that they require direct contact with the stimulus. A further distinction is then made between smell and taste, on the one hand, and touch on the other—for with smell and taste, the stimulus is said to "support" the perception of odors or flavors, whereas with touch there is no question of "supporting" a perception; instead, touch is reducible to nothing other than the perception of contact itself.[3] Touch is thereby positioned as the most direct mode of sense perception. Likewise, in explaining why the five senses are listed in a particular order, Vasubandhu's fourth-century treatise, the *Treasury of Abhidharma* (*Abhidharmakośabhāṣya*, hereafter *Kośa*), observes that sight can take place at a greater distance than hearing—"for one can see a river of which one cannot make out the sound"—thus, sight is listed before hearing. Similarly, smell can take place at a greater distance than taste—for "the organ of smell perceives the odor of food before the organ of taste perceives its taste"—thus, smell is listed before taste.[4] Interestingly, touch is not even included in this enumeration but clearly belongs last in the list because of its reliance on the most direct contact with the stimulus.

The diffuse nature of the sense organ responsible for touch, which in Buddhism is interpreted as the body (*kāya*) rather than the skin, is also conveyed in Abhidharma discourse. Thus, in the *Path of Purification*, the sense receptors responsible for sight, hearing, smell, and taste are located in very specific regions of the eye, ear, nose, and tongue, respectively. When it comes to touch, however, the sense receptors of the body are "found everywhere [on the body], like a liquid that soaks a layer of cotton. . ."[5] The *Kośa* similarly notes this diffuse nature of the sense organ responsible for touch, telling us that the sense receptors of the body do not have a precise location, but simply "have the shape of the body" itself.[6] Finally, the lowly status of the body as a sense organ is also suggested in the *Kośa*'s alternative explanation of why sight, hearing, smell, taste, and touch are always listed in this order: because the eyes are higher on the body than the ears, which are higher than the nose, which is higher than the tongue. "As for the place of the organ of touch, that is to say the body"—it concludes—"it is, for the most part, lower than the tongue."[7] We can also discern the degraded status of touch as a sense from a passage in the *Path of Purification* in which each sense organ's attraction to its appropriate sense object is compared to a different animal's attraction to its ideal habitat: thus, the eye's attraction to visible objects is like a snake drawn to a termite mound, the ear's attraction to audible objects is like a crocodile drawn to water, and so forth. Unsurprisingly, the body's attraction to tangibles is associated with the lowliest and most maligned animal of all: a flesh-eating jackal drawn to the charnel ground.[8] Buddhism thus seems to share with Western thought a perception of touch as lowly, primitive, and diffuse.

If it is true that touch constitutes the lowest of the senses, then what can we say of *sexual touch* in particular? Here, we are presented with something of a puzzle: on the one hand, touch of a sexual nature is consistently singled out as being especially dangerous and problematic, but on the other hand, there is no particular definition or theorization of sexual touch in Abhidharma sources. In fact, if we want to understand how sexual touch in particular was defined, we need to turn to the monastic code, the Vinaya, and especially the Vinaya rules regarding breaching the vow of celibacy. Here, one can do no better than to rely on José Ignacio Cabezón's masterful and definitive study of sexuality in classical South Asian Buddhism.[9] Drawing on a wide variety of Buddhist sources (but especially the Vinaya rules regarding breach of the vow of celibacy), Cabezón notes that sex, properly speaking, involves the genitals and consists of the pleasurable touch sensations resulting from physical contact with the body of another being, whether alive or dead, human or non-human. For men, the conception of sex is marked by "phallonormativity"[10] and emphasizes penile penetration of a bodily orifice (whether mouth, anus, or vagina), "even to the depth of a sesame seed,"[11] and regardless of the gender of the partner. For women, the paradigmatic sex act also involves penetration, but here the conception is marked more by "heteronormativity"[12] and emphasizes the presence of a male partner rather than penetration alone. Thus, a nun who "allows herself to be touched and rubbed below the shoulders and above the knees by a man who is impassioned"[13] is in violation of the vow of celibacy, requiring expulsion from the saṅgha, even absent the act of penetration. In contrast, a nun who allows herself to be penetrated "by another woman's fingers, or by a dildo"[14] commits only a minor infraction, since no male partner is involved. Thus, as Cabezón notes, "Monks can . . . get away with a lot *so long as it does not involve penetration*, and nuns can get away with a lot *so long as it is not with men*."[15] Beyond these technical matters, sexual touch, as a manifestation of sexual desire, "must involve a *pleasurable* sensation." Moreover, one must "take note of the pleasure by fixating on the sexual act," and there must be a volitional "attempt to prolong the sensation" (described in terms of "movement" or "exertion").[16] The necessity of *experiencing pleasure* and *seeking to prolong it* points to the fundamental nature of sexual touch as a manifestation of sexual *desire*, perhaps the most pernicious form of the desire that, according to Buddhism, ultimately leads to all suffering. It is this propensity to foster and fuel one's desire, of course, that gives sexual touch such a degraded status among the range of sensory experiences. Yet no explanation is offered for the special power of sexual touch to foster the greatest pleasure and fuel the most intense desire. As Cabezón has noted, "There is, to my knowledge, no explanation in Buddhist philosophical literature concerning why the sex organs and other erogenous zones of the body should produce the greater tactile sensation or pleasure than other parts of the body."[17]

While it is relatively easy (as Cabezón has shown) to formulate a Buddhist description or definition of sexual touch, the actual *sensory experience itself* does not seem to be subject to very detailed theorization. Here, we might first observe that when it comes to touch in general, Abhidharma discourse does attempt to provide a comprehensive account of what "touch" actually consists of, as well as what it might *feel like*. In Asaṅga's fourth-century treatise, the *Compendium of Abhidharma* (*Abhidharmasamuccaya*), for example, touch is described as the conjunction of the "body" (*kāya*), "tangibility" or a tangible object (*spraṣṭavya*), and the resulting "tactile consciousness" (*kāyavijñāna*). Each of these terms is precisely defined, and "tangibility" in particular is further classified as "softness, roughness, lightness, heaviness, flexibility, slowness, rapidity, cold, hot, hunger, thirst, satisfaction, strength, weakness, fading, itchiness, putrefaction, disease, aging, death, fatigue, rest, energy."[18] Similarly, the *Kośa*'s definition of "tangibility" tells us that it comes in eleven forms: "the [four] primary elements [of earth, water, fire, and wind], softness, hardness, weight, lightness, cold, hunger, and thirst"—further glossing several of these terms by explaining that "softness" is "smoothness," "hardness" is "roughness," "cold" is what produces "a desire for heat," and so on.[19] In other words, there does seem to be a real attempt here to get at the sensation itself. If we find this kind of attempt when it comes to touch in general, why don't we also find it when it comes to sexual touch in particular? The actual sensory experience of sexual touch seems oddly undertheorized, especially given the enormous power attributed to it in Buddhist discourse and the entire monastic disciplinary structure erected to guard against it.

What I would like to argue, however, is that it is precisely this monastic disciplinary structure—in other words, the many Vinaya rules legislating the sexual conduct of monks and nuns—that perhaps provides elements of a "science of sexual touch" *when such rules are read in reverse*. In other words, by looking at the details surrounding those sexual activities that are prohibited in the Vinaya, we might gain a sense of which actions were believed to be pleasurable and to stoke one's desire—which is, of course, the primary reason why those actions are prohibited in the first place. This type of "reverse engineering" has been a common hermeneutical strategy in the study and interpretation of Vinaya texts. Gregory Schopen, for example, in many of his publications,[20] has reconstructed the common economic and labor activities engaged in by Buddhist monks and nuns by looking at precisely which activities were prohibited—on the assumption that (as Amy Langenberg puts it) "rules prohibiting a certain behavior implies that behavior was common within a community of monks and nuns"[21] (or what Jan Nattier has termed "the principle of counter-argument").[22] Here, however, rather than arguing that prohibited sexual activities must have been activities that were actually engaged in by monks and nuns, I argue only that such activities must have been thought of as pleasurable by monastic redactors (regardless of whether they were engaged in or not).

The question I seek to answer, then, is: What kind of "rudimentary erotics"[23] or "science of pleasurable touch" might be discernible by examining some of the Vinaya regulations surrounding sex? A full analysis of this question would obviously require extensive and comparative study of all six extant Vinayas, which is far beyond the scope of this essay. Here, I offer only a few preliminary reflections, arranged under the two headings of "Cataloguing Touch" and "A Geometry of Contact."

Cataloguing Touch

We saw above that the Abhidharma discourse on touch seeks to catalogue the many types of sensations that might be included under the general category of "tangibility" (*spraṣṭavya*), using concepts that we ourselves might also invoke to describe the different sensations caused by the stroke of a feather on one's neck, the brush of sandpaper against the skin, or the whack of a palm against one's cheek—concepts such as "softness," "roughness," "lightness," "heaviness," "cold," "hot," and "itchiness." Is there an analogue to this cataloguing impulse in the special case of sexual touch?

In fact, cataloguing of various types is fundamental to the Vinaya project. One of the basic features of Vinaya jurisprudence, as many scholars have noted, is that it does not deal with broad, ethical principles; instead, it focuses on concrete and specific actions, prohibiting each inappropriate action (or slight variation of such an action) only as a specific instance of it arises within the monastic community. Thus, rather than prohibiting something as general as, say, masturbation, Vinaya law tends to imagine all of the different ways in which a person might masturbate, and then devises a specific narrative pertaining to each such variation, explaining how some monk or nun once masturbated in such a way and how the Buddha came to prohibit it. In this way, the Vinaya seeks to erect a comprehensive edifice of rules to follow, without leaving anything open to question. Yet if we take such catalogues of prohibited sexual touch and read them in reverse, they might be seen as offering a rudimentary categorization of the pleasures of sexual touch.

Let us take, for example, the first probationary offense (*saṅghādisesa*) for monks in the Theravāda or Pāli Vinaya,[24] which tells the delightful story of the dissatisfied monk Seyyasaka, who is "thin, haggard, and pale, his veins protruding all over his limbs"—until, that is, the monk Udāyī teaches him to make a habit of "emit[ting] semen with your hand," whereupon Seyyasaka becomes "handsome, his features rounded, his face a good color, his skin clear." This eventually leads the Buddha to promulgate a rule: "Intentional emission of semen is an offense entailing suspension" (later modified to include the phrase "except while dreaming"). Further legislation makes it clear that the particular *mode* of masturbation does not matter: as long as the monk "intends" to emit semen, "makes an effort" to emit semen, and then "emits semen," there is an offense entailing suspension—whereas without the intention and effort, there is no offense. Here, we see the Buddhist ethical primacy given to *intention*: it is the presence of the intention (and taking action upon this intention) that causes one to commit an offense, not the emission of semen per se. The rule seems complete as it stands. Nevertheless, the text then goes on to specify that this same general principle applies in each of the following cases—emitting semen while:[25]

dreaming	shaking the pelvis in the air
defecating	stretching the body
urinating	staring at a woman's genitals
thinking a sensual thought	inserting the penis into a keyhole
bathing in warm water	rubbing the penis against a piece of wood

applying medicine to a sore on the penis	bathing against the current
scratching the scrotum	playing in the mud
walking along a path	running in water
holding the foreskin and urinating	playing in the mud on the banks of a river
having one's belly heated in the sauna	running in a lotus grove
massaging a preceptor's back in the sauna	inserting the penis into sand
having the thigh massaged	inserting the penis into mud
having the penis held by a novice	sprinkling water on the penis
holding the penis of a sleeping novice	rubbing the penis against a bed
pressing the penis between the thighs	rubbing the penis with the thumb
pressing the penis with the fist	

Why is it necessary to provide such a list, when the general principle has been made clear? Some items on the list seem primarily concerned with *causation*: What *causes* arousal and ejaculation? The list tells us that such a response might be caused without any touch at all (*thinking a sensual thought, having a dream*); or it might be caused by direct stimulation of the penis (*applying medicine to a sore, holding the foreskin while urinating*); or it might be caused by stimulation of areas of the body close enough to the penis to have a similar effect (*defecating, scratching the scrotum, heating the belly in a sauna, having one's thigh massaged*); or it might be caused by natural substances brushing against the penis (*bathing in warm water, playing in the mud, running in a lotus grove*); or it might be caused by interaction with other people (*massaging the preceptor's back, holding the penis of a sleeping novice, staring at a woman's genitals*); or it might be caused by some other, unclear mechanism (*walking along a path*). Other items on the list, however, seem more directly concerned with *sensation*, and how different modes of masturbation might lead to different sensations (*pressing the penis between the thighs; inserting the penis into a keyhole, into sand, or into mud; sprinkling water on the penis; rubbing the penis with one's thumb*). Taken as a whole, the list provides a protoscience of pleasurable touch and a rudimentary catalogue of varying penile sensations.

While the first *saṅghādisesa* rule pertains to the monk himself being touched, the second *saṅghādisesa* rule (again from the Theravāda Vinaya) pertains to the monk touching others.[26] This rule—whose origin-story again features the lustful monk Udāyī—states: "If a lustful monk makes physical contact with a woman . . . he commits an offense entailing suspension." While the rule makes it clear that physical contact of any type constitutes an offense, it does not tell us what modes such contact might take or what these various modes might feel like. Perhaps this is why the rule is followed by a list of twelve different forms that physical contact might take: "physical contact, touching, stroking downwards, stroking upwards, pulling down, raising up, pulling, pushing, squeezing, pressing, taking hold of, contacting." It then goes on to further gloss each one of these terms: "physical contact" is "mere physical contact," "touching" is "touching here and there," "stroking downwards" is "lowering down," "stroking upwards" is "raising up," and so on. While such a list might simply be dismissed as a case of Vinaya scholasticism run amok, it is also possible to read it as a catalogue of bodily encounters, encompassing not only the sensation of touch but the kinesthetic and proprioceptive senses as well. I suspect that any monk who studies such a list not only learns which actions are forbidden but also mentally performs each type of movement—picturing to himself two bodies moving through space—and imagines its corresponding sensation.

One final example of the cataloguing impulse can be seen if we compare the same rule as it exists in two different Vinaya traditions. In the Mahāsāṅghika Vinaya (T 1425), the *pācattika* offenses for nuns (minor offenses requiring only expiation) include, as no. 133, the following: "If a *bhikṣuṇī* lets a man . . . cut open and sterilize [a] boil on her private parts below the shoulders and above the knees, without first making a motion and obtaining permission (from the Order), her act constitutes a *pācattika* offense."[27] The rule then goes on to specify that the nun should have a *woman* do this, rather than a man, suggesting that the action being prohibited is sexual in nature and might inflame the nun with passion. Yet beyond the phrase "cut open and sterilize," the rule does not go into great detail regarding the man's engagement with the nun's body.

If we look at the corresponding rule in the Pāli Vinaya, however, we find a fuller enumeration. *Pācittiya* no. 60 states: "Whatever nun, without having obtained permission from an Order or from a group, should together with a man, the one with the other, make a boil or a scab that has formed on the lower part of her body burst or break or let it be washed or smeared or bound up or unbound, there is an offence of expiation."[28] Here, we learn that there are multiple ways of engaging with a boil on one's body, including *bursting, breaking, washing, smearing, binding,* and *unbinding.* The basic idea that a nun is prohibited from having a man engage in any way with a wound on her genitals seems clear enough, yet the text here indulges us with a mini-catalogue of varying sensations. Anyone who has spent a pleasant childhood afternoon picking away at a hardened scab will likely recognize the pleasurable feelings that are here being invoked.

Perhaps the closest non-Buddhist analogue for these catalogues of prohibited sexual touch can be found in a text whose genre might otherwise be seen as the very opposite of Buddhist monastic disciplinary literature: Vatsyāyana's classic third-century manual of sex and love, the *Kāma Sūtra.* Here too we find the cataloguing impulse given free reign, for in the course of his discussion, the author Vatsyāyana enumerates, among other things, "12 embraces, 17 kisses, 16 bites and scratches, 17 [sexual] positions, 6 unusual acts, 16 slaps and screams, 10 sexual strokes of a man . . . 8 acts in oral sex, and, finally, 7 kinds of sex."[29] We can look at just a single passage to see that although Vatsyāyana's language is altogether more sensual than anything we might find in the Vinaya, the two genres are otherwise quite similar in their enumeration and cataloguing of sexual touch. Speaking of several different varieties of kissing, Vatsyāyana notes, "He grasps her upper lip while she is kissing him; this is called 'kissing the upper lip.' One partner grasps the other's two lips with the tongs made of the two lips; this is called the 'bowl' . . . one partner may rub the tongue over the other's teeth, palate, or tongue; and this is called the 'battle of tongues.' It may also involve giving and receiving hard blows on the mouth and teeth. Kisses may be applied moderately, with pressure, with curved lips, or gently . . . Those are the varieties of kisses."[30] Such enumerated lists, as Doniger and Kakar note, constitute a "quasi-scientific feature" typical of Hindu *śāstras* of all types—a feature whose purpose seems to be to convey "an aura of totality" to one's command over a particular body of knowledge.[31]

Why would celibate Buddhist monks be concerned with conveying "an aura of totality" to their command over sex? Perhaps we can speculate that the heightened danger attributed to sexual touch—its power to stoke a monk's passion and lead him down the path to destruction—led Buddhist monastic redactors to attempt to subject it to total control by giving it as thorough an accounting as possible. In place of a general prohibition against sexual behavior *en masse*, Buddhist authors felt compelled to imagine every mode and permutation of sexual touch—and the resulting sensations—judging each variety for its ability to generate pleasure and, thus, its corresponding degree of culpability. But of course, this effort to thoroughly legislate, prohibit, restrain, and tame the vast, wild country of sexual pleasure must ultimately be doomed to failure. The author of the *Kāma Sūtra* himself was under no such illusion, for as Vatsyāyana notes:

> This is no matter for numerical lists
> or textbook tables of contents.
> For people joined in sexual ecstasy,
> passion is what makes things happen.[32]

A Geometry of Contact

Touch, as a sensory phenomenon, always involves *direct physical contact* between the sense organ and its stimulating object; in fact, as we have already seen, "touch" is reducible to nothing other than the perception of this contact itself. If this is true, then perhaps in the case of sexual touch, we can judge the severity of a sexual offense by the degree to which it approaches, approximates, or achieves such contact—a matter that sometimes lends itself to the language of measurement, mathematics, or geometry. In other words, just as there is a quasi-scientific cataloguing impulse, there is also a quasi-scientific mathematical impulse in trying to legislate against sex.

To illustrate this point, we can consider the first *pārājika* offense for nuns in the Pāli Vinaya—that is, an offense requiring expulsion from the saṅgha.[33] It states: "Whatever nun, filled with desire, should consent to rubbing, or rubbing up against, or taking hold of or touching or pressing against a male person below the collar-bone, above the circle of the knees, if he is filled with desire, she also becomes one who is defeated. . ."[34] The rule thus designates *direct physical contact* between the nun's body and the man's body as an offense entailing expulsion. Following the rule itself, we are then told that if the nun makes contact not with the man's body but with *something attached to his body*, or if she makes contact between his body and *something attached to her body*—both of which might be described as direct physical contact once removed—she is guilty only of a "grave offense" (*thullaccaya*). Moreover, if she makes contact between *something attached to her body* and *something attached to his body*—in other words, direct physical contact twice removed—she is guilty only of an "offense of wrongdoing" (*dukkaṭa*). Also falling into this least-serious category (*dukkaṭa*) are the following cases: if *something cast away from her body* makes contact with the man's body, or makes contact with something attached to the man's body, or makes contact with something cast away from the man's body. In other words, as soon as the contact between the nun and a male involves anything "cast" and thus no longer in direct contact with the nun herself, it automatically falls to the level of the least-serious offense (regardless of the degree of contact the cast item makes with the body of the man).

Here, we are provided with a kind of geometry of direct physical contact, where the farther away an action is from the defining standard, the less serious is the offense—and the less culpable is the nun. How can we make sense of this mathematical impulse? If we keep in mind that the fundamental problem with sexual behavior of any type is its status as a manifestation of sexual *desire*—and if we recognize that desire is a mental and therefore invisible state—then perhaps there is an impulse within Buddhist monastic discourse to detect, measure, and quantify desire through its external manifestation: the geometry of physical bodies as they move through space. Thus, a woman who rubs up directly against a man can be presumed to be experiencing more desire than a woman who uses a stick or some other implement to touch the body of the man, who is herself experiencing more desire than a woman who throws some item to make contact with the man (or with something he is holding, or with something he has thrown). Granted, this is not an exact science—but when it comes to the vagaries of sexual desire and the practical need to legislate it, it is perhaps the best one can do.

A similar attempt to quantify sexual desire and reduce it to mathematical terms can be seen in the fifth *pācittiya* offense for nuns in the Pāli Vinaya.[35] Here, we are told that the Buddha's stepmother, the nun Mahāpajāpatī, approaches the Buddha one day and says, "Lord, the women smell nasty"—an indirect reference to their genitals—whereupon the Buddha says, "I allow an ablution with water for the nuns." Subsequently, one nun, out of sexual passion, gets carried away with her douching and ends up hurting her vagina. The Buddha then issues a formal ruling: "If a nun is taking an ablution with water, she may take at most (a measure of) two finger-joints. For whoever exceeds this, there is an offence of expiation." Presumably, this rule is based on the assumption that "two finger-joints" is the exact depth into the vagina one can allow water or fingers to penetrate before the practice becomes pleasurable and therefore problematic—a remarkably precise attempt to quantify female sexual pleasure. (It is interesting to note that the Mahāsāṅghika Vinaya has a similar rule, but disagrees slightly on the math, allowing insertion of a finger during douching "only up to the first knuckle.")[36]

The rule in the Pāli Vinaya then goes on to say that if the insertion is greater than two finger-joints, the nun is guilty of a *pācittiya* offense—regardless of whether she thought it was more, she was in doubt whether it was more, or she thought it was less. If the insertion is less than two finger-joints—but she thought it was more or was in doubt whether it was more—then she is not guilty of a *pācittiya* offense, but she is still guilty of an offense of wrong conduct (*dukkaṭa*) since she intended (or was in doubt about) an impermissible insertion. The only way to avoid any offense at all is for the insertion to be less than two finger-joints *and* for the nun to *believe* that it is less than two finger-joints. Here, there is an obvious attempt to correlate physical bodily measurements with one's internal state of mind and the degree of desire one is feeling—but of course, the correlation is not perfect and it cannot necessarily be trusted.

If we consider the intensely personal and intimate disciplinary regimen each individual nun is subjected to as a result of such a rule, then perhaps we can appreciate the full extent of the Buddhist monastic impulse to measure, quantify, and control the dangerous pleasures of sexual touch. Again, it is striking to note that just as the need to prevent such pleasures results in an impulse toward quantification and measurement, so also does the need to maximize it. For perhaps the closest analogue to this kind of language can again be found in the *Kāma Sūtra*: In its discussion of the relative sizes of penises and vaginas,[37] the *Kāma Sūtra* first classifies men into "hares," "bulls," and "stallions" (smallest to largest), and women into "does," "mares," and "elephant cows" (again, smallest to largest). Among the possible pairings of men and women in sexual intercourse, it then notes that the three equal couplings are the best; the two couplings with the greatest discrepancy in size between the two partners are the worst; and the remaining couplings are intermediate—although among the intermediate cases, "it is better for the man to be larger than the woman." Once again, we see an attempt to reduce sexual pleasure to a matter of math, measurement, and geometry (apparently size does matter). For Buddhist Vinaya literature, the attempt is to control and thus prevent such pleasure, whereas for the *Kāma Sūtra,* the attempt is to control and thus maximize it as much as possible.

Ultimately, of course, the human imagination motivating sexual touch and the endless varieties it might take can never be reduced to numerical terms, just as they cannot be enumerated in a catalogue. Once again, Vatsyāyana, the worldly author of the *Kāma Sūtra,* proves himself to be much more willing to recognize this fact than the monastic redactors of the Vinaya—for, as he states:

> The territory of the texts extends
> only so far as men have dull appetites;
> but when the wheel of sexual ecstasy is in full motion,
> there is no textbook at all, and no order.[38]

Conclusion: Technologies of the Self

How should we make sense of the strange confluence we find between Buddhist monastic discipline and the *Kāma Sūtra*? Why do sources that otherwise seem diametrically opposed to each other fall into similar varieties of discourse in their enumerations of sexual touch? In an intriguing article titled "Technologies of the Self: Courtly Artifice and Monastic Discipline in Early India," the historian Daud Ali addresses both the opposition and the parallelism between two new social categories that only developed with the waning of the Vedic sacrificial world: the Buddhist monk (*bhikṣu*) and the wealthy urban householder connected to the royal court (*nāgaraka*), the latter being the intended audience of the *Kāma Sūtra*. On the one hand, these two figures obviously stood in direct opposition to each other. As Ali notes, "the daily routine of the Buddhist monk formed a complete inversion of the courtier's life of pleasure."[39] In fact, all of the practices of beauty, adornment, and pleasure that were to be cultivated by the *nāgaraka* were precisely those practices that were forbidden by the monastic rules of the Buddhist *bhikṣu*.

On the other hand, however, this opposition was founded on a deeper commonality in which both figures were mutually imbricated: both were part of a new, urban society that was more individualistic in nature than Vedic society had been, and both came from the non-productive classes of urban society, far removed from the never-ending cycles of agricultural consumption, destruction, and generativity that had characterized the Vedic sacrificial world. According to Ali, within this newly-developing urban context, both figures seem to have shared an underlying conception of the external world as a series of surfaces characterized by complicated "marks (*lakṣaṇa*) and signs (*nimitta*),"[40] whose skillful interpretation and management were crucial for proper comportment and conduct: "Just as the monk was to disengage with the signs of phenomenal reality through withdrawal and analysis, the courtier was to engage with and manipulate these signs to make his way at court."[41] To manage their interactions with the marks and signs of the external world, both figures were concerned with developing what Michel Foucault has called "technologies of the self"—that is, bodies of practice that an individual agent can cultivate with the aim of self-transformation (into the proper monk, on the one hand, or the dapper man about town, on the other). "Monastic and courtly practice," Ali concludes, "can usefully be seen as inverse technologies of the self."[42] In both cases, moreover, the disciplinary regimens developed and cultivated by these figures appear to have lent themselves well to both *cataloguing* and *mathematical* discourses.

Ultimately, then, we might conclude that both the celibate Buddhist monk and the wealthy urban householder were equal partners in the enterprise of touch. By touching and dealing with gold and silver, wealthy merchant householders were able to support the Buddhist saṅgha economically—and by refraining from touching gold and silver, Buddhist monks fashioned themselves as great "fields of merit" (*puṇya-kṣetra*), or worthy recipients of such householders' donations, which would be more than repaid in the spiritual currency of merit. Similarly, by penetrating bodily orifices (to the depth of more than a sesame seed), wealthy urban householders were able to produce sons and daughters—and by refraining from such penetration, the Buddhist saṅgha made itself a worthy body to receive such sons and daughters as new monks and nuns to replenish their own ranks. In this way, the laity provided the saṅgha with material sustenance for this life, while the saṅgha provided the laity with spiritual sustenance for the next life. But both transactions were enacted through the medium of *touch*.

Notes

1. Oken's work, published in 1802, bore the title *Compendium of Nature Philosophy: The Theory of the Senses and a System of Animal Classification Based on the Senses.* The five classes of animals were skin animals (invertebrates), tongue animals (fish), nose animals (reptiles), ear animals (birds), and eye animals (mammals). See Mullen 1977, 383.
2. Classen 2012, xii.
3. Ñāṇamoli 2011, 443–44. The entire passage reads (in Ñāṇamoli's translation): "Now, among these [sensitivities] . . . the eye and the ear apprehend non-contiguous objective fields, since consciousness is caused even if the supporting [primaries] of the objective fields do not adhere to the [faculties'] own supporting primaries. The nose, tongue and body apprehend contiguous objective fields, because consciousness is caused only if their objective fields' [primaries] adhere to their own supporting [primaries], [that is to say, if the objective fields' primaries adhere] as support [in the case of odours and flavours], and themselves [directly in the case of tangible data. . .]."
4. La Vallée Poussin 1988, 1: 84.

5. Ñāṇamoli 2011, 445.
6. La Vallée Poussin 1988, 1: 123.
7. La Vallée Poussin 1988, 1: 85.
8. Ñāṇamoli 2011, 445. On the lowly status of the jackal in Buddhist sources, see Ohnuma 2019.
9. Cabezón 2017. Cabezón's definitions of sex, sexual touch, sexual desire, and "real sex" appear in several different sections of the book, depending on the particular angle from which he is approaching the topic. See, in particular, 114–31 (for sex as a manifestation of sexual desire), 132–38 and 185–92 (for sex as technically defined by the Vinaya), and 326–33 (for conceptions of male and female sexuality).
10. Cabezón 2017, 331.
11. Cabezón 2017, 185.
12. Cabezón 2017, 332.
13. Cabezón 2017, 190.
14. Cabezón 2017, 328.
15. Cabezón 2017, 333.
16. Cabezón 2017, 137.
17. Cabezón 2017, 130–31n340.
18. Rahula 2001, 6.
19. La Vallée Poussin 1988, 1: 66.
20. See especially the many papers gathered together in Schopen 2004 and Schopen 2014.
21. Langenberg 2020, 1132.
22. Nattier 2003, 67 (as cited in Langenberg 2020, 1132).
23. In a similar move, Cabezón (2017, 233–34) says of the Buddhist practice of "meditation on the foul" (*aśubha-bhāvanā*) that "even though the meditation focuses on the impurity of the body, it yields, through its negation, a kind of rudimentary erotics. It tells us what people found erotically arousing . . . and what portions of the body were fetishized."
24. *Saṅghādisesa* offenses (the second most serious category of offense) are those that require a formal meeting of the order and, if found responsible, result in the monk's suspension. The standard English translation of this particular rule is Horner 1992–93, 1: 192–98. However, much of the rule is not actually translated here, since Horner (writing in 1938) believed that much of it was "unsuitable for incorporation in a translation designed principally for Western readers" because of "the outspokenness and crudeness which it contains . . . which seem to be inseparable from early literatures" (197). The passages left untranslated by Horner are available in Kieffer-Pülz 2001. However, I have instead made use of the full translation of the rule by Bhikkhu Brahmali available on SuttaCentral.net (Bhikkhu Brahmali 2014a).
25. All quotations from Bhikkhu Brahmali 2014a.

26. For a translation of this rule, see Horner 1992–93, 1: 199–213. In this case, although Horner provides a complete translation, I have again made use of Bhikkhu Brahmali's translation (Bhikkhu Brahmali 2014b).
27. Hirakawa 1999, 357.
28. Horner 1992–93, 3: 359.
29. Doniger and Kakar 2002, xxiv.
30. Doniger and Kakar 2002, 44.
31. Doniger and Kakar 2002, xxi.
32. Doniger and Kakar 2002, 59.
33. Horner 1992–93, 3: 156–64. This can also be counted as the fifth *pārājika* offense for nuns, if the four *pārājika* offenses nuns share in common with monks (which are not included in the *Bhikkhunī Vibhaṅgha* of the Pāli Vinaya) are considered the first four.
34. Horner 1992–93, 3: 160.
35. Horner 1992–93, 3: 250–51.
36. Hirakawa 1999, 393. This rule, in the Mahāsāṅghika Vinaya, is not a *pācattika* offense and is not part of the *bhikṣuṇī-pratimokṣa*; instead, it appears in the *Bhikṣuṇī-Prakīrnaka* section containing various miscellaneous items.
37. Doniger and Kakar 2002, 28–29.
38. Doniger and Kakar 2002, 42.
39. Ali 1998, 178.
40. Ali 1998, 180.
41. Ali 1998, 181.
42. Ali 1998, 182.

Bibliography

Ali, Daud. 1998. "Technologies of the Self: Courtly Artifice and Monastic Discipline in Early India." *Journal of the Economic and Social History of the Orient* 41:2: 159–84.

Bhikkhu Brahmali, trans. 2014a. "1. The Training Rule on the Emission of Semen." (*Saṅghādisesa* 1 of the *Bhikkhu Vibhaṅga* of the Pāli Vinaya). https://suttacentral.net/pli-tv-bu-vb-ss1/en/brahmali.

———. 2014b. "2. The Training Rule on Physical Contact." (*Saṅghādisesa* 2 of the *Bhikkhu Vibhaṅgha* of the Pāli Vinaya). https://suttacentral.net/pli-tv-bu-vb-ss2/en/brahmali.

Cabezón, José Ignacio. 2017. *Sexuality in Classical South Asian Buddhism.* Somerville, MA: Wisdom Publications.

Classen, Constance. 2012. *The Deepest Sense: A Cultural History of Touch.* Urbana: University of Illinois Press.

Doniger, Wendy, and Sudhir Kakar, trans. 2002. *Kamasutra.* Oxford: Oxford University Press.

Foucault, Michel. 1988. *Technologies of the Self: A Seminar with Michel Foucault.* Edited by Luther H. Martin, Huck Gutman, and Patrick H. Hutton. Amherst: University of Massachusetts Press.

Hirakawa, Akira, trans. 1999 [1982]. *Monastic Discipline for the Buddhist Nuns: An English Translation of the Chinese Text of the Mahāsāṃghika-Bhiksuni-Vinaya.* 2nd ed. Tibetan Sanskrit Works Series 21. Patna: Kashi Prasad Jayaswal Research Institute.

Horner, I. B., trans. 1992–93 [1938–66]. *The Book of the Discipline (Vinaya-Piṭaka).* 6 vols. Oxford: Pali Text Society.

Kieffer-Pülz, Petra. 2001. "Pārājika I and Saṅghādisesa I: Hitherto Untranslated Passages from the Vinayapiṭaka of the Theravādins." *Traditional South Asian Medicine* 6: 62–84.

La Vallée Poussin, Louis de, trans. 1988. *Abhidharmakośabhāṣyam.* English translation from the French by Leo M. Pruden. 4 vols. Berkeley, CA: Asian Humanities Press.

Langenberg, Amy. 2020. "On Reading Buddhist Vinaya: Feminist History, Hermeneutics, and Translating Women's Bodies." *Journal of the American Academy of Religion* 88.4: 1121–53.

Mullen, Pierce C. 1977. "The Romantic as Scientist: Lorenz Oken." *Studies in Romanticism* 16.3: 381–99.

Ñāṇamoli, Bhikkhu, trans. 2011 [1956]. *Visuddhimagga: The Path of Purification. The Classic Manual of Buddhist Doctrine and Meditation.* Kandy, Sri Lanka: Buddhist Publication Society. https://www.accesstoinsight.org/lib/authors/nanamoli/PathofPurification2011.pdf.

Nattier, Jan. 2003. *A Few Good Men: The Bodhisattva Path according to The Inquiry of Ugra (Ugraparipṛcchā).* Honolulu: University of Hawai'i Press.

Ohnuma, Reiko. 2019. "The Heretical, Heterodox Howl: Jackals in Pāli Buddhist Literature." *Religions* 10.3: 221–36.

Rahula, Walpola, trans. 2001 [1971]. *Abhidharmasamuccaya: The Compendium of the Higher Teaching (Philosophy).* English translation from the French by Sara Boin-Webb. Fremont, CA: Asian Humanities Press.

Schopen, Gregory. 2004. *Buddhist Monks and Business Matters: Still More Papers on Monastic Buddhism in India.* Honolulu: University of Hawai'i Press.

———. 2014. *Buddhist Nuns, Monks, and Other Worldly Matters: Recent Papers on Monastic Buddhism in India.* Honolulu: University of Hawai'i Press.

Index

[Note: Page numbers in italics refer to the photographs and their captions.]

Abhidharma, 3–6
Abhidharmakośa (Kośa/Treasury of Abhidharma), 110, 159, 206–7, 209
Abhidharmanyāyānusāra Śāstra, 169
abhijñā, 10, 91–92
absence of the Buddha, 19–20, 23, 24–25, 31, 34, 35, 37, 47–48
Account of Origins, 6–7
Adhyāśayasañcodana Sūtra, 90–91
Advaita Vedānta school, 25
Aggañña Sutta, 6–7, 169
aggregates, 77–79
Āhāra Patikūlasaññā, 150
Ajaṇṭā caves, 37
alcohol, 113, 158, 159
Ali, Daud, 219
alms, 44, 54, 98. *See also* begging; offerings
ambrosia, 169–70, 178–79
Amitābha, 8, 78, 93
Amitatā, 53
amṛta, 169–70, 178–79
Ānanda, 14, 22, 48, 126, 128, 184, 187, 190–97
Anāthapiṇḍada, 95
Aṅguttara Nikāya, 90
Angyal, Andras, 147
animals, 3, 89, 205
anthropology, 146, 168, 172. *See also* anthropologists by name, e.g. Lévi-Strauss, Claude
aphrodisiacs, 113, 154, 156, 158
arhats, *xvi*, 97–100
art, xi–xii, 22, 43. *See also* statues; thangkas
Asaṅga, 209
asceticism, 98, 168, 169, 173
Asia, xii. *See also* particular regions and countries, e.g. East Asian Buddhism; Japanese Buddhism
Aśoka, 1, 2, 90
Aśokāvadāna, 2
aśubha meditations 116–17. *See also* corpse meditation
Aśvaghoṣa, 91
attachment, 7, 9, 10, 131, 169
Atthadassi, 129
attraction, 7, 150, 207
auditory sense. *See* hearing
Avadānaśataka, 152
Avalokiteśvara, 92
Avataṃsaka Sūtra, 109, 120, 167
Ayurveda, 154, 186
Ayutthaya period, 49–50, 53, 58

B

"bad," 15, 184. *See also under* food; smells; sounds; taste; touch
bahuśruta, 94
Baizhang Chan Monastic Regulations, 178
Bala, *27*
Baoding zan, 107
Baopuzi, 154
bardo, 16, 65–85
Becoming the Buddha, 48
Beggars and Buddhas, Of, 53–54
begging, 8, 13, 98, 103, 148–49, 150, 152, 172
Béjar, Arturo, xvii
Béjart, Maurice, 68, 69
Berger, John, 117
Besnagar, *27*
bewilderment, 67, 81, 82–85
Bhadrakalpika Sūtra, 130
Bhairāt, 90
bhakti, 25
Bharhut, 135
Bhikkhunīvibhaṅga, 113
Blue Cliff Record, 107, 108–9
Bodhgaya (Bodh Gayā), 49, 127–28. *See also* bodhi tree
bodhi tree, 128, 173
bodhisattvas, 26–27, *27*, 30, 91, 96–97, 99, 120, 129–30. *See also* Buddha (historical), past lives; and bodhisattvas by name, e.g., Avalokiteśvara
bodily fluids, 107, 117, 147, 152
body
- of Buddha. *See under* Buddha (historical)
- crystal, 11
- human, 13–15, 183. *See also* body odor; corpse meditation
- organ of touch, 3–4, 183, 206–7, 209

body odor, 111–12, 128–29, 131
bone-ornaments, 80–81
boundaries, crossing, 110, 113, 114, 116, 120
Bourdieu, Pierre, 146, 168
Bowie, Katherine, 53–54
Brahmā, 127, 194
Brahmanical rituals, 20, 31
Brāhmī, 27
brahmin community, 25
breath
- bad, 111–13, 129, 155, 186
- of Buddha, 126
- at death, 69, 71, 72
- meditating on, 14
- sounds of, 66, 69–72
- of spirits, 186

Brereton, Bonnie, 51, 52, 55
Brown, Robert L., 132
Buddha (historical; Gautama/Śākyamuni),
- body of, *xv*, 23, 90, 119, 126, 171
- chamber of, 134–36
- death of, 128, 149, 175
- departure from palace, 148
- enlightenment of, 127–28, 149, 173
- funeral of, 98, 128, 132
- human or godlike, 36, 130–31
- images of, 19–38, *29*, *30*, *34*, 43–44, 46–50, *50*, *57*, 58
- last meal, 3, 149, 175
- past lives of, 48, 58, 129
- senses of, 130, 171
- silence of, 89–90
- smell of, 126–28, 130–34, 136–37
- teachings of. *See* Dharma
- voice of, 89, 90–91
- youth (as Siddhartha), 95, 148–49
- *See also* absence of the Buddha; perfume womb; relics, of Buddha

Buddha images, *xv*. *See also under* Buddha (historical)
Buddha Subduing the Sandalwood Image, 58
Buddhaghosa, 13, 14, 49, 51, 59, 91, 152
buddhānusmṛti, 23
Buddhas. *See* Buddha (historical); future Buddhas; past Buddhas; Maitreya

Buddhism, 188. *See also* Dharma
Bun Phra Wet festival, 52, 54, 59. *See also* Vessantara Festival
Bunthong, Luang Poh, 54
Burke, Edmund, 146
Burmese Buddhism, 173
Burnouf, Eugène, 134
butchers, 45–46
butter, 167
Bynum, Caroline, 147

C

Cabezón, José Ignacio, 208–9
castes, 172
cause and effect, 4, 44. *See also* karma
cave shrines, 32, *32*, 33–34, 37
celestial music, 9, 96, 100
celibacy, 9, 14, 21–22, 91, 207–8
Cetiya Jātaka, 128–29
Ceylon, 125. *See also* Sri Lankan Buddhism
Chakri dynasty, 57–58
Chan tradition, 98. See also *Baizhang Chan Monastic Regulations*
chanting, 94–95
Chanyuan qinggui (*Qinggui*), 111, 151
charnel grounds, 2, 13–14
Chikū, 158
Chinese Buddhism, 13, 107–19, 150–51, 155–59, 160, 167, 174
Chion, Michel, 68, 73, 83
Chulalongkorn, 57, 58, 59
Citrasūtra, 33
class, social, 21, 56, 125, 146, 153, 172, 219
classification and smell, 125–26
clear light of reality, 70, 71
colors, 4–5, 77–79
concentration, 9, 14
Confucius, School Sayings of, 108–9
consciousness, 4, 79
consciousnesses, six, 150
consecration of images, 19, 173–74
contact, 183, 213, 215–18. *See also* touch
contagion, 184, 185–86
contamination, 110, 116, 120, 152
corpse meditation, 13–14, 111–12, 116–17
corpses, reviving, 188–89
coupling, 70, 71–72. *See also* sexual intercourse
covetousness, 80
craving, 168–69, 177
creation myth, 6–7, 8
cremation, 111–12, 128, 132
cremation-ground rituals, 189
crystal body, 11
Cūḷakammavibhaṅga Sutta, 46
Cullavagga, 154
culture and senses, 125, 145, 205
Cunda, 149, 175

D

dāna, 44, 46, 52. *See also* offerings
dancing, 81, 95, 96, 98–99
Daoshi, 113, 156
Daoxuan, 113
darśana, 43–44. *See also* eye contact
Darwin, Charles, 147
Daśāvatāra Temple, 35, *36*
dead, offerings to, 175–76
death
  of Buddha, 128, 149, 175
  of a god, 9–10
  of humans, 69–70, 71, 118
  smell of, 107, 114, 118. *See also* corpse meditation; cremation
deities, 77–78, 80, 127, 128. *See also* gods
  peaceful, 70, 71, 73–76, 77–82
  wrathful, 70, 71, 76, 77, 80, 81
delicacies, 3, 148, 150, 151, 159
delusion, 14
demons, 156, 186–87. *See also* zombies
Deogarh, 31, 35, *36*
desire, 55, 72, 150, 158–59, 169, 208, 209, 216–17
desire realm, 9
Devadatta, 153

devalakas, 25
devotion, 10–11, 32, 35, 37
dhāraṇī, 92, 187–97
Dharma (Dhamma),
  ability to preach, 11
  belief in, 44–45
  chanting, 94–95
  decline of, 49, 51–52, 59, 151
  sustaining, 43–44, 47–48
  taste of, 167
Dharmākara, 93
Diamond Sūtra, 12, 97
Dīpaṃkara, 129
Dīrghāgama, 116
disciples, 94, 97. *See also* disciples by name, e.g., Ānanda
discipline, monastic, 22, 209–10, 215–17. *See also* Vinaya
diseases, 13, 184–87, 189
disgust, 13–15, 146–47, 148, 149, 151–52
"distant" senses, 145, 150, 205–6
divine ear and eye, 10, 92
Divine Stories, 23. See also *Divyāvadāna*
Divyamauli, 96, 99
Divyāvadāna, 23, 43–46, 134
Dōgen, 159
douching, 217
Douglas, Mary, 110, 146, 168
"downfalls," 14
Droṇa, 132
Druma, 95, 96, 99–100
drums, 80–81, 114–15, 127
Durkheim, Émile, 145

E

ears, 3, 10, 13, 92
East Asian Buddhism, 13, 113–14, 128, 153–55, 158, 170, 172, 174, 176. *See also* traditions by country, e.g., Korean Buddhism
eating, 145, 147, 156. *See also* food; vegetarianism
elements, 77–79
emotions, 75, 77–79
emptiness, 96, 99–100. *See also* reality, nature of
Encountering the Buddha, xi–xvii, *xii–xvi*
enlightenment, 7, 91, 92, 127–28, 149, 173–74. *See also* path to enlightenment
Establishing Regulations, 155
ethics, 44–46, 152–53. *See also* morality
Evans-Wentz, W. Y., 65, 66, 79. See also *Tibetan Book of the Dead*
"evil," 184
excrement, 107, 111, 117, 126, 152, 176
experimental music, 68, 74, 75, 82
eye contact (*darśana*), 19–38
eyes, 3, 10, 13, 92. *See also* vision

F

Fabre-Vassas, Claudine, 146
faith, 44, 54
Farrer, Reginald, 125, 126
Faxian, 47
Fayuan zhulin, 156, 158
feasts, 12–13, 151, 172–73
feeling, 4, 7, 79, 83. *See also* emotions; touch
festivals, 54, 59, 95–96. *See also* Ghost festival; Vessantara festival
First Sermon, 34
flavors, 11. *See also* taste
flowers, 128, 129, 132–35
food, 6–7, 8, 146, 147–49, 150–61, 168–79
  "bad," 146, 149
  "good," 146, 149
  See also vegetarianism
form, 4, 7. *See also* musical form
form realm, 9
formless realm, 8–9
Foucault, Michel, 219
Four Treatises, 186–87
fragrances, 2, 128, 132. *See also* perfumes

funerals, 51, 188. *See also under* Buddha (historical)
future Buddhas, 129–30

G

gandhakuṭīs, 134–36
Gandhāran images, 26–30, 132
gandharvas, 2, 100, 130, 159
Gaṇḍī Sūtra, 101–2
garlic, 112–13, 115, 154–55. See also *wuxin*
Gautama. *See* Buddha (historical)
Gavāṃpati, 99
Ge Hong, 154
genitals, 6, 208, 210–14, 217–18
ghee (clarified butter), 150, 151, 167
Ghost festival, 13, 176
ghosts, 52, 192. *See also* hell-beings; hungry ghosts; spirits
giving (*dāna*), 44. *See also* alms; dāna; offerings
Glass, Philip, xv–xvii
gluttony, 150
gods, 9–10, 25, 30–33, 35, 131, 133. *See also* deities
gold, 45–46, 56, 132, 220
Gombrich, Richard, 19
"good," 15. *See also under* smells; sounds; taste
Goody, Jack, 168
Great Exegesis, 90
"Great Liberation through Hearing in the Intermediate State, The," 66
Greco-Roman religions, 133
greed, 150, 169
Gregory, William, 125, 126
Guanshiyin, 92
Gupta royalty, 20, 25–26, 30–32, 35
Gyurme Dorje, 82

H

handprints, 135
hearing, 3, 10, 12, 67, 71, 92, 126, 145. *See also* sounds
Heart Sūtra, 117
heavens, 9, 52, 56. *See also* formless realm; pure lands
hell-beings, 51, 52, 54–55, *55*. *See also* demons; ghosts; hungry ghosts
hell parks, 54–55, *55*, 56
Hell Scene, *55*
hells, 2, 16, 51, 52, 54–56, *55*, 156, 176
Henry, Pierre, 66–76, 80–85
"higher" senses, 3, 145, 168
Hīnayāna Buddhism, 96–97, 155. *See also* Thai Buddhism; Theravāda Buddhism
Hinduism, 25–26, 31, 32–33, 35, 146, 215
holy days, 54. *See also* festivals
honey, 151, 169–70, 173
horse feed, 172
Howes, David, 127
Hsüan Hua, 109, 114
human body. *See* body, human
Hume, David, 146
humor, 53–54
humors, 186
Hungry Ghost Scroll, *177*, *178*
hungry ghosts, 13, 45, 51, 52, *53*, 55, 112–13, 152, 156, 176–80

I

ignorance, 15, 79, 82
illness. *See* contagion; diseases; touch, infectious
images. *See under* Buddha (historical)
  created by monks, 22
  See also statues
immateriality, 4, 76, 109–10
immorality, 113. *See also* ethics; morality; sexual misconduct; theft
immortality, 36
impermanence, 7, 9–10, 94, 117, 120
in-between, the, 66, 76. *See also* bardo
incense, 2–3, 107, 110, 112, 133–34
Indian Buddhism, 25–26, 66, 126, 130, 134–37, 155, 169, 173
Indra, 51, *57*, 194

infectious touch, 183–97
insight, 12, 121
Inspiring Determination, 90–91
intention, 82, 211
intermediate states, 66. *See also* bardo

J

Jainism, 3, 93, 150, 154, 168
Japanese Buddhism, 158, 159, 160, 167, 174, 176–77, *177*, *178*
Jātakas, 57–58, 93. *See also* Jātakas by name, e.g., Vessantara Jātaka
Jay, Martin, 145
jealousy, 80
Jetavana monastery, 134
Jewish diet, 146
Jizō, 102
Jory, Patrick, 58
Jujaka, 53–54

K

kaiseki, 160
Kāma Sūtra, 214–15, 218–19
Kamnodo, 178–80, *180*
Kandy tooth relic, 125–26
Kaniṣka Reliquary, 132
kapardin-style figures, 26, *28*
karma
  effects on arhats, 99
  effects in bardo, 67, 71–72, 77, 80
  and illness, 186
  and merit-making, 43–46, 51–52, 135
  and rebirth, 6
  and sense experience, 7, 38
  from sexual misconduct, 54–55, *55*
  and smell, 109, 128–30
  and vegetarianism, 118
khakkhara, 102–3
Kharoṣṭhī, 27
killing, 2, 14, 44–45, 114–15, 118–19, 152–53, 159
kinnara, 95. See also *Questions of the Kinnara King Druma*
kissing, 214
knowledge, 11, 145, 215. *See also* super knowledge
knowledge-mantras, 192–93, 194–95
Kolnai, Aurel, 147
Korean Buddhism, 178–79, *180*
Kośa. See *Abhidharmakośa*
Kosalabimbavaṇṇanā, 46–48, 49
Koṭikarṇa, 45–46
Koṭikarṇa-avadāna, 45–46, 55
Kuṇāla, 1–2

L

La Fuente, Marguerite, 69, 76
Lakkhaṇa Sutta, 171
Lalitavistara Sūtra, 119, 148
Langenberg, Amy, 210
Laṅkāvatāra Sūtra, 114, 155
Laws of Manu, 25, 170
laypeople, Buddhist, 44, 112, 135–36, 172–73, 179–80, 220
leek, 154. See also *wuxin*
Lefferts, Leedom, 54
leftovers, 170–71, 179
legal rights of images, 24–25
Legend of Aśoka, 2
Lévi-Strauss, Claude, 168
liberation, 7, 70, 79, 92, 116–17, 167, 170
light, 70, 77–79
liminality, 16, 108–10, 127. *See also* bardo; boundaries, crossing
Lincoln, Bruce, 188
Linghu Yuangui, 158
lists, 4, 210–15
Lopez, Donald, 65
Lotus Sūtra, 10–12, 36, 92, 97, 130, 151, 167
lotuses, 129
"lower" senses, 168
lust, 1, 13–14, 213
lute music, 2, 95–96, 99–100
lying, 129

M

Maha Chat Kuam Luang, 53
Mahākāśyapa, 96, 97–100
Mahāpajāpatī, 217
Mahāparinirvāṇa Sūtra (Mahāparinibbāna Sutta), 22, 112, 114, 128, 149, 155, 167, 170, 175
Mahāratnakūṭa Sūtra, 171
Mahāsāṅghika Vinaya, 174–75, 213, 217
Mahāvaṃsa, 51
Mahāvastu, 149
Mahāvibhāṣa, 90
Mahāyāna Buddhism, 36, 96–100, 117, 129–30, 153, 155. *See also* bodhisattvas
maigre feasts, 12–13, 151
Maitreya, 51–52, 56, 59
Malaya, 51. *See also* Phra Malai
Māleyyadevathera-vattu, 51
Maṅgala, 129
Mañjughoṣa, 91
mantras, 79, 92–93, 191–96
Māra, 59, 119, 127–28, 184
masturbation, 210–13
materiality and smell, 109–10
Mathurān images, 26–30, *28*, *29*, 33
matter, 4, 79. *See also* form
Maudgalyāyana, 13, 99, 130, 176, 190–91
Māyā, 119, 131
McHugh, James, 110
meat, 114–16, 153, 155, 158–59
Medicine Buddha, 174
meditation, 9, 23, 54, 92, 96, 156. *See also* corpse meditation
merit-making, 43–46, 47, 50–54, 172–73, 220
Meru, Mount, 9, 51
Milinda, 91, 150
Milindapañha, 150, 170
milk, 167, 174
Miller, William Ian, 147
mind, 4, 9. *See also* consciousness
mind to mind transmission, 98
Ming dynasty sculptures, *xvi*
miracles, 107
miraculous food, 159–60, 172
miserliness, 80
monasteries (*vihāras*), 21–22, 37, 111–12, 134–37
monastic codes, 16, 21–23, 93–95, 111–14, 158, 168, 207–8. *See also* monastic food
monastic communities, 21–22, 111–14, 172–73, 179–80, 210. *See also* public perception of monastics; Saṅgha
monastic food, 147, 150–51, 153–59, 172–73
Monastic Purity Rules (*Qinggui*), 111
Mongkut, 57, 58, 59
monks, 8, 22, 102, 135–36, 150, 155, 208, 219–20. *See also* monastic codes; public perception of monastics
moral economy, 43–46, 172–73
morality, 52, 108–9, 184. *See also* ethics; immorality; masturbation
mortality, 117. *See also* impermanence
movement, 81–82
mudrās, 58, 190
Mukaliṅga, 31, *32*
Mūlasarvāstivāda Vinaya, 21, 95–96, 102, 112, 131, 135, 154, 173
music, 81, 93–96, 98–100. *See also* celestial music; *Voyage, Le*
musique concrète, 67–68, 74, 83
Muslim diet, 146
mythology, 58–59

N

Nāgasena, 91
Nālandā, 37
Nanda, 9, 135
Nangklao, 57, 58, 59
Nārada, 129
National Museum of Asian Art, xi–xvii, *xii–xvi*
Nattier, Jan, 210
Needham, Rodney, 127

Nidānakathā, 148
Nikāya Buddhism, 36
nirvāṇa, 4, 20, 29, 35, 36, 49, 91, 170
Nirvāṇa Sūtra, 167, 179
nonself, 7–8
nose, 3, 13
nuns, 8, 102, 113, 154–55, 208, 213–14, 216–18. *See also* monastic codes
Nyingma tradition, 66, 83

O

Obeyesekere, Gananath, 119
object condition, 4
objects, xi–xii, 4, 115
odor eaters (*gandharvas*), 2, 100, 130, 159
odors, 5, 107–8. *See also* body odor; smells
offerings, 46–47, 51, 95, 110, 127, 129, 132–34, 170, 172, 175–76. *See also* dāna; giving
Oken, Lorenz, 205
olfaction. *See* smell, sense of; smells
onion, 154. *See also wuxin*
oral tradition, 4, 12, 94
otherness, 115, 125–26

P

Padmasambhava, *xvi*
pain, 6, 168
Pakdeekham, Santi, 49
Pāli tradition, 23, 92, 133, 176
Pāli Vinaya, 22, 113, 211, 214, 216–17
Paramanuchit Chinorot, 58, 59
paribhāvita, 132
paripṛcchā, 95. See also *Questions of the Kinnara King Druma*
paritta, 93
Pasenadi, 46–47, 48
passions, 150. *See also* desire
past Buddhas, 129
past lives, 130. *See also under* Buddha (historical)
Path of Purification (*Visuddhimagga*), 13, 152, 206, 207
path to enlightenment, 12–14
Paṭhama Sambodhi, 58
Pathom Somphot, 59
peaceful deities, 70, 71, 73–76, 77–82
perfume womb, 107, 119, 127, 131
perfumes, 12, 127, 128, 134, 135–36. *See also* fragrances
Petavatthu, 152
pheromones, 111
philosophy, 3–4, 12, 25, 68, 90, 148, 150, 188, 205
Phra Malai, 44, 50–54, *53*, 59
Phra Malai Klon Suat, 44, 51–52, 54
"pig's delight," 3, 149, 175
Plato, 145
pleasure, 6, 7, 9, 10, 12, 168–69, 208, 217, 218. *See also* masturbation; sexual touch
Porridge Sūtra, 174
prasāda, 23–24
Prasenajit, 101
precepts, 44, 54, 109, 155
protection, 92, 187–88
public perception of monastics, 21–22, 37–38, 112, 168
pure lands, 2, 8, 93, 107. *See also* heavens
"Pure Rules for Chan Monasteries," 151
Pūrṇa, 134–35
Pūrva Mīmāṃsā school, 25
Puu Phraam, 54

Q

Qinggui (*Chanyuan qinggui*), 111, 151
questions, undetermined, 89–90
Questions of King Milinda, 150
Questions of the Kinnara King Druma, 95–96, 97, 99–100

R

Rattanakosin period, 49–50
rattling staff, 102–3
reality
  nature of, 70, 84, 97, 99–100

smell of, 108, 116–17, 120
sound of, 78–79
See also clear light of reality; emptiness
realms, 8–10, 77–79. *See also* realms by name, e.g., hells
rebirth, 7–10, 48, 66, 70–71, 77, 82, 119, 130–31, 175–76
refuge, 44
relationships and smell, 110–13, 120
relativity, 116–17
relics, of Buddha, 49, 50, 125–26, 132
religion and food, 146, 147. *See also* meat; monastic food; vegetarianism
reliquaries, 132
renunciation, 12
reverb (reverberation), 74, 78–79, 82
Rhi, Ju-Hyung, 26, 28
rice, 6–7, 148, 149
porridge, 174–75
sweet milk, 149, 173–74, 176
Rig Veda, 133
right speech and right view, 12
Rikyū, Sen no, 160
ringing staff, 102–3
rituals, 31–32, 188
robes, 8, 28, *29*, 47, 49, 51, 54, 98, 112
Rotman, Andy, 23–24, 45–46, 126
Rozin, Paul, 147
Ruwanwelisaya stūpa, *xii*, xiii, *xiv*

S

sacred food, 159–60
sacrifices, 19, 133, 153, 160, 170, 219
Śākyamuni. *See* Buddha (historical)
śāla trees, 128
Samdup, Kazi Dawa, 65, 79
saṃsāra, 9–10, 117, 119, 156
Saṃyutta Nikāya, 7–8
sandalwood, 3, 126, 127, 128, 129, 131, 134
sandalwood Buddha, 44, 46–50, 57
Saṅgha, 21–23, 44, 220. *See also* monastic communities; monks; nuns
saṅgīti, 94
Sāṅkhya school, 3
Śāntideva, 109
sarabhañña, 94
Śāriputra, 97, 154, 157, 190–91
Sarnath, 26, *27*, 29, *30*, 33, *34*, 37
Sarvagandhasugandhā, 160
Sarvāstivāda Vinaya, 21–22
satyavacana, 93
Schaeffer, Pierre, 67–68, 83
Schopen, Gregory, 21, 132, 135–36, 209–10
Scripture in Forty-Two Sections, 170
Scripture on the Fifty Contemplations, 8
sculptures. *See* statues
secret mantras, 193–94
seeing the Buddha, 23–26. *See also* eye contact
self-control, 22, 113
sensation, 212–13
sense experience, xiii, 3–6, 7, 16, 150
sense faculties, 10, 183
sense objects, 4, 7, 149–50, 207
sense organs, 3–4, 7, 149, 206–7
sense perception, 206
senses, 2–6
associations between, 161
of Buddha. *See under* Buddha (historical)
rankings of, 3, 9, 145, 168, 205–6
Seven Zombies Spell, 184–86, 187–97
sexual intercourse, 16, 113, 208. *See also* celibacy
sexual misconduct, 55, 208. *See also* celibacy; masturbation
sexual touch, 207–20
Seyyasaka, 211
Shen Yue, 151
shrines, *xiii*, xiii, *xvi*, 31–32, 37, 47
Shulman, David, 130
sickness. *See* contagion; diseases; infectious touch
Siddhārtha. *See under* Buddha (historical)

sight, 3, 91, 92. *See also* vision
silence, 89–90, 97
sin, original, 7, 169
singing, 2, 93, 94–95
sittaru, 19
skillful means, 97
Skilling, Peter, 49
skin, 13, 183, 206
smell, sense of, 11, 145
smells, 5, 107–21, 125–37
"bad," 107–8, 109, 111–13, 114, 115–21, 130
"good," 107–9, 116–17, 119, 120, 130
Smith, Mark, 133
sociality and smell, 111–13
somatic experience, xii
sound sources, 68, 73–74, 76, 81
sounds, 5, 65–85, 100
"bad," 67, 84, 94, 95, 100
"good," 93–103
See also under reality. *See also* hearing; music; voice
South Asian Buddhism, 19–38, 95, 113, 153, 172, 187–89, 208. *See also* Indian Buddhism; Sri Lankan Buddhism
Southeast Asian Buddhism, 37, 49, 95, 172. *See also* Thai Buddhism
speech, melodious, 90. *See also* voice
spirits, 187, 188. *See also* demons; zombies
sponsorship, 43, 47–48, 50
śrāvakas, 94, 96, 187
Śrāvastī, 134
Sri Lankan Buddhism, *xii*, xiii, 19, 50, 51, 133. *See also* Ceylon
Śroṇāparānta, 134–35
standing Buddha, *50*, 57, 58
Staniski, Stanley J., *xii*
statues, *xiii*, *xv*, 19–20, 26–38, *27–30*, *32*, *34*, *36*, 43. *See also* sandalwood Buddha; standing Buddha
stealing, 14, 44, 113
stimulus, distance from, 205–7
Strong, John, 174–76
stūpas, *xii*, xiii, *xiv*, 111–12, 130, 134
Subha, 46
Subhūti, 97
subject–object distinction, 82, 115
subjectivity, 107–8, 115
subjugation, 116
subtle food, 159
Sudinna, 14, 91
suffering, 6, 7, 9–10, 168–69, 170
Sugandhi, 129
Sujātā, 149, 173, 175
sūkaramaddava, 175
Sukhāvatī, 93
Sukhothai period, 58
Sumati, 129
Sunanda, 100
śūnyatā (emptiness), 96, 99–100. *See also* reality, nature of
super knowledge, 10, 91–92
supernatural abilities, 10–11, 91–92
Śūraṅgama Sūtra, 92, 155–56
Sūtra ... on the Bestowal of Food, 174
Sūtra Setting Forth the Inconceivable Secrets of the Tathāgata, 91
sutras, chanting, 94–95
Swearer, Donald, 48
"sweet dew," 151, 170, 178–79
Sweet Dew paintings, 178–80, *180*
sweetness, 146, 151, 169–70, 173–74, 178–80

T

Taibei Fajie, 117–19
Taiwanese Buddhism, 117–19
Tamālapatracandanagandha, 130
"tangibility," 209, 210
tantric Buddhism, 3, 16, 92–93, 117, 179, *180*, 189
taste, 5, 11, 145, 151, 152, 158–59, 167–72
as aesthetic judgment, 146, 168
"bad," 146–49, 150, 151–52, 159
of Buddha, 171–72

of Dharma, 167
"good," 150, 151, 159, 168
See also sweetness
Tathāgatācintyaguhyanirdeśa Sūtra, 91
tea ceremony, 160
teachings. *See* Dharma
temple-based Hinduism, 25, 31
Tenzo kyōkun, 159
terror, 71, 80
Texture of Practice, The, *xii*, *xiv*
Thai Buddhism, 43–59, *50*, *53*, *55*, *57*, 173–74
Thai Tellings of the Phra Malai, 51
Thammayut nikai, 59
theft, 14, 44, 113
Theravāda Buddhism, 44, 49, 58. *See also* Hīnayāna Buddhism; Thai Buddhism
Thet Maha Chat festival, 52, 59. *See also* Vessantara festival
Three Jewels, 44
Three Thousand Regulations for Great Bhiksus, 112
Thullanandā, 113
Thus Have I Seen, 45–46, 126
Tibetan Book of the Dead, The, 65–66, 69–73, 75–84
Tibetan Buddhism, *xiii*, *xiv*, *xvi*, 66, 93, 95, 100–102, 184–90
tofu, 158
tongue, 3, 11
of Buddha, 90
touch, 5–6, 183–86, 205–7, 210
active and passive, 185
aggregate, 79
"bad," 183–85
infectious, 183–97
See also contact; sexual touch
Trailok, 53, 58
transitions, 127–28, 130, 131, 136. *See also* boundaries, crossing; liminality
translation, 2, 94
Trāyastriṃśa Heaven, 51, 56, 131, 169
Treasury of Abhidharma (*Abhidharmakośa/Kośa*), 110, 159, 206–7, 209
truth, 79, 145
truth power, 93, 187
truth-telling, 128–29
Tuṣita Heaven, 131

U

Udayagiri, 31–32, *32*
Udāyī, 211, 213
Upāli, 95–96
Upananda, 150
upāya, 97

V

Vaiṣṇava temples, 31, 35
Vajrayana shrine, xiii, *xiii*
Vakkali, 43
van Lohuizen-de Leeuw, Johanna, 28
Varaha, 32
Vasubandhu, 110, 130, 159, 206
Vatsyāyana, 214–15, 218
Vaṭṭaṅgulirāja Jātaka, 48–49
Vedānta, 25
Vedic tradition, 25, 32, 95, 133, 170, 219
vegetables, pungent (*wuxin*), 112–13, 115, 153–58
vegetarianism, 114, 117–19, 147, 152–53, 155
Vessantara festival, 51–54. *See also* Bun Pra Wet festival; Thet Maha Chat festival
Vessantara Jātaka, 51, 52–54, *53*, 58, 59
vetāla, 188–89. *See also* zombies
vihāras, 37. *See also* monasteries
Vimalakīrti, 97, 170
Vimalakīrti Sutra, 97, 98, 160, 170
Vinaya, 21–23, 111–14, 207–8. *See also* monastic codes; and Vinayas by name, e.g., Pāli Vinaya
violence, 114–15. *See also* killing
vipassanā, 12
Vipaśyi, 129

vision, 22, 24, 38, 77–79, 126, 145. *See also* sight
Viṣṇu, 35, *36*, 194
visualization, 23
Viśvakarman, 157
voice, 89–93
vows. *See* celibacy; precepts
Voyage, Le, 66, 67–76, 80, 81–85

W
"Wanglei," 117–18
Warren, Henry Clarke, 90
Wat Saen Suk, *55*, 55, 56
womb, perfume, 107, 119, 127, 131
wrathful deities, 70, 71, 76, 77, 80, 81
wuxin, 112, 153–58

X
Xuedou Chongxian, 108–9

Y
yakṣas, 26, *27*
Yijing, 37
Yuanwu Keqin, 108–9
Yuanzhao, 112–13
Yuga Sutta, 174
Yunmen, 117

Z
Zen Buddhism, 108–9, 117, 159, 160
Zhigong, 114–15
Zhiyi, 155
zombies, 184–97

Contributors

Bryan J. Cuevas
John F. Priest Professor of Religion and Director of Buddhist and Tibetan Studies at Florida State University. His research specialties include Tibetan religious history and hagiography, Buddhist ritual magic and sorcery, and Tibetan Buddhist narrative literature on death and the dead. He is the author and translator of several books on these subjects, including most recently *The All-Pervading Melodious Drumbeat: The Life of Ra Lotsawa*.

Robert DeCaroli
Professor of South and Southeast Asian Art History at George Mason University. He is the author of *Haunting the Buddha: Indian Popular Religions and the Formation of Buddhism*, *Image Problems: The Origin and Development of the Buddha's Image in Early South Asia*, as well as numerous articles and book chapters. Recently, he co-curated *Encountering the Buddha: Art and Practice across Asia* at the National Museum of Asian Art. He has been awarded a Getty Research Institute Fellowship and the Robert H. N. Ho Family Foundation Research Fellowship.

Debra Diamond
Elizabeth Moynihan Curator for South and Southeast Asian Art at the Smithsonian's National Museum of Asian Art. She is a specialist in Indian painting, the visual culture of yoga, and exhibiting religions. Her Smithsonian exhibitions include *Encountering the Buddha: Art and Practice across Asia* and *Yoga: The Art of Transformation*. She is the coordinating editor for *Paths to Perfection*, the museum's first handbook of its Buddhist collection.

She received scholarship awards for the publications *Yoga* and *Garden and Cosmos: The Royal Paintings of Jodhpur*.

Donald S. Lopez Jr.

Arthur E. Link Distinguished University Professor of Buddhist and Tibetan Studies in the Department of Asian Languages and Cultures at the University of Michigan. He is the author of numerous monographs, translations, and edited volumes on South Asian Buddhism, Tibetan Buddhism, and the European encounter with Buddhism. In 2014 his *Princeton Dictionary of Buddhism* (with Robert Buswell) was awarded the Dartmouth Medal of the American Library Association for best reference work of the year. In 2002 he was elected to the American Academy of Arts and Sciences.

D. Max Moerman

Professor and Chair in the Department of Asian and Middle Eastern Cultures, Barnard College, Columbia University, and Co-Chair of the Columbia University Seminar in Buddhist Studies. His research interests lie in the visual and material culture of pre-modern Japanese Buddhism. He is the author of *Localizing Paradise: Kumano Pilgrimage and the Religious Landscape of Premodern Japan* and *The Japanese Buddhist World Map: Religious Vision and the Cartographic Imagination*.

Reiko Ohnuma

The Robert 1932 and Barbara Black Professor of Religion and Chair of the Department of Religion at Dartmouth College. She specializes in South Asian Buddhism and is the author of *Head, Eyes, Flesh, and Blood: Giving Away the Body in Indian Buddhist Literature*, *Ties That Bind: Maternal Imagery and Discourse in Indian Buddhism*, and *Unfortunate Destiny: Animals in the Indian Buddhist Imagination*.

James Robson

The James C. Kralik and Yunli Lou Professor of East Asian Languages and Civilizations at Harvard University and the Victor and William Fung Director of the Harvard Asia Center. He is the author of the *Power of*

Place: The Religious Landscape of the Southern Sacred Peak [Nanyue 南嶽] in Medieval China, the editor of the *Norton Anthology of World Religions: Daoism*, and has published widely on sacred geography, local religious history, the development of Chan Buddhism, and the contents of religious images. He is currently a co-editor of *T'oung-Pao*.

Melody Rod-ari

Associate Professor of Art History at Loyola Marymount University. She is the Southeast Asian content editor for *Smarthistory* as well as an active curator who has organized exhibitions and permanent galleries for the Norton Simon Museum and the University of Southern California Pacific Asia Museum. Her research investigates Buddhist visual culture in Thailand and the history of collecting South and Southeast Asian art. Her work has been published by various journals and university presses, including *Amerasia Journal*, the *Journal of the History of Collections*, and the National University of Singapore Press.

Kurtis R. Schaeffer

The Frances Myers Ball Professor in the Department of Religious Studies at the University of Virginia, where he co-directs the program in Tibetan Buddhist studies. He is a student of the cultural history of Tibet and is particularly engaged in the biographical and poetic literature of Tibet. He is the author of *Himalayan Hermitess: The Life of a Tibetan Buddhist Nun*, *The Life of the Buddha by Tenzin Chögyel*, and the co-editor of *Sources of Tibetan Tradition*, among other works.

John S. Strong

Charles A. Dana Professor Emeritus of Religious Studies and Asian Studies at Bates College. During his forty years of teaching there, he has also had visiting appointments at the University of Peradeniya (Sri Lanka), the University of Chicago, and at Stanford, Princeton, and Harvard Universities. His books include *The Buddha: A Beginner's Guide*, *Relics of the Buddha*, *Buddhisms: An Introduction*, and most recently *The Buddha's Tooth*. Happily retired, he lives in a woods by a lake in Maine.

Lina Verchery
Scholar of Chinese Buddhism and an independent filmmaker who teaches at the University of Otago in New Zealand Aotearoa. She received her PhD in Buddhist studies from Harvard University's Committee on the Study of Religion, where she specialized in the ethnographic study of contemporary Buddhist monastic life in China and throughout the global Chinese diaspora. An award-winning filmmaker, her documentary, experimental, and educational films about Buddhism and connected topics have been screened in festivals and on television networks around the world.

About Wisdom Publications

Wisdom Publications is the leading publisher of classic and contemporary Buddhist books and practical works on mindfulness. To learn more about us or to explore our other books, please visit our website at wisdomexperience.org or contact us at the address below.

Wisdom Publications
132 Perry Street
New York, NY 10014 USA

Wisdom Publications is affiliated with the Foundation for the Preservation of the Mahayana Tradition (FPMT).